# Talk in Two Languages

# Talk in Two Languages

Joseph Gafaranga
*The University of Edinburgh*

© Joseph Gafaranga 2007

All rights reserved. No reproduction, copy or transmission of this publication may be made without written permission.

No paragraph of this publication may be reproduced, copied or transmitted save with written permission or in accordance with the provisions of the Copyright, Designs and Patents Act 1988, or under the terms of any licence permitting limited copying issued by the Copyright Licensing Agency, 90 Tottenham Court Road, London W1T 4LP.

Any person who does any unauthorized act in relation to this publication may be liable to criminal prosecution and civil claims for damages.

The author has asserted his right to be identified as the author of this work in accordance with the Copyright, Designs and Patents Act 1988.

First published 2007 by
PALGRAVE MACMILLAN
Houndmills, Basingstoke, Hampshire RG21 6XS and
175 Fifth Avenue, New York, N.Y. 10010
Companies and representatives throughout the world

PALGRAVE MACMILLAN is the global academic imprint of the Palgrave Macmillan division of St. Martin's Press, LLC and of Palgrave Macmillan Ltd. Macmillan® is a registered trademark in the United States, United Kingdom and other countries. Palgrave is a registered trademark in the European Union and other countries.

ISBN-13: 978–1–4039–4861–8 hardback
ISBN-10: 1–4039–4861–5 hardback

This book is printed on paper suitable for recycling and made from fully managed and sustained forest sources. Logging, pulping and manufacturing processes are expected to conform to the environmental regulations of the country of origin.

A catalogue record for this book is available from the British Library.

A catalog record for this book is available from the Library of Congress.

10  9  8  7  6  5  4  3  2  1
16  15  14  13  12  11  10  09  08  07

Printed and bound in Great Britain by
Antony Rowe Ltd, Chippenham and Eastbourne

*For Shany, Sandrine, Nickita and Benitha*

# Contents

| | |
|---|---|
| List of Tables | x |
| Acknowledgements | xi |

**1 Introduction**     1
   1.1  Bilingualism, talk in two languages and Linguistics     1
   1.2  From order in practical social action to order in talk in two languages     3
   1.3  In search for common grounds in studies of talk in two languages     5
   1.4  Focus and structure of the book     7
   1.5  A word on data     8

**2 Some quasi-theories of order in talk in two languages**     10
   2.1  Introduction     10
   2.2  Lay explanations of language alternation     11
   2.3  Some 'en-résumé' practices by linguists     17
       2.3.1  Borrowing vs code-switching     18
       2.3.2  Code-mixing vs code-switching     22
       2.3.3  Insertional vs alternational language mixing     27
   2.4  Conclusion     32

**3 Grammatical order in talk in two languages**     34
   3.1  Introduction     34
   3.2  Grammar as an issue of order     34
   3.3  An alternational model of language alternation     38
       3.3.1  Original constraints model     38
       3.3.2  Later developments     41
            3.3.2.1  Lone L2 incorporations     41
            3.3.2.2  Constituent insertion     44
   3.4  An insertional model of language alternation     47
       3.4.1  A mentalistic model of language alternation     47
       3.4.2  The asymmetry principle in language alternation     49
            3.4.2.1  Morpheme order principle     51
            3.4.2.2  System morpheme principle     55

|  |  |  |
|---|---|---|
| | 3.4.3 Predictions of the MLF | 57 |
| 3.5 | Conclusion | 60 |

## 4 Using the models: Class agreement in Kinyarwanda–French language alternation — 62
    4.1 Introduction — 62
    4.2 Grammatical agreement in Kinyarwanda and in French — 64
    4.3 Class agreement in Kinyarwanda–French language alternation — 66
        4.3.1 French adjectives and verbs in agreement-governed position — 66
        4.3.2 French nouns in agreement-commanding position — 70
        4.3.3 Class agreement and multi-word fragments — 76
    4.4 Conclusion — 79

## 5 Interactional order in talk in two languages: identity-related accounts — 83
    5.1 Introduction — 83
    5.2 Diglossia: language alternation and/in the Sociology of Language — 85
    5.3 We-/they-codes: language alternation and/in Interactional Sociolinguistics — 91
        5.3.1 Interactional Sociolinguistics — 91
        5.3.2 Language alternation in Interactional Sociolinguistics — 94
    5.4 Markedness: a rational choice model of language alternation — 102
        5.4.1 Language choice as a rational act — 102
        5.4.2 The markedness model — 104
            5.4.2.1 Some premises — 104
            5.4.2.2 Types of language choices — 108
    5.5 Conclusion — 114

## 6 Interactional order in talk in two languages: organisational explanation — 116
    6.1 Introduction — 116
    6.2 The notion of 'preference' in Conversation Analysis — 117
    6.3 Local order in bilingual conversation — 120
        6.3.1 Some premises — 120
        6.3.2 Preference for same language talk — 123

|  |  |  |  |
|---|---|---|---|
|  | 6.3.3 | Language preference | 128 |
|  | 6.3.4 | Categories of code alternation | 131 |
| 6.4 | Overall order in bilingual conversation | | 135 |
|  | 6.4.1 | Overall order in talk-in-interaction | 135 |
|  | 6.4.2 | Preference for same medium | 138 |
|  | 6.4.3 | Categories of language alternation | 145 |
| 6.5 | Conclusion | | 149 |

## 7 Using the models: direct speech reporting in talk in two languages — 151

7.1 Introduction — 151
7.2 Language choice in direct speech reporting as an issue of order — 151
7.3 Direct speech reporting as demonstration — 157
7.4 Language choice and direct speech reporting among bilingual speakers — 164
    7.4.1 Language choice as the depictive element — 164
    7.4.2 Language choice as a supportive element — 168
7.5 Conclusion — 172

## 8 Applying language alternation studies — 174

8.1 Introduction — 174
8.2 From applied Linguistics to applied language alternation studies — 175
8.3 Investigating language shift and maintenance among bilingual Rwandans in Belgium — 179
    8.3.1 Language shift as a real world concern — 179
    8.3.2 Research design — 181
    8.3.3 Language alternation, language shift and maintenance — 182
    8.3.4 Language choice and language shift among the Rwandans in Belgium — 188
        8.3.4.1 Initiation of conversation in French — 188
        8.3.4.2 Accommodation in French — 191
        8.3.4.3 The parallel mode — 194
8.4 Conclusion — 196

## 9 Summary and conclusion — 198

*References* — 209

*Index* — 219

# List of Tables

| | | |
|---|---|---|
| 3.1 | Studies of language alternation (i) | 35 |
| 3.2 | Grammatical perspectives on language alternation | 35 |
| 3.3 | A model of language production | 48 |
| 3.4 | A model of language production for language alternation | 48 |
| 4.1 | Noun classes in Kinyarwanda | 65 |
| 5.1 | Studies of language alternation (ii) | 85 |
| 5.2 | Functional differentiation of language varieties in diglossia | 87 |
| 5.3 | Diglossia and bilingualism | 89 |
| 6.1 | Categories of code alternation | 131 |
| 6.2 | Categories of language alternation | 145 |
| 6.3 | Language alternation as an aspect of the overall order in talk in two languages | 148 |
| 7.1 | Language choice and direct speech reporting among bilingual Rwandans | 153 |
| 8.1 | Stages of reversing language shift | 184 |
| 8.2 | Strategies for language maintenance in bilingual families | 187 |

# Acknowledgements

This book can be thought of as a step on a journey, and it is right to look back and acknowledge the various people and institutions who have contributed to it. During the academic year 1982–83, Dr Robert Botney, then at the National University of Rwanda, introduced me to the field of Sociolinguistics and made me to think about language use in bilingual settings. I owe him a debt of gratitude as I do to my six classmates on that year's *Licence en Anglais*, many of whom have unfortunately passed away because of the war and genocide in 1990–94. Interest in Bilingualism was then strengthened through participation in the various research groups: the Bilingualism Research Group at Lancaster University, the Language Research Group at Edge Hill University College and the Language in Context at the University of Edinburgh. I would like to say 'Thanks' to members of these groups, to Professor Marilyn Martin-Jones, Dr Mark Sebba, Dr Jo Arthur and Dr M. C. Torras, in particular. I have also immensely benefited from formal and less formal discussions with scholars in Bilingualism, including Professor Peter Auer, Professor Carol Myers-Scotton, Professor Li Wei, Professor Peter W. Martin, to name but a few.

Three research funding bodies have contributed to this project and I would like to acknowledge them. The Economic and Social Research Council has supported the collection of some of the data used (RES-00-22-1165). The Research Trust Fund at the University of Edinburgh has supported the transcription of some of the data. And AHRC, through their Research Leave Scheme, has supported the writing up of the project (AID Number 112778). I would like to thank my commissioning editor at Palgrave Macmillan, Jill Lake, for her patience and understanding. To the anonymous reviewers, I would like to say 'thank you for your comments on the proposal'. And I would like to thank my colleague Dr Erik Schleef who has read through the manuscript with utmost care. Mistakes and other infelicities may be found in this book and I would like them to be blamed only on me.

I owe a huge debt of gratitude to bilingual Rwandans and to the Rwandan community in Belgium, in particular. Without their unlimited co-operation, my interest in Bilingualism would have been impossible to sustain. However, my greatest debt is to my family for their support over the years, especially during those years when the future looked less than certain. 'Girls, you've been wonderful and I am proud of the four of you.'

# 1
# Introduction

## 1.1. Bilingualism, talk in two languages and Linguistics

Let me open with what is now a truism. Bilingualism[1] is a world-wide phenomenon. A simple analysis of the world map reveals that only very few countries, if any at all, can claim to be monolingual. And this should not be surprising as, notwithstanding the current unprecedented loss of the world languages, there are still far more languages in the world than there are countries. Of course, one could argue that bilingualism is unevenly distributed and therefore that some countries can rightly claim to be monolingual. There is some truth in this. Most of the world languages are found in the developing world, but this does not mean that developed countries are linguistically homogeneous. For example, a country like the United Kingdom may claim to be monolingual in English simply because English is its 'official' language. However, this does not correspond to reality at all. The Ethnologue lists 14 living languages for the United Kingdom, and these do not include the languages of the so-called 'immigrant' minority groups such as Urdu, Bengali, Chinese and so on. Closer to home, a recent survey revealed that 106 languages were represented in schools in Scotland (Murray, 2006). Finally, another country which is often claimed to be monolingual is France, but even here, the situation is more complex than this. The Ethnologue lists 29 living languages, not including the languages of immigrant groups.

The situation becomes even more complex if one takes account of the fact that the boundary between a language and a dialect is a fuzzy one (Haugen, 1966). There is no objective difference between a language and a dialect. Dutch and Flemish are different languages and so are Kinyarwanda and Kirundi even though the languages in each pair are mutually intelligible. On the other hand, Cantonese and Mandarin are two dialects of Chinese even though they are not mutually intelligible. In fact, some people even find it difficult to accept that Mandarin is a dialect, given its social prestige. So if there is no strictly objective difference between a language and a dialect, the many cases of bidialectalism may be included in the count when one wants to determine whether a country is monolingual or whether it is bilingual. Thus, the overall picture is that of bilingualism being the norm rather than the exception. In that sense, Jakobson (1953) was ever so right in maintaining that 'bilingualism is [...] the fundamental problem of Linguistics' (cited in Romaine, 1995: 1).

To be sure, the need for Linguistics to concern itself with bilingualism should not be seen as a matter of casual interest, but rather as a priority. A number of scholars have clearly indicated that a good understanding of bilingual phenomena uniquely improves our understanding of language in general and of the way it works. For example, according to Muysken, the study of code-switching (hereafter referred to alternatively as 'language alternation'/'talk in two languages' for reasons I will specify in Chapter 2) 'is crucial for linguistics as a scientific discipline', for it 'can uniquely contribute to elucidating and perhaps ultimately resolving' some of the most crucial issues in modern linguistics, including that of 'the division of labour between the lexicon and the grammar of a language' (1995: 178). Likewise, according to Myers-Scotton, 'bilingualism offers a unique opportunity to understand the structures of a particular language when we see how they pattern when in contact with the structures of another language' (2006: 12). For example, as we will see in Chapter 4, in Kinyarwanda, there are 16 classes of nouns, each one of which dictates agreement at the level of relevant verbs (subject-verb) and adjectives (head noun + modifier/complement). However, when in contact with French, this structure of Kinyarwanda patterns differently. While French verbs consistently show class agreement with Kinyarwanda noun-subjects, French adjectives do not show class agreement with relevant Kinyarwanda nouns. Thus, on this basis, it might be possible to say that class agreement in Kinyarwanda is stronger between the noun-subject and the verb than between nouns and adjectives. Clearly, this intimate understanding of the structure of Kinyarwanda can only be achieved by studying Kinyarwanda–French bilingualism.

One of the most noticeable aspects of bilingualism is the phenomenon of language alternation. Sometimes to the amazement of their monolingual counterparts, bilinguals all over the world are often seen to be using two or more languages within the same conversation. That is they are found to be conducting talk in two languages. And this happens independently of the language pairs involved. As indicated above, bilingualism can be studied for the contribution it makes to our understanding of language in general. In addition to this and probably prior to it, bilingualism, and talk in two languages in particular, is interesting in its own right and must be studied as such. For example, from Saussure (1995), we know that language is a 'system *où tout se tient*' (Muysken, 1995: 196). A more recent formulation of this is what Myers-Scotton (2002, 2006) calls the 'Uniform Structure Principle', the principle according to which 'a given constituent type in any language has a uniform abstract structure and the requirements of well-formedness for this type must be observed whenever the constituent appears' (2006: 243). Given this, it is clear that language alternation is 'impossible in principle' (Muysken, 1995: 196). Because of this theoretical impossibility, an issue arises, how can its occurrence in specific instances of talk in two languages be accounted for? This is what I will be referring to in this book as the 'problem of order' in talk in two languages. Therefore, talk in two languages can be studied, as a phenomenon in its own right, in order to resolve this problem of order. This book is an account of how this problem of order can, and indeed has been, addressed.

## 1.2. From order in practical social action to order in talk in two languages

To view and speak of language alternation in terms of order implies a specific perspective from which it is viewed. In this book, I will adopt the sociological perspective of Ethnomethodology (Garfinkel, 1967, 1968). Roughly defined, the object of Sociology is to account for the social order, however this is defined. Within Sociology, Ethnomethodology proposes accounts of the orderliness of practical social action, and does so, in Garfinkel's own words, from a 'member's perspective'. This is also known as an 'emic orientation' (Ten Have, 1999). Thus, Ethnomethodology describes community members of a community (ethnos) use to produce order in practical social action (Garfinkel, 1968). From this perspective, order is the very possibility of social action. Any action which has been accomplished must be assumed to be orderly, to have been made possible by a particular order. The practical impossibility of disorderly action was established by Garfinkel in his 'breaching experiments'. In these experiments, students were asked to 'suspend' the natural order (e.g. not to return greetings) and see what happens. When students attempted to act as instructed, they either found that they actually could not do it, that their behaviour was interpreted as somehow strange and in need of an account, or simply that interaction broke down.

Central to the Ethnomethodological notion of order is the view that social action takes place in a normative framework. Any action which has been accomplished refers (indexicality of social action) to a particular 'social norm' which has made it possible and with reference to which it is interpreted as meaningful. In turn, with reference to a particular norm, three types of acts can be identified. First, an act is a direct application of the norm (normative action) or it is an instance of deviance from it. In the second possibility, an act consists of functional deviance or it consists of repairable deviance (Garfinkel, 1967; Heritage, 1984). Take the social activity (referred to above) known as the exchange of greetings. In most societies, there appears to be a norm that a greeting calls for a return greeting. This norm accounts for the orderliness of the many cases where a greeting receives a return greeting, but it also accounts for the few cases where a greeting is not returned. If a greeting is not returned, members customarily interpret the situation as 'he/she did not hear me' and go on to attempt to make themselves be heard (repairable deviance). Alternatively, if there is evidence that hearing has taken place, members develop the further interpretation that 'he/she is ignoring me' (functional deviance). Thus, not returning a greeting is in no way taken as a challenge to the norm, but rather as further evidence that the norm exists.

One particular area of practical social action which has attracted most attention is that of 'talk-in-interaction' (Schegloff, 1968), resulting in the specific name of Conversation Analysis (hereafter CA). The aim of CA is to describe the orderliness of talk-in-interaction. Thanks to CA, talk-in-interaction has been demonstrated to be highly orderly and at different levels. It has been demonstrated to be orderly at the level of turn-taking (Sacks *et al.*, 1978); actions in conversations have been demonstrated to come in pairs (adjacency pairs – Schegloff and Sacks, 1973), entry into the conversation has been found to be orderly (Schegloff, 1968) and so on. To illustrate the kind of order that CA describes, take the opening sequence in general practice consultation as described by Gafaranga and Britten (2003, 2005). General practice consultations, in the British context at least, open with a 'concern elicitor' of the type 'what can I do for you?' or 'How are you?'. Gafaranga and Britten show that there is order here for 'What can I do for you?' is used when the doctor defines the encounter as a new consultation (i.e. a visit in which the patient is to report a new problem) and 'How are you?' is used when the consultation is viewed as a follow-up (i.e. a visit about an on-going problem). In the great majority of cases, this pattern is followed, but there are also a few cases in which it is not. The example below (from Gafaranga and Britten, 2005: 83) illustrates a case of repairable deviance. In the example, the doctor uses 'What can I do for you?' thereby indicating that she sees current consultation as a new one. In turn 2, P produces talk which is visibly disturbed (recycles, hesitation) and even laughs. As Haakana (2001) shows, in doctor–patient interaction, laughter often indicates 'a delicate object'. All these seem to be signalling that a problem has arisen. In addition, P uses the possessive adjective 'my' which works as a 'retrospective tying device' (Firth, 1995) as if to tell the doctor, of course without stating it so many words, that he is actually consulting about an ongoing problem, and therefore that the consultation has to be seen as a follow-up. In turn 3, D acknowledges P's work and accepts the correction saying 'Yes. Yes. Yes'.

*Example 1.1*

1. Doctor: Right. Okay. And what can I do for you today?
2. Patient: You – my blood test er from er my gout ((laughs))
3. Doctor: Right. Yes. Yes. Yes. Th:e uric acid is – is high
4. Patient: Is it. Yeah

The point to be made here is that the need to repair D's action indicates that, for participants, there is order in the opening sequence in general practice consultation and that this order cannot be freely violated. If there is no functional motivation for violating it, deviance must be repaired, otherwise communication becomes impossible.

## 1.3. In search for common grounds in studies of talk in two languages

In the study of language alternation, the CA methodology has already been used, particularly by researchers such as Auer, Wei, Gafaranga and others (see Chapter 6). These researchers have convincingly demonstrated that, among bilingual speakers, language alternation is 'a significant aspect of talk organisation' (Gafaranga, 1999), that bilingual speakers use language alternation to structure the conversational activity in which they are engaged. Consider the following instance from Milroy and Wei (1995: 151). One aspect of conversational organisation that conversation analysts have described is repair organisation (Schegloff et al., 1977). They have noted, among other things, that repair can be either 'self-initiated' or 'other-initiated', preference going for 'self-initiated self-repair'. On the other hand, research in talk in two languages shows that language alternation can be used to signal dispreference (Wei, 1994; Milroy and Wei, 1995; Shin and Milroy, 2000). Thus, in the following instance, alternation between Chinese and English, corresponding to the repair initiator, can be seen as contributing to the organisation of repair, marking the other-repair initiation as dispreferred.

*Example 1.2*

> A: Da m do. Koeige telephone gonggan. Koei dang yatjan joi da.
> [Can't get through. Her telephone is engaged. She'll ring again in a short while]
> B: She'll ring?
> A: Hai a, ngaw da.
> [Yes, I'll ring.]

However, because it has co-occurred with other research paradigms, the CA methodology has often been misunderstood as if standing in competition with them. Commentators such as Sebba and Wootton (1998) and Wei (1998, 2002, 2005) explicitly contrast the CA methodology with other approaches, the Markedness Model of Codeswitching (see Chapter 5) in particular. To be sure, competition between the models is not to be blamed on commentators in the first instance; rather it seems to be the motivation for the development of alternative models. For example, one of the most central statements by Auer is that 'any theory of conversational code-alternation is bound to fail if it does not take into account that the meaning of code-alternation depends in essential ways on its "*sequential environment*"' (original emphasis) (1995: 116). Starting from this position, Auer argues for a 'sequential (i.e. CA) approach to code-switching' which sees the meaning of language alternation as a local accomplishment. However, not everybody shares these views. For example, Myers-Scotton (1993b: 109–110) writes,

I cannot agree with those researchers who see the social meaning of (language) choices as largely generated by the dynamics of the interaction. It is true that a part of the social meaning does develop in the actual turn-taking of a conversation, but most of the interpretation depends on the markedness framework which is provided by societal norms.

Wei (1998) nicely puts this disagreement saying that the CA model sees meaning in language alternation as essentially 'brought about' in the interaction, while rational choice models, including the Markedness Model, see it as 'brought along' from the community. This book is a search for common grounds. It argues that all approaches to language alternation, not just the above two, address the same issue, that of order in talk in two languages, although they approach it from different perspectives.

## 1.4. Focus and structure of the book

As indicated above, this book is a search for common grounds for current approaches to language alternation. To help the reader make up their mind as to whether to go on reading, it is important to make it clear exactly what to expect, what the book is about and what it is not about. The book does not purport to present any new theory of language alternation. Every model of language alternation which will be discussed has already been published in some form or other. However, the book is not a simple review of the literature. In fact, an exhaustive review of the literature on language alternation is not a humanly possible task given the amount of literature that is currently available. Rather, in the following chapters, I want to do two things: First, I will identify the main approaches to language alternation, select representative work in each approach and propose a reading of it as an account of order in talk in two languages. Secondly, I will propose case studies in which I show how ideas, concepts and methodologies discussed in the review of approaches can be used to address specific issues of order in talk in two languages.

Thus, the structure of this book is as follows. Chapter 2, entitled 'Quasi-theories of language alternation', covers the various ways in which language alternation is talked about and explained in non-technical terms. Particularly, the chapter discusses lay people's accounts, including bilinguals themselves, of language alternation. The chapter then moves on to survey the various ways in which 'linguists' refer to language alternation in a short-hand fashion. Chapter 3, entitled 'Grammatical order in talk in two languages', shows that and how, from a grammatical perspective, the issue of language alternation must be seen as that order. As Muysken (2000) and Auer (1999, 2000) argue, from a grammatical view, two general patterns of language alternation can be found. Language alternation is either 'insertional' or it is 'alternational'. Either way, however, language alternation can be seen as an issue of order because, in principle, it runs against the Structural Uniformity Principle (see above). The chapter goes on then to examine two approaches which account for the orderliness of language alternation, one from the alternational end and the other from the insertional end of the spectrum. Ideas developed in the survey are then used, in Chapter 4, to address a specific issue of order in talk in two languages, namely class agreement in Kinyarwanda–French language alternation. In Chapters 5 and 6, emphasis shifts from the grammatical perspective to the socio-functional perspective. Chapter 5 looks at language alternation from an 'identity-related' perspective (Sebba and Wootton, 1998), while Chapter 6 looks at it from an 'organisational' perspective (Torras and Gafaranga, 2002; Gafaranga, 2007). In each case, a principle or a set of principles which allow(s) us to view language alternation as an issue of order is identified before each perspective is inspected for the account it proposes for the identified issue of order. Following on from this, Chapter 7 uses ideas, concepts and methodologies identified and develops an account of a specific issue of order in talk in two languages, namely language alternation and direct speech reporting in talk in two languages. Finally, in line with Heap's (1990: 42) view that 'any serious piece of scholarship presumes the existence of a compelling answer to the twin questions of Why Speak/Listen and Why Write/Read', Chapter 8 shows how the study of language alternation as a problem of order can be used to address a real-life issue. The specific issue used by way of an illustration is that of language shift in the Rwandan community in Belgium, an issue which, as we will see, is of significant concern for community members themselves.

### 1.5. A word on data

Data for my discussion will come mainly from my own corpus of Kinyarwanda–French bilingual conversations and, where appropriate, I will complement this data set with examples from a variety of sources which, if published, will be explicitly acknowledged.[2] In particular, the three case studies are based on bilingual conversations I have collected among the Rwandans in Belgium, first as part of my PhD in 1996, and secondly as part of an ESRC-funded project on language shift and maintenance in 2006 (Res 00-22-1165)[3]. The Rwandans in Belgium, among whom data were collected, settled in Belgium, mostly after 1994, following the Rwandan civil war (1990–1994) and the ensuing genocide. However, even before they arrived in Belgium, these Rwandans were bilingual in French and Kinyarwanda (literally the language of Rwanda) because of the then Rwandan language policies. In Rwanda, both French and Kinyarwanda had been declared official languages, with Kinyarwanda enjoying the further status of national language (Constitution de la République Rwandaise, 1985). While everybody acquired Kinyarwanda as a first language, French could only be learned later through formal education (age 10 onwards). Actual language use in Rwanda was such that monolingual Kinyarwanda, just like monolingual French, was used only in very formal contexts or when interacting with monolinguals. Otherwise, among bilingual Rwandans, language alternation was the norm. This has led me to argue that Kinyarwanda–French language alternation could be seen as a bilinguals' vernacular (Gafaranga, 1987a). At the level of grammar, Kinyarwanda was the 'matrix language' (see Chapter 3) and this has led me to argue that Kinyarwanda–French language alternation could be seen as 'Kinyarwanda-for-all-practical purposes' (Gafaranga, 1997a, 1998, 2001a).

## Notes

1. The term 'Bilingualism' will be used generically to mean access to more than one language.
2. I am particularly indebted to Dr M. C. Torras for allowing me to access her data of Catalan–Castilian and Catalan–Castilian–English service encounters. As I have previously worked on these data sets in the context of joint publications, no further acknowledgement will be needed.
3. The following conventions were used to transcribe these audio recordings:

    Plain: Kinyarwanda
    *Italics: French*
    <u>Underlining: Other languages</u>
    **Bold: Target element**
    (.) perceptible pause
    ba-: interruption
    [overlapping talk
    ((laughter)) non-verbal vocal action
    ( ) inaudible

    Free translation in English follows from original extracts.
    Extracts from other data sets follow, except where indicated, original transcription conventions.

# 2
# Some Quasi-Theories of Order in Talk in Two Languages

## 2.1. Introduction

The use of two languages within the same conversation has always been a very noticeable phenomenon for lay people and linguists alike, even though bilingual speakers themselves may not be aware of it while talking. Therefore, it may safely be assumed that both linguists and non-linguists have developed ways of dealing with the issue of its orderliness. For the sake of organising this discussion of the ways in which the issue of order in talk in two languages has been addressed, I will adopt a distinction made by Peräkylä and Vehveläinen (2003) in relation to doctor–patient interaction. Peräkylä and Vehveläinen note that conversation analysts and health professionals have ways of talking about doctor–patient interaction, ways which are not always equivalent. In the case of professionals, Peräkylä and Vehveläinen speak of 'professional stocks of interactional knowledge' or 'quasi-theories' about social interaction. Conversely, they imply that conversation analysts develop 'fully-fledged theories' of social interaction. In this book, I want to adopt a similar distinction in respect of language alternation as an issue of order in talk in two languages. On the one hand, there are views and accounts of language alternation as held and expressed by professional analysts, that is people whose attention is firmly focused on addressing the issue of order in language alternation. I will refer to these views and accounts as fully-fledged theories of language alternation and deal with them from Chapter 3 onwards. On the other hand, there are views and ways of talking about language alternation as observed among non-specialists. In turn, these divide into two categories. First, there are views held by lay everyday people. I will refer to these as 'lay explanations'. Secondly, there are what I will refer to as 'en-résumé' practices. These are ways of referring to language alternation data in a short-hand fashion by linguists. En-résumé practices are ways of organising the data before a fully-fledged account is developed. As the title suggests, this chapter deals with quasi-theories of order in talk in two languages and covers both lay explanations and 'en-résumé' practices among linguists.

## 2.2. Lay explanations of language alternation

As indicated above, given the salient nature of language alternation, both analysts and ordinary everyday people have ways of dealing with the issue of its orderliness. Lay explanations of language alternation fall in at least two categories, namely the use of derogatory names and the use of pseudo-scientific terms. A constant behind these two ways, as the discussion below shows, is the view that language alternation is a disorderly phenomenon. Wherever language alternation is a salient feature of social interaction, a name is coined by the way of identifying this mode of speech. Such names include 'Spanglish' (Spanish and English in the United States), 'Franglais' (French and English in France), Kinyafrançais (Kinyarwanda and French in Rwanda), Singlish (English and Chinese in China) and so on. This naming practice conveys two important meanings. First, it shows that language alternation, where it occurs as a significant means of communication, is a very visible phenomenon. Secondly and following from the above, because language alternation is visible, people react to it, often negatively, depending on prevalent language ideologies. According to Jones and Wareing (1999: 34), an ideology is 'any set of beliefs which, to those who hold them, appear to be logical and "natural"'. Or, as Myers-Scotton (2006: 135) puts it, 'ideologies are patterns of belief and practice, which make some existing arrangements appear normal and others not'.

On the whole and across the world, the dominant language ideology is that monolingualism is the norm. Beliefs such as 'one country/people–one language' are deeply engrained in people's minds. The most explicit form of this monolingual ideology can be found in the various policies of assimilation as practised in many countries, especially towards the so-called 'immigrant minorities' and their languages, but less explicit forms exist as well, often without the holders' conscious awareness. As a consequence of this monolingual ideology, attitudes towards some forms of bilingualism are often negative. Note that I am deliberately talking about some forms of bilingualism. There is evidence that bilingualism involving two prestigious languages, say English and French, is highly regarded. There is even evidence that, in some contexts, bilingualism involving one of these highly valued languages and a local language, also known as 'elite bilingualism' (e.g. Kinyarwanda and French bilingualism in Rwanda), is seen as an asset. However, there are other forms of bilingualism which, if not completely unnoticed, are met with negative attitudes. The first possibility is found in many countries in Africa, Asia and Latin America where competence in two or more languages is a pre-requisite for any significant participation in social life. For members of these communities, bilingualism is the norm and, therefore, is not particularly noticeable. The second possibility obtains in the so-called 'immigrant situations'. In these contexts, bilingualism is looked down upon and is blamed, falsely of course, for social exclusion of all kinds.

Independently of whether bilingualism in general is viewed positively or negatively, attitudes towards language alternation are on the whole negative. And this is so because of what Gardner-Chloros (1995) has referred to as 'the myth of the discreteness of linguistic systems' (also see Gafaranga, 2000a). This myth has it that the bilingual's languages are and ought to be kept separate, that, in talk, a bilingual person speaks either language A or language B. Because of this myth or language ideology of language separateness, the alternate use of two languages within the same conversation is felt to be a problem, to be a disorderly phenomenon. An example of such negative attitudes towards language alternation is the following statement from a Rwandan 'linguist' regarding Kinyarwandan–French language alternation

> Pour nous le français c'est la langue française véhicule de la culture française et ses corollaires belges, canadiennes et suisses. Le kinyarwanda est la langue bantu véhicule de la culture rwandaise. Le français dilué, qu'il se nomme 'Rwandisme' et autre 'Africanisme' cultive en nous un phénomène de rejet. *Il en est de même du kinyarwanda dilué que certains dénomment déjà 'ikinyafaransa', characterisé par un mélange grossier et par des emprunts inopportuns.* (Gasana, 1984: 224)[1]

These negative views can also be found in accounts of the motivations for language alternation, often by bilingual speakers themselves. Language alternation is said to occur because of laziness, lack of attention or because of inadequate mastery of the language. The following statements by bilinguals themselves (reported in Grosjean, 1982) are by no means unusual:

> A French–English bilingual: This whole process of code-switching is done mostly out of laziness, for if I searched long enough for the correct word, I would eventually find it... (p. 148)
>
> A Russian–English bilingual: When I speak to another Russian–English bilingual, I don't speak as carefully and often the languages blend. This also happens when I am tired or excited or angry. (p. 150)

That is to say, according to these views, language alternation is simply a disorderly phenomenon, and names such as Franglais, Kinyafrançais and Spanglish translate these views.

The second form that lay explanations of language alternation take is the use of pseudo-scientific terms. Two such pseudo-scientific terms are discussed below. The first term that non-specialists use to refer to the use of two languages within the same conversation is 'interference'. To be sure, there was a time when specialists in bilingualism themselves used the term although, nowadays, it has largely fallen into disuse. Examples of otherwise distinguished scholars who have used the term are Haugen (1956), Weinreich (1953), Mackey (1962), to name just a few. The term 'interference' comes from the area of Second Language Acquisition (SLA). In the SLA literature, 'interference' is used to mean the negative effect of learners' 1st language on their performance in L2, an effect which can be observed at any level of language description: grammar, lexis, accent, spelling and so on.[2] In interference, because L1 is seen to affect negatively the learner's production in L2, the simultaneous use of both languages is viewed as disorderly and to be avoided. Two problems can be noted with respect to the use of the term 'interference' when referring to the alternate use of two languages within the same conversation as observed in bilingual communities. First, the term is either inappropriate or outright wrong. An important dimension in interference as studied in SLA is directionality. L1 interferes with L2 and not the other way round. In the case of language alternation in the same conversation, this is not necessarily the case. In fact, in most cases of language alternation described in the literature, the base language[3] is the speaker's L1. The direction of switch would therefore be from L1 to L2 and not the other way round. Secondly, the negative connotations that interference is associated with in SLA are carried over when the term 'interference' is uncritically used as a short-hand, outside the SLA context, to refer to the use of two languages within the same conversation.

The second pseudo-scientific term I can consider here is 'borrowing' (but see below). Like interference, the term 'borrowing' implies more or less clear boundaries between the two languages involved (see language separateness above). One variety is the borrowing language while the other is the lending language.[4] Behind this metaphor is an issue not only of attitudes to and views about the languages involved but also about the linguistic repertoire of the bilingual speaker. One language is seen as impoverished, as incapable of expressing the totality of the speaker's experience, hence the need to borrow from the other. Of course, nobody disputes the fact that there is a relationship between language and its speakers', monolinguals and bilinguals alike, experiences. The wider the experiences, the larger the linguistic tools to express them. For bilinguals, specifically, experiences are lived in both/all of their languages. The notion of 'diglossia' (Ferguson, 1959; Fishman, 1967; see Chapter 5) has been used to describe this state of affairs. A key feature of diglossia is what Fishman calls 'domain congruency' between social situations, including topics, and language varieties. As a result, on some occasions, especially where self-control is not very high, aspects of experiences are talked about using the language they are associated with. Consider the following account by a French–English bilingual, who lives in the United States, of why she uses both French and English (reported in Grosjean, 1982: 150).

> The reason why I use so many words in English when I speak with French speaking people is because I find it very hard to convey certain ideas or information about my daily life in this country (the U.S) in a language other than English. Notions such as 'day care center', 'finger food', 'window shopping', 'pot-luck dinners', need a few sentences to explain in French.

That is, used to speaking about some realities of her everyday life in English, the speaker finds it difficult to express them in French. Among bilinguals, this is a very common reality.

But is 'borrowing' the appropriate term for describing this reality? Consider the following example from my Kinyarwanda–French bilingual data. The conversation was recorded at Lancaster University where participants B and C, coming from Brussels, were visiting participant A (the author), then a PhD student. Right before the example, participants B and C have invited A to reciprocate the visit, but A hesitates to accept the invitation saying that it would be better if he could combine the visit and his fieldwork. In the example, the French item '*documentation*' as well as the integrated form 'wakwi*documenta*', used in the specific sense of library research, may be said to have been used here because participants are talking about the specific activity of doing research. As in Rwanda, French was the medium of higher education and research (see Section I.5), one could speak of borrowing, of 'cultural borrowing' (Myers-Scotton, 2006), to be sure. However, this cannot explain the occurrence of the many other French items (italics) in the example, items which do not refer to any specific area of experience.

*Example 2.1*

A: ndibw (.) *enfin donc* hari ibyo ngomba gu*combin*a (.) sinzi niba ngomba kujya kubikorera iBuruscli cyangwa se niba ngomba kujya iNairobi. Ariko di iBuruseri niho heza niho hari n'ibitabo.
B: Niho hari **documentation**
C: niho hari **documentation** naho iNairobi se wakora *sur quelle base*
B: **wakwidocumenta** ute (.) ibitabo byava he?

A: I think (.) well there are things I must combine (.) I don't know if I must do it in Brussels or in Nairobi. Wait a minute it's better I go to Brussels for there are also books
B: that's where there are library resources
C: that's where there are library resources as for Nairobi how can you work
B: what library resources would you use (.) where would you find books

On the other hand, at the psycholinguistic level, the term 'borrowing' reflects a particular view of the linguistic repertoire of the bilingual person. The linguistic repertoire of the bilingual speaker is seen as compartimentalised between the two languages (see language separateness above). The poorer section of the repertoire borrows from the richer section. It is from such views that the now discarded notions of 'semilingualism' and 'balanced bilingualism' originate. Cummins defined semilingualism as the situation where a speaker has 'less than native-like skills in both languages' (1979: 228). As it is clear in the definition, for proponents of semilingualism, the yardstick for measuring bilingual competence is monolingual competence. A balanced bilingual is one with monolingual competence in both languages. Anybody short of this ideal is said to be semilingual, either in one language or in both languages. In the latter case, authors have spoken of 'double semilingualism'. Because of this lack of 'full' competence in one of the languages in contact, in actual situations of use, bilingual speakers would borrow from their stronger language while speaking the weaker one. Consider the following example from a service encounter in Barcelona. In the example, there is indeed a problem of competence in the language-of-interaction (Auer, 1984), namely Catalan, and it is signalled as such by participants. Therefore, one could say that CU1 borrows from Castilian (italics) while speaking Catalan (plain). However, among bilingual speakers, most cases of the use of two languages within the same conversation do not follow this pattern.

*Example 2.2*

1. CU1: allò que se'n diu- que se'n diu espera' t t'ho haig de dir en castellà perquè sé com es diu en català
2. OWN: *viva la gracia*!
3. CU1: és greu eh?
4. OWN: [digues
5. CU1: [*codillos*
6. OWN: si (.) *codillos*
7. CU2: ah no sé com es diu en cataá [*codillos*
8. CU1:                                             [jo tompoc

1. CU1: that which is called- chich is called hang on I've got to tell you in Castilian because I don't know what it's called in Catalan
2. OWN: hurray!
3. CU1: it's awful isn't it?
4. OWN: say it
5. CU1: shanks
6. OWN: yes shanks
7. CU2: oh I don't know how to say 'shanks' in Catalan
8. CU1: me neither

To be sure, the notion of semilingualism itself has now been rejected, especially by Martin-Jones and Romaine (1985), Romaine (1995) who have referred to it as a 'half-baked theory of communicative competence' and 'a container view of competence'. An alternative view of the bilingual repertoire is the one proposed by Grosjean (1986) according to whom 'the bilingual person is a competent but specific speaker-hearer'. In Grosjean, the linguistic repertoire of a bilingual person is seen as consisting of a continuum, the end points of which are the two languages and, along the continuum, a variety of language alternation styles. In that sense, Grosjean rejects any attempt to see the bilingual as consisting of 'two monolinguals in one person' (1989). In this case, if the bilingual's linguistic repertoire is seen as fully integrated, it does not make sense to say that, in talk, there is borrowing. At best, as Muysken suggests, there is 'sharing' (2000: 69).

Briefly, the issue of language alternation among bilingual speakers, wherever it is observed, is a real concern. Wherever language alternation is a significant social practice, people develop ways of making sense of it. Drawing on prevalent language ideologies, they often view it as a disorderly phenomenon and express those views in a variety of ways, including the use of derogatory names and pseudo-scientific terms such as 'interference' and 'borrowing'. These lay explanations, according to which language alternation is a disorderly phenomenon, clearly miss a very important point. They fail to account for the very possibility of talk in two languages. If language alternation were a disorderly phenomenon, talk in two languages would simply be impossible. One may assume that it is because lay explanations fail to account for the possibility of language alternation that analysts have had to focus on it and develop what I have referred to above as fully-fledged theories.

## 2.3. Some 'en-résumé' practices by linguists

As I have said above, the use of two languages within the same conversation is very noticeable. Therefore, linguists themselves have not failed to notice it. Having noticed language alternation, linguists deal with it in either of two ways. Either they develop fully-fledged theories of its orderliness or they adopt en-résumé practices. As I have already indicated, en-résumé practices consist of the various ways in which analysts refer to language alternation in a short-hand fashion, usually before a fully-fledged theory is developed. Such practices are adopted by way of organising the data before analysis, identifying what is interesting to follow up and what is not. Different practices may be found in the literature and it is not my intention to review them all here. Rather, by way of an illustration, I will discuss the three most common ones, namely the distinction between 'borrowing' and 'code-switching', that between 'code-mixing' and 'code-switching' and that between 'alternational' and 'insertional code-switching'.

### 2.3.1. Borrowing vs code-switching

The first way of categorising language alternation data is in terms of borrowing vs code-switching. When this scheme is employed, the aim is invariably to leave out those cases of language alternation which are categorised as borrowing in order to focus on those which are categorised as code-switching. Among language alternation specialists, the term 'borrowing' often has a specific meaning different from the one we have discussed above. According to Grosjean (1982), a distinction ought to be made between 'language borrowing' and 'speech borrowing' while other researchers such as Poplack *et al.*'s (1988) distinguish between 'established loans' and 'nonce borrowing' respectively. By language borrowing, Grosjean means items which, although originally from language A, have come to be integrated into language B such that speakers of language B use them without any awareness of their foreign origin. In English, for example, such established loans include words such as 'paper', 'table', 'beef' and so on. Myers-Scotton (2006: 208–232) is a good account of this process of language borrowing as is Romaine (1995: 51–67). Speech borrowing or nonce borrowing, on the other hand, refers to the use by bilingual speakers of elements from language A in a discourse mainly in language B. While language borrowing passes unnoticed, speech borrowing is noticeable and the negative attitudes I have mentioned above apply to it. Consider the following instance of talk among two bilingual Rwandans:

*Example 2.3*

    A: noneho rero nka bariya b'impunzi ukuntu bigenda (.) ba bagira ba- a **amashuri** hano ni *privé quoi* (.) ni *privé* mbega (.) kuburyo rero kugirango aze muri iyi **université** agomba kwishyura.

    A: As for refugees the way it works (.) they have- schools here are *private* (.) they are *private* (.) so for him to attend this *university* he must pay

In this example, two languages are involved, namely Kinyarwanda and French. Assuming Kinyarwanda to be the base language, we could say that the elements in italics are all candidates for the category 'speech borrowing'. However, the element *'amashuri'* (schools) is not originally Kinyarwanda either. Originally, it is German and could have entered Kinyarwanda during the brief period of German colonisation of Rwanda (1890–1916). Alternatively, it could be seen as having come into Kinyarwanda via Swahili where the word 'shuli' (school) is attested. Either way, the point to note is that, nowadays, it is fully Kinyarwanda. In this respect, it is interesting to compare it to the item *'université'*, which I have noted as French. Equivalent expressions exist in Kinyarwanda, notably 'amashuri makuru' and 'kaminuza'. Briefly, in the example, 'université' would be a case of speech borrowing, while 'amashuri' is a case of language borrowing.

While everybody agrees on the idea of language borrowing, in the literature, there is very little agreement about the category of speech borrowing or nonce borrowing and how it differs from code-switching. While some researchers (e.g. Boeschton, 1990; Poplack, 1990) distinguish between (nonce) borrowing and code-switching, others (e.g. Treffers-Daller, 1990; Myer-Scotton, 1993a; Muysken, 2000) do not. Thus, Poplack and Meechan (1995: 200) write,

> 'Code-switching' may be defined as the juxtaposition of sentences or sentence fragments, each of which is internally consistent with the morphological and syntactic (and optionally phonological) rules of its lexifier language.... 'Borrowing' is the adaptation of lexical material to the morphological and syntactic (and usually phonological) patterns of the recipient language.

Consider Example 2.4 below. In the example, the elements 'ku-ku-*embrouill*-a' and 'u-mu-*génocidaire*' are mixed, have been adapted in the sense that the morphemes that make them up come from both French and Kinyarwanda. In the case of 'ku-ku-*embrouill*-a', French has provided the content morpheme (embrouill-) and Kinyarwanda has provided the system morphemes (ku-, ku-, and –a) (see Chapter 3). In that sense, according to Poplack and associates, these two words would be instances of nonce borrowing.

*Example 2.4*

A: ubungubu ujya ahantu bashaka kukw*embrouilla* no kuguturumbanya bakavuga ngo uri umu*génocidaire*
B: ngo uri *génocidaire*

A: Now if people want to mistreat you they say you are a 'genocider'
B: saying you are genocider

On the other hand, consider Example 2.5. In this example, again assuming that Kinyarwanda is the base language, all the highlighted items are code-switching for they consistently observe the syntax of French. Take for example turn 3. In the element 'vous privileg-iez', French morphology is applied as the verb agrees in number with the subject (2nd PL).

*Example 2.5*

1. A: ni wowe nanjye turi kuvugana
2. B: hmm
3. C: *en fait vous privilé[giez-*
4. A:                                *la notion de langue déjà*
5. C: ihita igenda
6. A: *tu mets la notion de langue*
7. C: igenda
8. A: *dans mon travail je la mets en cause*

1. A: It's you and me who are talking
2. B: hmm
3. C: in fact you focus on-
4. A:                                the notion of language
5. C: disappears
6. A: you put (in bracket) the notion of language
7. C: disappears
8. A: in my work I question it

Researchers disagree as to whether borrowing and code-switching are different, evoking a variety of arguments. By way of illustrating how controversial the distinction can be, consider Example 2.4 again, particularly the pair of words 'umu*génocidaire*' and '*génocidaire*'. Both words are equivalent semantically, for they have the same content morpheme. They both mean, 'someone who killed people in the context of the Rwandan genocide'. From a grammatical point of view, they are obviously different, for one is integrated in the morphological system of Kinyarwanda while the other is not. Therefore, depending on whether one sees these processes of integration as important or not, a decision will have to be made whether to include both in their analysis or not. Also consider Example 2.5 again, especially turns 4 and 5. In turn 5, C completes the sentence that A has started in turn 4. So for all practical purposes, this is one sentence. However, note that A's talk is in French, while C's talk is in Kinyarwanda. This example is interesting because the element *'la notion de langue'* could be seen as borrowing and as code-switching depending on where one stands. From one position, the noticeable aspect will be the fact that the Kinyarwanda verb forms 'i-hit-a' and 'i- gend-a' have a noun class morpheme i-, and therefore that the whole French expression *'la notion de langue'* has actually been integrated in the Kinyarwanda syntactic frame (see Chapter 4). That is, from this position, the element behaves like borrowing. From another position, however, the noticeable aspect of this piece of talk is that, internally, the element is consistent with the grammar of French. From this position, it would be seen as code-switching (see constituent insertion and internal island in Chapter 3). In other words, even from a grammatical point of view, the distinction borrowing vs code-switching cannot be taken for granted.

For those researchers who investigate the socio-functional dimension of language alternation, the problem is felt and expressed differently. The issue is not whether a particular word is or is not integrated, but rather whether it expresses a function that it would not express depending on whether it was integrated or not. In the case of 'u-mu-*génociadire*' and '*génocidaire*' in Example 2.4, the two words contribute to the conversational strategy of repetition for agreement (Pomerantz, 1984). By repeating what an interlocutor has just said, a speaker expresses strong agreement with their interlocutor. From this perspective, '*génocidaire*' is a repetition of 'umu*genocidaire*' for all practical purposes. In other words, from this perspective, integration or lack of it is not an issue.

In short, the disagreement among researchers as to whether to distinguish between borrowing and code-switching is important, for it is consequential for the kind of analysis they proceed to do. The distinction or lack of it is a pre-theoretical issue. Those who make the distinction do so in order to organise the data before analysis can begin in a particular way and they do so because of the particular research interests they have. Thus, once they have categorised some elements as code-switching and some others as borrowing, they go on to analyse only those elements they consider to be code-switching. On the other hand, those who do not make the distinction look at the totality of the data, whether elements have been integrated or whether they have not, with important implications for the final results. In other words, the distinction should not be seen merely as a technicality, as a mere way of talking about language alternation. Rather, it significantly affects the final account of the orderliness of language alternation analysts end up with.

### 2.3.2. Code-mixing vs code-switching

The distinction between code-mixing and code-switching is even more complex. The first difficulty resides at the level of the term 'code' itself. For some researchers, the notion of code and that of language are equivalent such that they can be used one for the other. This is the most traditional view and I need not dwell on it. The very definition of code-switching as the use of two languages within the same conversation assumes such a view of the notion of language and that of code. For those in this category, there is no difference between code mixing and language mixing. Consider the following statement from Muysken (2000: 1):

> The question discussed here is: how can a bilingual speaker combine elements from two languages when processing mixed sentences? I am using the term **code-mixing** to refer to all cases where items and grammatical features from **two languages** appear in one sentence.

Conversely, Morimoto (1999) entitles her paper 'Making words in two languages: A prosodic account of Japanese–English **language mixing**', defining language mixing as 'a phenomenon in which morphemes from two languages – Japanese and English – are combined to form a word (or phrase)' (1999: 23).

Other researchers (Alvarez-Caccamo, 1998; Meeuwis and Blommaert, 1998; Gafaranga and Torras, 2001), however, see the notion of 'language' and that of 'code' as different. 'Language' is a grammatical notion while 'code' is a semiotic notion. A 'communicative code' may, but need not, be linguistic. For example, communication may well take place without the use of language, for example by means of gestures. Researchers in this category argue that the use of two languages itself may be the code for participants on specific occasions (see Chapter 6). Thus, in this understanding, language mixing and code-switching are different. This is precisely Auer's (1999) position when he chooses to use the term 'language mixing' instead of 'code mixing' in the title 'From codeswitching via **language mixing** to fused lects'. As we will see below, for Auer, a code is oriented to as such by participants in a conversation. In language mixing, although two languages are used, they are not oriented to by participants as separate entities. Therefore, it would not be adequate to speak of code-mixing in this case.[5]

The second difficulty is that of the relationship between code-switching and code-mixing. First, in some cases, the term 'code-switching' is used with a generalising meaning to refer to actually different types of language contact phenomena and, in some other cases, 'language/code-mixing' is. Consider the following title by Wei (2001): 'Lemma congruence checking between language as an organizing principle in intrasentential **codeswitching**'. In this title, the term 'codeswitching' is used as an umbrella for possibly different phenomena, but what is being taken as relevant is the fact that two languages are involved. In that sense, the term 'code/language mixing' could have been equally valid. Or consider the following statement from Auer (1998: 1):

> Thus, **code-switching** has developed from what used to be looked upon as 'possibly a somewhat peculiar... act' (Luckmann, 1983: 97) into a subject matter which is recognised to be able to shed light on fundamental linguistic issues.

Here the term 'code-switching' is used to refer to the whole subject area within which various phenomena of language contact are investigated. It is in this sense that the term 'code-mixing' is used by Muysken (2000) and 'language mixing' is used by Wei (2001).

Second, in some cases, code-switching and language/code-mixing are seen as two different phenomena. For example, in his study of language use in Johannesburgh, Herbert (2001: 225–226), makes the following three-way distinction which involves both code-mixing and code-switching:

> the present model [...] employs a three-way distinction between **borrowing, code-mixing** and **codeswitching**. Borrowings and code mixes are incorporated lexical items, which vary along temporal and spatial considerations. Borrowed forms are typically known and used by both bilingual and monolingual speakers, they are widely distributed through the community and they typically reveal a process of historical incorporation. Code mixes on the other hand are synchronic incorporation of lexical material from one language into a second. The term codeswitching is thus reserved for instances in which the operative grammar in conversation changes.

Thus, according to this view, in Example 2.3, the word 'amashuri' would be a case of borrowing, in Example 2.4, the item 'umugénocidaire' would be a case of code-mixing and, in the same example, the item 'génocidaire' would be a case of code-switching. Example 2.5 can be used to show some of the difficulties in maintaining the distinction between code-mixing and code-switching on grammatical grounds. In this example, the element 'la notion de langue' is obviously consistent with French grammar. Therefore, it could be said to be a case of code-switching. However, as we have seen, participants in the interaction have actually taken it to be integrated into Kinyarwanda and assigned it to a particular noun class as revealed by the class morpheme [i-] in 'i-hita' and 'i-genda'). Therefore, the question is, which of the two categories to retain?

Herbert and many others like him distinguish code-switching from code-mixing on grammatical grounds. Others make the same distinction, but on functional grounds. Right after Blom and Gumperz (1972) had claimed that code-switching (generalising sense) was functional, Sankoff (1972) questioned the idea that every instance of language alternation was functional. Later, Kachru (1978) referred to cases where no specific function could be attributed to specific instances as code-mixing. However, a more explicit account of the difference between code-switching and code-mixing, from a functional perspective, is given in Auer (1999) and I shall spend some time clarifying the issues involved from Auer's perspective. Remember that, as we have said, Auer is one of the researchers who refrain from equating the notion of language and that of code. Speaking of the difference between language mixing and code-switching, Auer (1999: 310) writes,

> CS (code-switching) will be reserved for those cases in which the juxtaposition of two languages is perceived and interpreted as a locally meaningful event by participants. The term 'LM' (language mixing), on the other hand, will be used for those cases of the juxtaposition of two languages in which the use of two languages is meaningful (to participants) not in a local but only in a more global sense, that is, when seen as a recurrent pattern.

Elsewhere, he goes on: 'Mixed codes (language mixing) contain numerous and frequent cases of alternation between two languages when seen from the linguist's point of view, but these singular occurrences of alternation do not carry meaning qua language choice'

(1998: 16). That is, the difference between language mixing and code-switching is that code-switching is locally functional while language mixing is not. Consider Example 2.6 below:

Example 2.6

1. A: ubu rero ab (.) buretse (.) abazayuruwa bagiye gutangira ngo (.) **fukuza munyarwanda** (.) [( )
2. B:                             [ *avec raison (.)* [ *puisque* turi imbwa
3. A:                                     [( ) ((laughter)) ariko
4. C: *avec raison* (.) none se none wanzanira ibibazo iwanjye

1. A: now Zairians Zair (.) wait a minute (.) Zairians are going to start saying **kick out Rwandan** (.) [( )
2. B:                                 [*rightly so (.) [as* we do not deserve any respect
3. A:                                     [( ) ((laughter)) but
4. C: *rightly so* (.) if you bring problems to my door

In the example, the Swahili element '*fukuza munyarwannda*' is locally functional and is oriented to as such by participants themselves. It is meant to document the identity Zairian (see Chapter 7 for a full analysis of the example). On the other hand, no specific interactional motivation can be attached to the elements '*avec raison quisque*' in turn 2 and '*avec raison*' in turn 4. Therefore, while '*fukuza munyarwanda*' would be an instance of code-switching, these other items would be instances of language mixing.

The notion of functionality as a criterion for telling code-mixing and code-switching needs to be made very clear. It is beyond doubt that, within the so-called code-mixing, local functionality can be observed. Consider Example 2.7 below:

Example 2.7

1. A: izo *bus* zagarutse-
2. B:                   *vides*
3. A: *vides*
4. C: *c' est vrai?*

1. A: those buses came back
2. B: empty
3. A: empty
4. C: really?

In this instance, we have a case of what Lerner (1991) calls 'sentence completion', that is the case of the joint construction of utterances. A's sentence (turn 1) is completed by B in turn 2. By completing A's sentence, B shows strong agreement (Pomerantz, 1984). And as the transcript shows, in this particular case, this process of utterance completion involves language alternation. Therefore, we will say that, in the example, a local conversational function is accomplished and coincides with language alternation. The question is, is this code-switching or code-mixing?

A second reading of Auer's statement makes it clear what he means. One can speak of code-switching if and only if a local function is accomplished by virtue of the 'languageness' of the relevant element. Consider Example 2.6 above. As we have seen, the function of the Swahili item '*fukuza munyarwanda*' is to identify the reported speaker as Zairian. This effect is achieved, not because of what is said, but because of the very use of Swahili. Note that use of any other language, Kinyarwanda for example, would not achieve the same effect. In Example 2.7, on the other hand, the same function of agreement could have been served independently of the language used. An example is Example 2.5. As we have seen, in this example, C starts a sentence in turn 3 using French, and A completes it in turn 4 using Kinyarwanda. In other words, the direction of the switch in the joint production of utterances does not matter. Would the fact that there is a switch be in itself the significant factor? The answer has to be 'No'. As Example 2.8 below shows, utterance completion need not involve language alternation. Participants are saying that, here in Europe, unlike in Africa, it would be expensive to have someone to help with housework. In turn 1, A starts a sentence, B completes it in turn 2 and the completion is acknowledged in turn 3. In the process, no language alternation occurs. The whole sequence is accomplished in Kinyarwanda.

*Example 2.8*

1. A: ba u- ushatse umuntu ugute[era
2. B:                                  [**wamuhemba**
3. A: **wamuhemba** (.) ibihumbi mirongo euh itanu intadatu

1. A: if you looked for somebody to cook for you
2. B: you'd pay them
3. A: you'd pay them (.) fifty to sixty thousand

Therefore, according to Auer, while the use of Swahili in Example 2.6 is a case of code-switching, the use of Kinyarwanda in Example 2.5 and that of French in Example 2.7 are instances of code-mixing even though, in all three cases, a local function is accomplished.

Also consider Example 2.9 below. In this example, as in the whole data set, both French and Kinyarwanda are used. Therefore, one would be tempted to disregard language choice in this instance as yet another case of code-mixing. However, a close observation reveals that something else is going on. In turn 1, there is a process of attribution (icyo bita – what they call) which makes the use of French look like a case of direct speech reporting, with the possibility of it being medium reporting (Gafaranga, 1998; Chapter 7). Following this, French is used (*ordre établi*). Secondly, in turn 3, A goes on to explain the meaning of '*ordre établi*' in a manner similar to what happens in the case of what Gafaranga (2000b) calls 'medium repair'. As argued in Gafaranga (2000b), medium repair occurs when an element perceived as alien to the code participants are currently using slips in the talk. Therefore, we will say that, by applying the same process, A constructs the item '*ordre établi*' as alien, as an instance of other-language. And he does so in order to put emphasis on what he is saying.

*Example 2.9*

1. A: bagira icyo bita (.) **order pre-établi**
2. B: hmm ino aha
3. A: *order* ita- udashobora gukoza ho n' umutwe w'urutoki

1. A: they have what they call (.) pre-determined system
2. B: Hmm over here
3. A: a system you cannot touch

Briefly, other-languageness itself, and by implication its functionality, is a local accomplishment. Thus, from a functional perspective, the distinction code-switching vs code-mixing cannot be established a priori. It is a discoverable object.

### 2.3.3. Insertional vs alternational language mixing

Another distinction which is often made in language alternation studies is between 'insertional' and 'alternational' types. This distinction is important because it is sometimes believed to relate in some ways to the one between mixing and switching (see above). According to Auer (1999: 313), prototypical code-switching is alternational, while 'it is a typical feature of LM (language mixing) that alternational and insertional strategies converge' (p. 315). In addition to structural differences, there also would be a psycholinguistic and, more importantly, a sociolinguistic basis for the distinction between insertional and alternational bilingual language use (Muysken, 2000: 8–9). Altenational language use would be 'frequent in stable bilingual communities with a tradition of language separation ... (while) insertion is frequent in colonial settings and recent immigrants, where there is considerable asymmetry in the speakers' proficiency in the two languages' (Muysken, 2000: 8–9). In both cases, it would not be far-fetched to read an implication that insertional language alternation is disorderly.

For all the above reasons, researchers often feel the need to state, by way of describing their data, that the language contact phenomena in them are either insertional or alternational. Thus, in Backus and Van Hout (1995: 17–18), one reads,

> Three conversations from our Turkish–Dutch data were selected for analysis in this paper. Earlier studies of CS patterns in the Dutch–Turkish community (cf Backus, 1993) revealed that two different types of CS are in use. Members of the first and intermediate generations showed mainly **insertional CS**, ... On the other hand, members of the second generation tended towards **alternational CS**.

Backus and Van Hout define alternational code-switching as the one occurring 'at clause or sentence boundary' (1995: 18). Conversely, insertional code-switching is understood as one occurring within the clause or sentence. This corresponds to an earlier distinction by Poplack (1980) between what she called inter-sentential code-switching and intrasentential code-switching respectively. Because of this correspondence, researchers also describe their data either as intra- or extrasential code-switching, often without specifying exactly what this means. Thus, a title by Wei (2001) reads, 'Lemma congruence checking between languages as an organizing principle in intrasentential codeswitching'. Throughout the paper, this notion of intrasentential code-switching is used without any attempt to define it. Conversely, describing their data, Shin and Milroy (2000: 357) write,

> the entire corpus for the Korean–Korean pairs consisted of approximately 8,000 utterances, unevenly distributed across subject and activity types. Figure 1 shows the percentage of **extrasentential codeswitching** (e.g. codeswitching across utterance boundaries) for each subject for each of the three activity types.

And, in a note attached to the above statement, one reads,

> Unlike extrasentential codeswitching, **intrasentential switching** has often received attention of researchers attempting to formulate grammatical constraints on codeswitching.

That is to say, for these authors, data can be categorised either as intra or as extra (inter) sentential. However, also note that, here, the notion of 'sentence' and that of 'utterance' seem to be equated.

Other ways of signalling the distinction insertion–alternation include reference to the main language and subordinate language as in:

> The present paper is concerned with codeswitching in two minority languages: Yiddish in Israel and Low German in Northwest Germany. Both are spoken languages used mainly for private communication. Both are in contact with dominant written languages,... The study is based on data of spoken Yiddish recorded in Israel...and Low German... **In the corpora, Yiddish and Low German are the main languages of communication (L1) with codeswitching into Hebrew/German (L2)**. (Reershemius, 2001: 177)

By signalling that Yiddish and Low German are the main languages of communication, Reershemius might be seen as indicating that the use of Hebrew/High German is insertional.

Finally, some researchers, in describing their data, exhibit the same ideas of insertion–alternation using terms which refer to talk organisation as in:

> The discussion in this paper will be conducted on the basis of three sets of data, namely Kinyarwanda-French data, Catalan-Castilian data and Catalan/Castilina-English data. [...] The Kinyarwanda-French data come from an African postcolonial context [...] while the Catalan-Castilian data come from Catalonia,... As a consequence, in the first set of data, frequent alternation is observed and it obtains both **within turns and between turns**.... On the other hand, in the second set of data,..., language alternation is less frequent and is mainly of the **interturn type**. (Gafaranga and Torras, 2002: 2–3)

Here, the idea that some instances of language alternation occur within turns while some other occur between turns suggests some notion of insertion vs alternation although the unit is no longer the clause or sentence, but rather the turn.

Briefly, the notion that language alternation is either insertional or alternational is very incipient, and researchers express it in various ways. However, it is important to realise that all these are short-hand ways of describing the data and no more than that. To start with, the various ways are not really equivalent. As we have seen above, some view their data in terms of sentences, some view them in terms of utterances and some others still view them in terms of turns. Thus, for example, alternation across turns may, if looked at from the sentence perspective, turn out to be insertional. Take the following Kinyarwanda–French bilingual data. A is the editor of the Rwandan Refugee Newsletter. He is telling co-participants that the publisher of the newsletter takes his time in printing the newsletter.

*Example 2.10*

1. A: ni mukuru (.) nta ibi bya *compétivité* ashyiramo
2. B: hmm
3. A: agakora- aga*tourn*a uko ashaka
4. B: *à son rythme*
5. A: *à son rythme*

1. A; he's mature (.) he's not into competition
2. B: hum
3. A: he works- prints as he wants
4. B: on his own pace
5. A: on his own pace

In the example, it is fairly uncontroversial that the French elements '*compétivité*' and '*tourn-*' are instances of insertion. However, the same cannot be said of the item '*à son rythme*'. From a turn-organisation perspective, this would be a case of alternational language choice across turns. However, from a sentence perspective, this could be intrasentential switching as B's actual sentence is 'aga*tourn*a *à son rythme*'.

In addition, even within the same perspective, the situation might actually be more complex than a simple distinction between alternation and insertion. Muysken (2000) has looked closely at the typology of what he calls 'code-mixing' from a grammatical perspective and came up with a three-way distinction: 'insertion' vs 'alternation' vs 'congruent lexicalisation' (see below). Furthermore, according to Muysken, these distinctions are not absolute ones, but rather end points of three related continua (2000: 9). Finally, according to Muysken (2000: 238–243), all three processes can be found in the same corpus of data and even within the same sentence. Consider the following piece of talk. Participants in this interaction are saying that the fact of leaving huge numbers of people in refugee camps is not likely to help in the Rwandan reconciliation process.

*Example 2.11*

A: oya (.) bariya bo bari muri *camp- camp* yo- *quelque soit le camp-* iyo ari yo yose ni *pépinière* (.) y'intuza- *du d d'une guerre*

A: No (.) as for those in (refugee) camp- as for the camp- whatever camp – whatever camp- is a breeding ground (.) for something- for war

Muysken (2000: 69–95) demonstrates convincingly that singly occurring bare nouns are to be analysed as insertions. On this basis, we take the two occurrences of 'camp' in 'muri *camp*' and '*camp* yo' respectively and that of '*pépinière*' to be insertions. As for the noun phrase '*du d d'une guerre*', it is a case of congruent lexicalisation as it occupies exactly the same syntactic slot as 'y'intuza', of which it is a recycle, without any effect on the overall syntactic structure of the sentence (see 'fragment insertion' in Chapter 3). Finally, the clause '*quelque soit le camp*' is a case of alternation. Occurring in a parenthetical construction just like its Kinyarwanda equivalent coming right after it, the clause is peripheral to the main sentence '*camp* yo ni *pépinière*...'. Evidence such as this indicates that it would be too simplistic to describe my Kinyarwanda–French data simply either as insertional or as alternational.

Briefly, researchers have developed a number of practices whereby they deal with issues of the orderliness of language alternation in a short-hand fashion. Faced with the complex task of accounting for the orderliness of language alternation, researchers order the data in terms of dichotomous categories such as borrowing vs code-switching, code-mixing vs code-switching, alternational vs insertional code-switching, and so on. In so doing, they actually mean that the orderliness of some pieces of data can be taken for granted and therefore is uninteresting, while that of some other data is interesting and worth the analyst's attention. A close inspection of these categories shows that they are actually very fuzzy, and especially that actual data does not come pre-packaged into these categories. Therefore, the value of these practices as accounts of the orderliness of language alternation is limited and this is the reason I have labelled them as 'quasi-theories of order' even though their value as 'en-résumé' practices in the practical task of developing accounts for the orderliness of language alternation cannot be doubted.

## 2.4. Conclusion

In this chapter, we have begun to look at the various ways in which the issue of order in language alternation among bilingual speakers can be addressed. First, we said that lay people view language alternation as a disorderly phenomenon. Evidence used to support this includes pejorative names, negative attitudes and the use of terms such as borrowing and interference, both of which suggest either inadequate mastery of one of the languages involved or negative influence of one language on the other. A major problem with this view is that it is actually unsupportable. If language alternation was random, it would not be observed, that is it would be impossible. Secondly, we looked at what I have called 'en-résumé' practices by linguists. These are short-hand ways linguists use to describe language alternation data, before they go on to develop fully-fledged accounts of the data. These practices consist of categorising language alternation data, of ordering it, in terms of dichotomies such as borrowing vs code-switching, code-switching vs code-mixing, alternational vs insertional language alternation. I have demonstrated that these categories, although useful as short-hand tools, do not necessarily correspond to what actually happens in the data, that they are inadequate as accounts of the orderliness of language alternation. In the remaining chapters, I will look at fully-fledged theories of language alternation, starting, in the next chapter, with grammatical accounts of order in talk in two languages.

## Notes

1. [For us, French is the French language, vehicle for the French culture and its Belgian, Canadian and Swiss corollaries. Kinyarwanda is the Bantu language, vehicle for the Rwandan culture. Diluted French, whether it is referred to as 'Rwandisme' or any other 'Africanism', evokes a feeling of repulsion. The same feeling is experienced with diluted Kinyarwanda that some are already referring to as 'Ikinyafransa', which consists of a rude mixture and inopportune borrowings.]
2. A more positive view of this effect is usually referred to as (positive) *transfer*.

3. A more technical discussion of issues regarding the notion of base language can be found in Auer (2000). Related issues will be dealt with as appropriate throughout the book. For the purpose of the discussion here, 'base language' can be defined as the language used as the default and from which alternation is a switch from.
4. A supposedly more positive way of talking about this is in terms of 'guest' and 'host' language.
5. It is precisely because I am of the view that the notion of language and of code are different that I prefer the term 'language alternation' rather than 'code-switching' as the umbrella term.

# 3
# Grammatical Order in Talk in Two Languages

## 3.1. Introduction

As I have indicated in Section 1.2, order is the possibility of social action. Without order, social action is impossible. We have also seen that language alternation can be seen as an issue of order in talk as social action. Therefore, the role of analysts is to account for its orderliness. As indicated in Torras and Gafaranga (2002) and expanded on in Gafaranga (2007), the territory of research on language alternation can be represented, in the form of a flow chart, as in Table 3.1.

In the chart, each terminal node represents an approach to language alternation. In this chapter, I will be concerned with the first terminal node, namely the grammatical perspective on language alternation. According to Muysken (1995: 180–181; 2000: 3–4), the grammatical perspective on language alternation divides into two, namely alternational approaches and insertional approaches. Alternational approaches are also sometimes referred to as 'equivalance' approaches, because they assume equivalence between the two languages, while insertional approaches are referred to as 'dominance/asymmetrical' approaches, because they assume that one language is dominant while the other is subordinate. Therefore, in the representation above, the node 'grammatical perspective' details as shown in Table 3.2.

In this chapter, I will discuss and illustrate each of these two approaches.

## 3.2. Grammar as an issue of order

The starting point for any grammatical account of language alternation is that, as Muysken states, if we take 'a strong system-oriented view'

Table 3.1 Studies of language alternation (i)

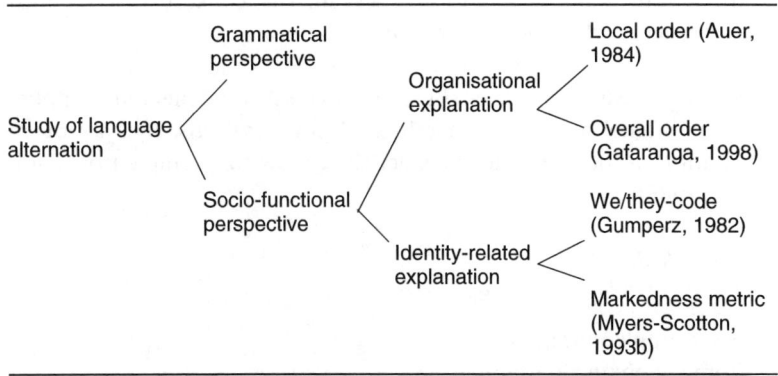

Table 3.2 Grammatical perspectives on language alternation

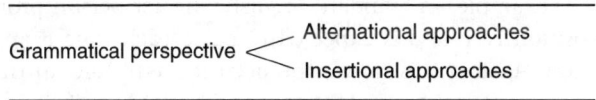

and conceive of 'the grammar of each single language as a system *où tout se tient* (everything holds together) (then)...*code-switching is impossible in principle*...' (1995: 195–96) (my emphasis). That is to say, the starting point for any grammatical account is the view that, at the level of grammar, language alternation is an issue of order. To begin to appreciate this, it is necessary to remind ourselves that talk, whether monolingual or bilingual, is organised at different levels. For example, studies in Conversation Analysis have shown that talk is an orderly activity at the level of turn-taking (Sacks *et al.*, 1978), the level of the chaining of actions (Schegloff and Sacks, 1973), repair (Schegloff *et al.*, 1977) and so on. However, there is yet another level of talk organisation which is of most relevance for the study of language alternation. As we have seen in Chapter 2, Auer (1999) argues that, in talk in two languages, functions can be served by virtue of the languageness of the elements used. Behind this claim is, of course, the assumption that talk is orderly at the level of its languageness, at the level of language choice. Indeed, according to Gafaranga (1999), language choice itself is 'a significant aspect of talk organisation'.

At the level of grammar, these ideas that talk is organised at the level of its languageness are best expressed in Myers-Scotton's (2002: 120) Uniform Structure Principle. The principle provides that

A given constituent type in any language has a uniform structure and the requirements of well-formedness for this constituent type must be observed whenever the constituent appears.

According to Myers-Scotton, this is a universal principle and it applies in monolingual as well as in bilingual conversations. By way of an illustration of the principle, consider the following example from John Agard (1985):

*Example 3.1*

Me not no Oxford don,
me a simple immigrant
from Clapham Common.

Any speaker of Standard English will recognise this sentence as ungrammatical. For example, in Standard English, the 1st person pronoun in subject position is 'I' and is expected to be so each time it appears in that position. Against this norm, the occurrence of 'me' in the above sentence is noticed as deviant. Likewise, in Standard English, the copula is required. Against this background, its absence in the sentence above is noticeable. In Standard English, negation in the form of 'not' cannot be followed by another. Here again, this norm renders the double negation visible. That is to say, to a speaker of Standard English, the sentence is striking because it repeatedly violates the Uniform Structure Principle. Faced with these violations, speakers of Standard English will interpret them either as a problem to be repaired or as functionally motivated. It is actually this latter possibility which has allowed John Agard (1985) to write the sentence above in his poem 'Listen Mr Oxford Don', confident that readers would see it, not as evidence of lack of competence in English on his part, but as intentionally conveying a specific meaning. That is to say, John Agar was able to produce the sentence only because the Uniform Structure Principle is used as a scheme of interpretation by speakers of Standard English. In other words, the orderliness of the sentence above, that is its possibility, is accountable with reference to the Uniform Structure Principle.

In talk in two languages, as Myers-Scotton says (2006: 242–243), structural uniformity cannot be taken for granted and this is the reason why, according to Muysken (1995: 195–196), language alternation is 'impossible in principle'. Mismatches between the systems in contact may appear at different levels. Consider Example 3.2 below.

*Example 3.2*

A: *la notion de language déjà-*
B:                       ihita igenda

A: the notion of language-
B:                       disappears

In this jointly constructed sentence, there is equivalence between the syntax of French and that of Kinyarwanda, for both are S+V languages and this would appear to be the reason alternation at the level of the subject has been possible. At another level, however, there is no congruence. In Kinyarwanda, the verb must agree in class with its subject (see Chapter 4) while, French not being a class language, no such agreement exists in this language. Therefore, the juxtaposition of French and Kinyarwanda at this point could run against the Uniform Structure Principle at this level of class agreement and therefore make the sentence impossible. As the sentence has actually been produced, the aim of grammar would be to describe the methods participants have used to overcome this impossibility. Also consider the clause 'abapowa batanga *leurs candidats'* in Example 3.3 below.

*Example 3.3*

1. A: ((laugh)). *Bon,* haza igihe cyo ku*noma les Ministres* (.) *du Gouvernement à base élargi,* irimo na FPR.
2. B: hmm
3. A: abapowa batanga ***leurs candidats***

1. A: ((laugh)). So time came to appoint ministers for the enlarged Government, in which the RPF would be represented
2. B: hmm
3. A: the Powa faction gave their candidates

This sentence can be analysed into major constituents as follows:

| ABAPOWA | BATANGA | LEURS CANDIDATS |
|---|---|---|
| subject: | VERB | OBJ |

As the analysis shows, in the sentence, there is structural uniformity because, although two languages are involved, both have the same constituent order, namely Subj + Verb + Obj. At another level, however, the two languages are divergent. In French, the structure of NP (noun phrase), such as the Obj., is QUANTIFIER + N. On the other hand, NPs in Kinyarwanda follow the structure N + QUANTIFIER. Therefore, in principle, alternation at the level of Obj. is impossible. A grammatical account of the orderliness of language alternation in the sentence would explain why, despite this in-principle impossibility, the sentence has been produced. Presumably, cross-linguistic differences such as those illustrated in these examples are common. Therefore, the aim of grammatical accounts of language alternation should be to demonstrate how bilingual speakers achieve a sense of uniformity despite diversity, how they use linguistic resources available to maintain a sense of structural orderliness. My aim in this chapter is to see how current grammatical accounts address this essential issue of order.

## 3.3. An alternational model of language alternation

Above, we have seen that grammatical accounts of language alternation are either alternational or insertional. The most popular alternational model of language alternation has been developed by Poplack and associates in a series of publications since the 1980s. However, it is important to note that, although the model is generally said to be alternational, from its conception, it contained an element of insertion (see, for example, the notion of 'borrowing'). And recent developments of the model, especially in collaboration with Meechan (Meechan and Poplack, 1995; Poplack and Meechan, 1995), have added further weight to this dimension of the model.

### 3.3.1. Original constraints model

As we have seen, Poplack makes a distinction between code-switching and nonce borrowing. In Chapter 2, we have seen that nonce borrowing consists of elements of language A which have been integrated morphologically (and maybe phonologically) into the system of language B. Usually such elements consist of singly occurring lexical items. To account for the difference between borrowing and code-switching, Poplack postulates her first constraint, namely the 'free morpheme constraint'. This constraint has it that, 'codes may be switched after any constituent in discourse provided that constituent is not a bound morpheme' (1980/2000: 227). That is, when there appears to be a language switch at the level of bound morphemes, say between an affix and a stem, one is dealing, not with code-switching, but rather with borrowing. Thus, in Example 3.4, the lexical items 'gu-*combin-*a' and ku-i-*document-*a' are nonce borrowings, because Kinyarwanda-bound morphemes (gu- / ku-, i- a) have been added to French stems (*combin-* and *document-*).

*Example 3.4*

1. A: ndibw- *enfin donc* hari ibyo ngomba **gu*combin*a** (.) sinzi niba ngomba kujya iBuruseri cyangwa niba ngomba kujya iNairobi. (.) Ariko di iBuruseri niho heza niho hari n'ibitabo
2. B: niho hari *documentation* (.)
3. C: niho hari *documentation*. Naho iNairobi se wakora (.) *sur quelle base?*
4. B: **wakwi*documenta*** ute- ibitabo byava he?

1. A: I think- well there are things I must combine (.) I don't know whether I must go to Brussels or whether I must go to Nairobi. (.) wait a minute it's better I go to Brussels for there are also books
2. B: There are library resources
3. C: (.) there are library resources. As for Nairobi how can you work
4. B: what library resources can you use (.) what books?

Poplack's second constraint, namely the 'equivalence constraint', specifies the possibility of code-switching and reads,

> Code-switches will tend to occur at points in the discourse where juxtaposition of L1 and L2 elements does not violate a syntactic rule of either language, i.e. at points around which the surface structures of the two languages map onto each other. According to this simple constraint, a switch is inhibited from occurring within a constituent generated by a rule from one language that is not shared by the other. (1980/2000: 228)

Elsewhere, she emphasises this point as in:

> Code-switching may be defined as the juxtaposition of sentences or sentence fragments, each of which is internally consistent with the morphological and syntactic (and optionally, phonological) rules of

its lexifier language. Intra-sentential switching may occur feely at 'equivalence sites', i.e. points around which constituent order in the two languages is homologous. (Poplack and Meechan, 1995: 200)

In these relatively simple statements, Poplack makes it absolutely clear how her model addresses the issue of order. According to this model, language alternation, at least the type she refers to as 'code-switching', is possible because it does not violate the grammar of either language. At the left of the switch point, the grammar of one language is observed, and at its right, the grammar of the other is followed. Clyne (1987) refers to this as the 'structural integrity principle'. Here is an example. Two Rwandan participants are talking about the whereabouts of another Rwandan and his skills in the French language (*the language of Molière*). Talk proceeds as follows:

Example 3.5

1. A: *à un moment donné* yabaga mu ntuuza (.) [mu mu Busuwisi
2. B: [yicaga *la langue de Molière* rwose
3. C: agenda hose T ntawamenya aho aba

1. A: at one point he was living in (.) [in in Switzerland
2. B: [he really killed the language of Molière
3. C: T travels a lot and you cannot pin him down to one point

Take the clause '*à un moment donné* yabaga mu Busuwisi' in turn 1. In this clause, the switch occurs between '*donné*' and '*yabaga*'. On the left of the switch, talk is consistently in French (see gender agreement, for example), and on its right, talk is Kinyarwanda. Furthermore, alternation between French and Kinyarwanda occurs at an identifiable syntactic point for the French fragment is an adjunct. Finally, there is congruence between French and Kinyarwanda as regards the position of such adjuncts. Indeed a sentence in Kinyarwanda could read, '**mu minsi ishize** yabaga mu Buswisi' (a few days ago, he was living in Switzerland), where 'mu minsi ishize' is an adjunct. Likewise the French fragment '*la langue de Molière*' would be code-switching because, internally consistent with the grammar of French, it appears at a point where the 'surface structures of the two languages match onto each other'. The fragment is an object and both French and Kinyarwanda are V + O languages. Briefly, according to Poplack, code-switching is possible because it does not violate the Uniform Structure Principle. Structural uniformity is maintained trough equivalence.

### 3.3.2. Later developments

*3.3.2.1. Lone L2 incorporations*

Poplack's model has been criticised with counter-examples being found for both the free morpheme constraint and the equivalence constraint (Berk-Seligson, 1986; Nortier, 1990; Treffers-Daller, 1990; Bentahila and Davies, 1991; Muysken, 2000). As Poplack herself recognises, the biggest challenge for the model 'resides in the status of lone L2 incorporations into otherwise L1 discourse' (Meechan and Poplack, 1995: 181; Poplack and Meechan, 1995: 200). The issue here is whether bare L2 incorporations should or should not be considered, like integrated lexical items, borrowings. Consider Example 3.6 below:

*Example 3.6*

1. A: ubungubu ujya ahantu bashaka **kukw*embrouilla*** no kuguturutumbya bakavuga ngo uri *génocidaire*
2. B: ngo uri **umu*génocidaire***

1. A: now if you go somewhere and that they wanted to mistreat you, they say you are a genocider
2. B: say you are a genocider

In this example, it is relatively uncontroversial that, in Poplack's view, the items 'ku-ku-*embrouill*-a' and 'u-mu-*génocidaire*' are borrowings, for they show morphological integration into the Kinyarwanda system with French stems. The issue is with the bare form '*génocidaire*' in turn 2. Likewise, in Example 3.7, the items 'a-ga-*tourn*-a' and '*à son rythme*' are clearly borrowing and code-switching respectively. The problem is the status of '*compétitivité*'.

*Example 3.7*

1. A: eh akaba nta- nta ibi bya *compétitivité* arimo (.) ni mukuru (.) aga- **agatourna** [uko ashaka
2. B:                             [*à son rythme*
3. A: *à son rythme*

1. A: he's not not into competition (.) he prints as (fast/slow) as he wants
2. B: [at his own pace
3. A: at his own pace

In a study of 'nominal structure in Wolof–French and Fongbe–French bilingual discourse', Poplack and Meechan (1995) seem to have found a solution to this problem. Such lone lexical items must be seen as borrowings.

Should all lone L2 lexical items be seen as borrowings then? All the above lone L2 items are nouns. How about other lexical categories? In another study, Meechan and Poplack (1995) have focused on 'adjective structures involving elements from French' and Wolof on the one hand and French and Fongbe on the other. An example involving Wolof from Meechan and Poplack (1995: 183) is

*Example 3.8*

Danga    y      *écoeuré*
STAT    HAB   disgusted
(You are disgusted)

In my own data, similar adjectival constructions can be found in clauses such as 'amashuri hano ni *privées*' (Schools here are private) and 'izo ni *publiques*' (those are public) extracted from Examples 3.9 and 3.10 respectively.

*Example 3.9*

A: noneho rero nka bariya b'impunzi uko bigenda- babagira ba- a **amashuri hano ni *privées*** quoi (.) ni *privées* mbega (.) kuburyo rero kugirango aze muri iyi *université*

A: as for refugees like him (.) the way it goes- they do- schools here are private (.) they are private (.) so in order to be able to attend this university...

*Example 3.10*

A: Kenya Kenya (.) ifite bya *universités*- ifite *universités* zirenga eshanu (.) **izo ni *publiques***

A: Kenya Kenya (.) has universities (.) has over five universities (.) those are public

After analysis of the data, Meechan and Poplack (1995) concluded that, in the case of French–Wolof bilingual discourse, 'lone French-origin adjectives are functioning as loan words' (p. 184), that is they are borrowings, but that, in the case French–Fongbe bilingual discourse, 'French adjectives... are virtually all code-switches...' (p. 188). The results from both studies are highly revealing. The categories 'borrowing' and 'code-switching' cannot be taken for granted (see Chapter 2). The same lexical category, 'adjective' for example, can be seen as code-switching or as borrowing depending on the language pair involved. If such is the case, it is not surprising that counter-examples to Poplack's original claims have cropped up as soon as data sets other than her original one (Spanish/English) were examined.

More important for our concern is the issue that lone L2 lexical items raise for Poplack's model as an account of order in talk in two languages. Recall that the model includes an aspect Winford (2003: 129) refers to as the 'blocking hypothesis', according to which 'switching is blocked where there is a mismatch in constituency between the two languages'. For the model to be complete, that is for the distinction 'code-switching' vs 'borrowing' to be usable as 'a scheme of interpretation' (Garfinkel, 1967), a reverse blocking hypothesis would be needed, one which would predict that borrowing will be blocked if there is equivalence. As we have just seen, L2 lexical items are sometimes integrated in the morphological system of L1, and some other times they are not. One could argue that, since language alternation is in principle impossible, in the absence of equivalence, integration of lexical items is a strategy that bilingual speakers use to achieve congruence (Sebba, 1998), to make the juxtaposition of two languages 'less offensive' (Muysken, 1995: 197). If such is the case, how can the occurrence of bare forms be accounted for? Consider Example 3.6 again. In the example, there is no equivalence between French and Kinyarwanda as Kinyarwanda is a class language while French is not. In this case, alternation would have been rendered 'less offensive', that is possible, through borrowing (u-mu-*génocidaire*). From this angle of lack of congruence, the occurrence of the bare form '*génocidaire*' would have been blocked. On the other hand, as regards the place of the complement, the syntax of Kinyarwanda and that of French 'map onto each other'. They both use the structure 'copula "be"+ complement'. Under this view, '*génocidaire*' would be a case of code-switching and the integrated form (umu*génocidaire*) should have been blocked. Briefly, at the level of singly occurring lexical items, Poplack's model as an account of order is under-specified. It cannot explain why, in the same example, the same content has taken two different forms in the same syntactic position. That is to say, in this case, the model does not show how a sense of structural uniformity is maintained.

*3.3.2.2. Constituent insertion*

As we have seen, Poplack herself accepts that lone L2 incorporations into discourse in L1 are a challenge for her model. Would L2 multi-word fragments be more predictable? Are they all code-switching? We have observed typical examples of code-switching in Examples 3.5 and 3.7. A third example of code-switching is the French fragment '*sur quelle base*' in turn 3 in Example 3.4. However, not all multi-word fragments are so easily categorised as code-switching. Poplack herself has come up with yet another category of language alternation, namely 'constituent insertion'. According to Poplack and Meechan (1995), constituent insertions are L2 multiword fragments which are 'incorporated unanalysed' into the discourse in L1. Occurring at non-equivalence sites,

> constituent insertion imposes weaker constraints on the languages involved than switching under equivalence. While it too requires that the internal grammaticality of the switched fragment is preserved, for its placement it need only refer to the word order of the language into which it is inserted. (1995: 225)

That is to say, in constituent insertion, the grammar of L2 is observed internally and may be violated externally. Here is an example:

*Example 3.11*

A: *ils ont* **des des des institutions d'enseignement supérieur nyinshi cyane** (.) bafite abanyeshuri barenga *cinquante mille*

A: they have many higher education institutions (.) they have more than fifty thousand students

In the extract, the interesting constituent is '*des institutions d'enseignement supérieur* nyinshi cyane' (many higher education institutions). In the sentence, this is the object NP. In turn, this NP can be analysed as comprising two constituents, namely a quantifier phrase (nyinshi cyane) and the noun group it modifies (*des institutions d'enseignement supérieur*). At the point of switch, there is no equivalence between French and Kinyarwanda. In French, word order would be QUANT+NP as in 'beaucoup d' /de nombreux/ une multitude de institutions d'enseignemnt supérieur). In Kinyarwanda, on the other hand, the structure is NP+QUANT as in 'ibigo by' amashuri makuru menshi cyane' (many higher education institutions). Because there is no equivalence, one cannot speak of code-switching here. And as word order is that of Kinyarwanda, we have a case of constituent insertion.

However, the above distinction between code-switching and constituent insertion seems to be based on a limited view of syntax, namely that of syntax as word order. If syntax is viewed more broadly as 'the study of the rules, or "patterned relations" that govern the way the words in a sentence come together' (http://en.wikipedia.org/wiki/Syntax), it becomes obvious that, in some languages, word order is not enough. Well-formed sentences must show appropriate word order, but they also must respect relevant conventions regarding aspects such as case marking and class agreement. In Kinyarwanda, for example, as we have seen, verbs must show class agreement with their subjects, otherwise they are not well-formed. Under this view, the French fragment *'tout le village'* in turn 3 in Example 3.12 will be seen as a case of constituent insertion. Indeed internally, the fragment is consistent with the grammar of French, but externally, the grammar of Kinyarwanda is observed. The French fragment has been assigned to a particular noun class (CL 9) for the purpose of class agreement between the subject and the verb as obtains in Kinyarwanda and not in French.

*Example 3.12*

1. A: n'iyo akoroye -
2. B: hmm
3. A *tout le village* irabimenya
4. C: oui (unclear)

1. A: when he coughs-
2. B: hmm
3. A: the whole village notices it
4. C: *yes* (unclear)

Thus, the above definition may be rephrased:

Constituent insertion imposes weaker constraints on the languages involved than switching under equivalence. While it too requires that the internal grammaticality of the switched fragment is preserved, for its placement 'and other syntactically relevant surface features', it need only refer 'to the structure' of the language into which it is inserted.

Although the model thus recognises the possibility of multi-word language alternation which is different from code-switching, it nevertheless leaves a serious issue of order unaccounted for. As we have seen, according to this model, code-switching is possible because it does not violate the structural uniformity principle. Constituent insertion, on the other hand, violates the principle. More precisely, violation of the principle is a defining criterion for this category of language alternation. The question therefore is, if there is a blocking principle built into the model, why does it not block such violations? The only way the model could be salvaged would be to claim that pragmatic motivations license this violation of structural uniformity. As Poplack does not go as far as formulating this proposal, a proposal which in any case would be problematic, I will not comment on it any further.

To summarise, Poplack's model of language alternation proposes three categories of language alternation, namely borrowing, code-switching and constituent insertion. Borrowing consists of singly occurring items from language A in talk in language B. That is, borrowing assumes 'an unequal partnership' (Bentahila and Davies, 1998) between the two languages. Such elements may or may not be integrated. Constituent insertion consists of multi-word fragments from language A in talk in language B. Internally, the fragment is consistent with the grammar of language A and, externally, it complies with the syntax of language B. Here again, there is dominance of one language over the other. Between these two is code-switching. Like borrowing, code-switching may consist of singly occurring items from language A in talk in language B and, like constituent insertion, it may consist of multiword fragments. The key difference between code-switching and these other contact phenomena is that code-switching, unlike the other two, occurs at 'equivalence sites'.

As we have seen, while the model accounts for the orderliness of language alternation in the form of code-switching, it fails to account for that of borrowing and constituent insertion. According to the model, code-switching is orderly because, occurring at equivalence sites, it does not violate the Uniform Structure Principle. In the case of borrowing, as we have seen, the model is under-specified and allows it to occur both at equivalence sites and at non-equivalent ones. To be sure, in the case of borrowing, equivalence or lack of it ceases to be a defining criterion.

Thus, the distinction code-switching vs borrowing cannot be used as a scheme of interpretation, as they do not use the same interpretive parameters. As for the orderliness of language alternation in the form of constituent insertion, it too is not accounted for, but for different reasons. Unlike code-switching, constituent insertion is explicitly said to occur at non-equivalent sites. That is equivalence or lack of it is a defining criterion. However, the model does not indicate why this violation of the norm of equivalence, hence of structural uniformity, is not blocked. In my view, in both cases, the problem derives from the lack of a sufficient recognition of the insertional nature of language alternation on the part of the model. Section 3.4 looks at a model of language alternation which accounts for order in talk in two languages explicitly in terms of insertion.

## 3.4. An insertional model of language alternation

### 3.4.1. A mentalistic model of language alternation

The Matrix Language Frame (MLF) model was developed by Myers-Scotton (1993a) and expanded and refined by Myers-Scotton and associates over a series of publications (1995, 1998a, 2001, 2002, 2006, etc.). In terms of theoretical background, unlike Poplack's model reviewed above which is surface-based, the MLF model of code-switching can be said to be 'mentalistic' in the Chomskyian sense (Chomsky, 1965: 4). Myers-Scotton (1995: 234) writes,

> The proposition supported is that intra-sentential CS is governed by **abstract principles** which apply to CS data sets across different communities and therefore are apparently **cognitively based**. (my emphasis)

That the MLF is a mentalistic perspective can also be seen in the recently introduced notion of 'classic codeswitching'. Classic code-switching is defined as

> ...alternation between two varieties in the same constituent by **speakers who have sufficient proficiency in the two varieties to produce monolingual well-formed utterances in either variety.** This implies that speakers have sufficient access to the abstract grammars of both varieties to use them to structure codeswitching utterances. (Myers-Scotton, 2001: 23) (my emphasis)

Influence from the notion of 'balanced bilingualism', and, by implication, that from the Chomskyan 'ideal speaker-hearer' is obvious. Thus, the MLF is primarily a model of the ideal 'bilingual language competence' (Myers-Scotton and Jake, 1995/2000), although it may be extended and applied to 'language contact phenomena for which speakers do not have such full access to abstract grammatical structures' (Myers-Scotton, 2001: 23).

The MLF is also known as a production-based model of Code-Switching, for it focuses 'on what happens during language production' (1995: 235). The model of language production adopted by the MLF comprises three stages as in Table 3.3.

Applied to language alternation, this model looks as in Table 3.4.

*Table 3.3* A model of language production (reproduced from Myers-Scotton, 1995: 237)

| | |
|---|---|
| Conceptual level: | Speaker's intention regarding referential information and pragmatic and socio-pragmatic messages |
| Functional level: | Select lemmas from mental lexicon (congruent with intentions) |
| | Lemmas send directions to the formulator (regarding morpho-syntactic procedures) |
| | (Result: basic sentential frame is set) |
| Positional level: | Select phonological representations |
| | (Result: lexemes are realised) |
| | Direct positioning of lexemes |

*Table 3.4* A model of language production for language alternation (adapted from Myers-Scotton and Jake, 1995/2000: 287)

| | |
|---|---|
| Conceptual level: | universally present lexical-conceptual structure in the conceptualizer. 'Choices' made: |
| | If discourse includes CS, then select ML (Matrix Language- see below) and semantic/pragmatic feature bundles |
| | Language-specific semantic/pragmatic feature bundles activate entries in the mental lexicon (language-specific lemmas) |
| | Language-specific lemmas send directions to formulator |
| Functional level: | The 'activated' formulator projects |
| | Predicate-argument structures (e.g. thematic roles) and Morphological realizations (e.g. word order, case marking, etc.) |
| Positional level: | Morphological realization (surface structure after move-alpha, agreement inflections, etc.) |

In other words, some of the decisions regarding code-switching are taken very early on in the language production process. For example, as early as the conceptual level, speakers 'decide' whether to use language alternation or not and which of the two languages involved to adopt as the Matrix Language (see below) for that alternation (1995/2000: 289–290).

Because the MLF is such a mentalistic view of language choice among bilingual speakers, it may be unfair to examine it in terms of order in social action. As I have already indicated, the notion of 'order' I have adopted in this book refers to practical social action. However, in its own words, the model claims to be an account of order and it is for this reason that I propose to look at it as such. Myers-Scotton (1993a: 75) writes,

> The MLF [...] seeks to predict the form of CS utterances. There are two complementary predictions:
>
> It predicts which utterances containing CS forms will be considered well-formed (and which, therefore, are predicted to be **possible occurrences**).
>
> It predicts which such utterances are not well-formed and therefore **will not occur, unless they are stylistically marked** (in order to serve some socio-pragmatic purpose, such as emphasis). (my emphasis)

As we have seen, order is the possibility of social action. Any act which has been accomplished is either a direct application of the norm or it is a case of deviance from the norm. If deviant, an act is either repairable or marked and functional. The above quotation comprises these very same ideas with specific reference to language alternation. Elsewhere, in a statement that echoes the ethnomethodologists Ryave and Schenkein (1974), Myers-Scotton (2006: 249) affirms that the principles of the MLF are 'an answer to the question: is there "traffic control" in bilingual clauses in codeswitching?'. Therefore, by looking at the MLF, my aim is to see to what extent it achieves the goals it set itself as an account of order in talk in two languages.

### 3.4.2. The asymmetry principle in language alternation

As we have seen, Poplack's model accounts for language alternation, especially language alternation in the form of code-switching, in terms of structural equivalence between the two languages involved (see equivalence constraint). The central claim of the MLF model, on the other hand, is that of asymmetry between the two languages. According to Myers-Scotton, one of the premises of the MLF is the 'Asymmetry Principle' (2002: 9). One of the languages involved is dominant, the other is subordinate. In this respect, Myers-Scotton and Jake write,

> Central to our discussion of intrasentential CS is the claim that the two languages involved do not participate equally. One language, which we will call the Matrix Language (ML), is more dominant [...]. (1995/2000: 282)

Elsewhere Myers-Scotton writes,

> Bilingual speech is characterised by asymmetry in terms of the participation of the languages concerned. In what I now call classic codeswitching, only one of the participating languages is the source of the Matrix Language. In other contact phenomena (such as composite codeswitching), the Matrix Language may be a composite of abstract features from more than one language, but asymmetry still marks the contributory roles of the participating languages. (2002: 9)

As indicated in the above quotations, the dominant language is referred to as the 'Matrix Language' and the less dominant one is referred to as the 'Embedded Language'. However, both the notion of Matrix Language and that of Embedded Language must be clearly understood. And this is so because, in Myers-Scotton's own words, the notion of Matrix Language is 'the most misunderstood part of the Matrix Language Frame model' (2001: 32). The Matrix Language should not be confused with a natural language such as English or French. Rather, it should be understood as 'an abstract frame, the source of grammatical structures for the bilingual CP (complementiser phrase)' (2001: 32), as 'a label for the abstract morphosyntactic frame for an utterance' (2002: 58). As the Matrix Language and the Embedded Language co-define each other (2001: 35), presumably, the Embedded Language must be seen as an abstract system as well (2002: 131).

Why asymmetry and what does the asymmetry between the ML and the EL consist in then? Myers-Scotton sees the asymmetry between the Matrix Language and the Embedded Language as responding to the Uniform Structure Principle. She writes,

This asymmetry is evidence of the universal drive in language to achieve uniformity in the structural frame of any variety, to avoid meaningless variation – although this outcome never entirely exists in any language. Still, the drive is there, and, in bilingual speech it is especially expressed as part of the movement toward the morphosyntactic dominance of one variety in the frame. (2002: 9)

That is to say, the role of the Matrix Language is to ensure that, in talk in two languages, uniformity is observed. To put it in other words, according to Myers-Scotton, order in talk in two languages is achieved through the dominance of the Matrix Language.

As for the asymmetry itself, it is captured through the two main principles of the MLF, namely the 'Morpheme-Order Principle' and the 'System Morpheme Principle'.

> The Morpheme-Order Principle: In ML+EL constituents [mixed constituents] consisting of singly occurring EL lexemes and any number of ML morphemes, surface morpheme order (reflecting surface syntactic relations) will be in the ML.

> The System Morpheme Principle: In ML+EL constituents [mixed constituents], all system morphemes which have grammatical relations outside their head constituent (which participate in the sentence's thematic role grid) will come from the ML (1993a: 83)

In the following, I discuss and illustrate each of these principles in turn.

### 3.4.2.1. Morpheme order principle

The morpheme order principle provides that, in mixed constituents, the syntactic frame comes from the ML. Myers-Scotton (2006: 248) illustrates this by the following example from her Nairobi corpus involving Swahili (plain type) and English (italics):

*Example 3.13*

A-li-nunu-a gari **ya** *red*
3s-past-buy car of red
(He bought a red car)

As the translation shows, in English, the attributive adjective 'red' would normally come before the noun it modifies. In Swahili, attributive modifiers follow the noun they modify and they normally consist of prepositional phrases introduced by a relating element ('ya' in the example) because Swahili, like other Bantu languages, has very few adjectives. Thus, in the example, the syntactic frame is clearly that of Swahili. In other words, in this example, Swahili is the Matrix Language and English is the Embedded Language. Also consider the following Chinese–English sentence from Wei (2001).

*Example 3.14*

Ni   nei-pian ARTICLE hai mei FINISH a?
you   that-CL         yet not          PART./AFFIRM. –QUE?
(You haven't finished that article yet?)

Here, even considering only the position of the two English items 'article' and 'finish', it is clear that word order in the sentence is not that of English.

Therefore, according to the morpheme order principle, language alternation is orderly because it does not violate the syntactic structure of the Matrix Language. Two situations may be observed: language alternation occurs at points where there is equivalence between the two languages, but it may also occur at non-equivalence sites (see above). Either way the structure of the ML is followed. Consider the sentence '*à un moment donné* yabaga mu Busuwisi' in Example 3.4 again. As we have seen, there is equivalence between French and Kinyarwanda as regards the placement of adjuncts such as '*à un moment donné*' at the head of the sentence and this is the reason Poplack would see the clause as involving code-switching. Myers-Scotton, on the other hand, would explain the orderliness of language alternation in the sentence, not in terms of equivalence between French and Kinyarwanda, but rather in terms of the grammar of Kinyarwanda, the Matrix Language, being respected; whether that of French is or is not respected is not an issue.

However, that, in language alternation, the Matrix Language provides the syntactic frame does not mean that it legislates at every point. While the general frame will be that of the Matrix Language, there may also be 'EL islands'. These are EL multiword fragments whose internal structure remains consistent with EL grammar. Remember the notions of code-switching and constituent insertion as introduced in the discussion of Poplack. According to MLF, the Matrix Language still dominates as it determines the syntactic position of such items (2006: 264). Consider Example 3.7, reproduced below as 3.15 for convenience:

*Example 3.15*
1. A: eh akaba nta- nta ibi bya *compétitivité* arimo (.) ni mukuru (.) aga- aga*tourna* [**uko ashaka**
2. B: [*à son rythme*
3. A: *à son rythme*

1. A: he's not not into competition (.) he prints as [as he wants
2. B: [at his own pace
3. A: at his own pace

In the clause 'aga*tourna à son rythme*', the PP (prepositional phrase) '*à son rythme*' is internally consistent with French grammar. For example, the modifier '*son*' is pre-positioned while, if the grammar of Kinyarwanda was followed, it would have to be post-positioned. In other words, Kinyarwanda, the Matrix Language, does not legislate inside the PP. However, outside the PP, Kinyarwanda is still the norm as regards the position of the PP.

Regarding EL islands, Myers-Scotton (1995: 249–251; 2006: 260–266) notes that there are two types of them, 'Internal Embedded Language Islands' and what one might call 'peripheral EL islands'. These are alternatively described as follows:

> EL islands that are not internal islands [...] are well-formed maximal projections (e.g. NP, PP) in the EL; internal islands may or may not be maximal projections. (Myers-Scotton and Jake, 1995/2000: 306)

> that an internal EL island must be well formed in the EL [...] is not enough. Rather, its particular form is governed by the constituent frame projected by the ML maximal projection containing it. (Myers-Scotton and Jake, 1995/2000: 310)

> Internal embedded language islands include a Matrix Language element to frame the Embedded Language Phrase. That is they are part of a larger phrase. (2006: 265).

Peripheral EL islands 'are "add-ons" to the main structure/semantic elements of the clause' (2006: 264), are 'structurally peripheral' (1995: 250).

Consider, the NP '*des des des institutions d'enseignement supérieur nyinshi cyane*' from Example 3.11. The fragment '*des institutions d'enseignement supérieur*' is an island because internally it is consistent with the grammar of French. However, this French island is part of a larger NP, does not form a maximal projection on its own. Therefore, it must be seen as an internal EL island. On the other hand, in Example 3.16 below, all the highlighted French fragments are instances of peripheral EL islands.

*Example 3.16*

A: X nawe ati *non, ça ne peux pas marcher comme ça*! Nawe **avec sa faction** baravuga bati **pour commencer**, bariya bantu b'abadepite, bariya batowe, ntuza ariya matora yabo turaya*nuye* **puisque ils se sont méconduits (.) à l'égard du parti**

A: then X said no, it can't work like that. With his faction they said, to start with, those deputy elects, we invalidate their election as they have misbehaved (.) vis-à-vis the party

All the above are 'add-ons'. For example, deleting '*pour commencer*' and '*puisqu'ils se sont méconduits à l'égard du parti*' would not change the structure of the sentence in any way. They are adjuncts.

However, things are not always this easy. Consider the French fragment '*tout le village*' in the sentence '*tout le village* irabimenya' in Example 3.12. This French fragment is internally consistent with the grammar of French (position of the modifier 'tout' and even the article 'le'). As the phrase is a full NP, a maximal projection, it is not an internal EL island. However, as the subject of the sentence, the fragment is central to its main structure. Note that the sentence includes a framing element in the form a class marker (i-) in 'i-rabimenya' to show agreement between the verb and its subject. Also consider the EL island '*la faction dissidente*' in Example 3.17:

*Example 3.17*

A: Turafata, twafata baa X *d'accord*, ariko Y aravaho (.) *puisque* naho turajya gufata **la faction dissidente**.

A: we will take, we can take those from X no problem, but Y will have to go (.) as on his side as well we will have to retain those from the dissident faction

The EL island '*la faction dissidente*' is a complete NP. At the same time, it cannot be seen as an 'add-on' vis-à-vis the predicate-argument structure of the clause 'turajya gufata *la faction dissidente*' in which it is the object. If it were removed, the clause would be meaningless. Finally, consider the EL island '*très faible*' in Example 3.18:

Example 3.18

A: *Donc* ubwo, euh, *côté* ya X iba **très faible** kuburyo ntiyashoboraga gukoresha meeting. Ntibishoboka.

A: So X's side became so week that he could not even organise a public rally (meeting). It was impossible

The adjectival group is so central to the clause '*côté* ya X iba **très faible**' that, if it were removed, the sentence as a whole would become meaningless. Yet as in the above, it is a complete maximal projection (AdjP).

The issue therefore is: what counts as an internal embedded island and what as a peripheral EL island? In my view, the problem seems to be that, in the model, two different levels of talk organisation are not clearly kept separate, namely the predicate–argument level and the languageness level. In other words, issues of language choice (languageness) and those of content organisation (predicate-argument) are compounded. An alternative approach would be to identify centrality or lack of it with reference not to content organisation, but rather to the organisation of talk at the level of its languageness. For example, the difference between 17 and 18, on one hand, and 12, on the other, is not that one French fragment is central to the argument–predicate structure, but rather that, at the level of language choice, one (12) participates in class agreement, while the others (17) and (18) do not. Likewise, the similarity between (17) and (18) on one hand and (16) on the other, even though one is an adjunct while the others are not, is that, in all three cases, class agreement is not involved. In other words, in these cases, it might be more fruitful to consider class agreement, rather than predicate-argument, as the structure with respect to which centrality/peripherality of EL islands is defined. As Myers-Scotton has not contemplated the possibility of defining the centrality/peripherality of islands with reference to specific structures at the level of language choice, I will not pursue the argument here (but see Chapter 4).

### 3.4.2.2. *System morpheme principle*

As for the system morpheme principle, in order to understand it, the distinction between 'content morpheme' and 'system morpheme' is crucial. In traditional grammar, we are familiar with the distinction between function words and content words. This distinction more or less parallels the one between content morpheme and system morpheme, as all content words include content morphemes while some function words are system morphemes. For the sake of a definition, we will say that 'content morphemes are those that either assign or receive thematic roles [...] (while) system morphemes are those which neither assign nor receive thematic roles' (Myers-Scotton, 2006: 244–245). Typical content morphemes are content words such as verbs, nouns and adjectives while typical system morphemes are affixes.

In turn, three types of system morphemes are identified, namely 'early system morphemes', 'bridge late system morphemes' and 'outsider late system morphemes'. Thus, Myers-Scotton and Jake (2000) speak of the '4-M model' in reference to the four types of morphemes. Early system morphemes 'are always realized without going outside the maximal projection of the content morpheme that elects them.' (Myers-Scotton, 2001: 43). On the other hand, 'outsider late system morphemes depend on grammatical information outside of their own maximal projection' (Myers-Scotton, 2001: 44). Consider the sentence 'umwirabura muri abo bazungu *ça se remarque*' jointly produced by two Rwandan bilingual speakers as in Example 3.19:

Example 3.19

1. A: bon (.) **umwirabura muri abo bazungu** (.) [*c'est*
2. B: [*ça se remarque*
3. A: *ça se remarque* ntumbaze

1. A: right (.) a black person among so many whites (.) [it is
2. B: [it is noticeable
3. A: it is noticeable indeed

In the Kinyarwanda component of the sentence, a number of system morphemes have been used, including the class markers mu- in 'u-mu-irabura'and ba- in 'ba-zungu'. Both of these are early system morphemes, for they are directly attached to the content morphemes the class of which they indicate. The totality of the information needed for their well-formedness is found within the content morpheme to which they are attached. On the other hand, the demonstrative 'abo' is analysable as 'a-ba-o', the [a] of 'ba' disappearing in front of [o] for morphophonological reasons. In 'a-ba-o', the ba- refers to the class marker ba- in 'a-ba-zungu'. That is, there is agreement between the demonstrative and the head noun it modifies. The same demonstrative, if used with a noun from a different class, would be different (e.g. a-*ka*-o *ka*–gabo = that small man). In this sense, we will say that ba- in 'abo' is an outsider late system morpheme, for it depends for its well-formedness on information outside its maximal projection. In fact, in the same item, a- is another outsider late system morpheme, but I will not dwell on it. As for bridge late system morphemes,

> they are similar to early system morphemes in that they depend on information within the maximal projection in which they occur. Yet, they differ in that they do not add conceptual structure to a content morpheme; rather, what they do is unite elements in a maximal projection. (Myers-Scotton 2001: 43)

In the example above, the item 'muri' (among) is a bridge late system morpheme. For its well-formedness it does not depend on anything else. It is invariable. In the sentence, its function is to relate 'umwirabura' and 'abo bazungu'. Thus, according to the system morpheme principle, language alternation is orderly because all outsider late system morphemes, that is all syntactically relevant system morphemes, come from the Matrix Language. To summarise, according to the MLF model, in language alternation, structural uniformity, that is orderliness, obtains because both the syntactic frame and all outsider late system morphemes come from the same source, the Matrix Language.

### 3.4.3. Predictions of the MLF

The MLF framework as discussed above led Myers-Scotton to recognise three types of language alternation: 'ML +EL constituents' or 'mixed constituents', 'EL bare forms' and 'EL islands'. As we have seen, the category EL island divides into two, namely, internal EL islands and peripheral EL islands. According to MLF as an abstract level model, these types result from a matching process between ML and EL elements at the three level of language production (see above). Also, because the model is lexically based (Myers-Scotton, 1995), it claims that matching takes place at the level of singly occurring items. Thus of the three types of constituents, mixed constituents, that is singly occurring mixed items, are normative for they occur when there is maximal congruence between an EL and an ML item.

> ...the premise of the Abstract Level model is that when Embedded Language singly occurring forms occur with morphosyntactic integration into a mixed constituent in a Matrix Language frame, they have passed checking for congruence at all three levels of abstract grammatical structure. (2002: 97)

Since mixed constituents are normative, the other two types must be seen as deviant. Indeed Myers-Scotton accounts for them in terms of functional deviance as follows. A bare form consists of

> an EL content morpheme which, although it occurs in the constituent slot project by the ML, it lacks the ML system morphemes to make it completely well-formed according to the ML morphosyntax... EL uninflected content morphemes occur because there is not sufficient congruence at some level. (Myers-Scotton and Jake, 1995/2000: 293)

Elsewhere she writes,

> I argue that many Embedded Language islands [...] occur for the same reason that singly occurring Embedded Language elements occur. That is, **there is a semantic or pragmatic mismatch between the two languages at the lexical-conceptual level and the speaker's intentions are better satisfied by producing the Embedded Language element or Embedded language island.** (2002: 145) (my emphasis)

Myers-Scotton does not develop this idea of functional deviance any further (but see Myers-Scotton, 2006: 265–266). Thus, the MLF model as an account of order in talk in two languages is formally complete for it provides for normative conduct as well as for deviance from the norm.

However, when looked at closely, the MLF is soon found to present some difficulties. We have seen above that the MLF accounts for order in language alternation in terms of the asymmetry between the two languages involved. We have also seen that the Matrix Language must be seen as an abstract morphosyntactic frame rather than a particular language. This frame may change from one CP to the next and it may come from one of the languages involved just as it may also come from both languages. In the latter case, Myers-Scotton speaks of a

'Composite Matrix'. Consider the clause *'l'individu* aba *obligé d'expliquer'* from Example 3.20:

*Example 3.20*

A: Hanyuma kuri iyi ngiyi bikagaragara ko *à un certain moment*, *l'individu* aba *obligé d'expliquer.*

A: then it becomes clear that at some point the person must explain

In this clause, both French and Kinyarwanda have provided outsider late system morphemes. The subject of the sentence consists of the French island *'l'individu'*. In the verb form 'aba', there is class agreement with the subject in accordance with Kinyarwanda syntactic structure (see Chapter 4). On the other hand, the adjective *'obligé'* agrees in gender and number with *'individu'* in accordance with French syntax. Therefore, in this case, the Matrix Language is neither French nor Kinyarwanda. It is a combination of both. None of the languages is dominant for both provide outsider late system morphemes. The question therefore is, how the orderliness of cases like this can be accounted for as there is no asymmetry between the languages involved? Myers-Scotton's answer would be that this is not a case of classic codeswitching, an answer which leaves the issue of order entirely unresolved. To be sure, as soon as the Matrix Language is seen as an abstract grammatical frame different from an existing language, the idea of asymmetry between the languages becomes obsolete. If order in language alternation is accountable in terms of an abstract grammatical frame, it does not matter which language contributes what and in what proportion to that Matrix. What matters is that, for each case, the actual matrix is identified.

Secondly, as either of the languages involved can potentially contribute to the grammatical frame, the Matrix Language cannot be taken for granted. It must be discovered. Over the years, different types of evidence have been used, including sociolinguistic and psycholinguistic evidence, but it is currently accepted that only the grammatical evidence generated by the two main principles is reliable. In other words, to tell the Matrix Language, one observes word order in the CP and late system morphemes. In my opinion, this is a very limited view of order in bilingual conversation. Reflecting the grammatical assumption that the sentence, in this case the CP, is the highest unit of analysis, this view does not capture generalities which are observable across whole data sets. For example, Fuller and Lehnert have investigated the structure of gender assignment in a corpus of German–English bilingual conversation, interestingly using concepts and ideas from MLF, and identified general patterns such as 'the use of the gender of the German cognate of the codeswitched English noun' (2000: 401). Such general patterns would be difficult to account for if the Matrix Language was seen as limited to individual CPs. Likewise, Myers-Scotton (1998a) herself speaks of the 'Matrix Language Turnover' phenomena in situations of language shift, but these are difficult to conceptualise if the Matrix Language is seen as applying to individual CPs only.

To summarise, the MLF model of codeswitching accounts for the orderliness of language alternation in terms of the asymmetry between the languages involved. Language alternation is orderly because it does not violate the morphosyntactic structure of one of the languages involved, the Matrix Language. For this to be possible, the norm is for singly occurring Embedded Language elements to occur in the morphosyntactic frame set by the Matrix Language. This dominance of the Matrix Language is captured through two principles, namely the morpheme order principle and the system morpheme principle. However, that the Matrix Language sets the frame does not mean it is not deviated from. Rather it means that deviance from it is accountable, especially in terms of functional deviance. In turn, deviance at the morphological level gives rise to bare forms, while deviance at the syntactic level gives rise to EL islands. Thus, at a formal level at least, the MLF is a complete account of order. However, when the model is looked at closely, a few shortcomings become apparent, especially as regards the central theoretical construct of Matrix Language. Because the Matrix Language is viewed as the abstract moprhosyntactic frame for bilingual CPs, it is questionable whether the asymmetry principle, as a premise for the model, is needed or whether one should approach the data 'indifferently' and discover the Matrix Frame of each CP. Also, because the Matrix Language is limited to individual CPs, it becomes difficult to capture important generalities which may be observed either overtime in the same society or synchronically across a data set.

## 3.5. Conclusion

At the grammatical level, talk in two languages represents an issue of order, for language alternation potentially clashes with the Uniform

Structure Principle. Starting from the observation that language alternation is either insertional or alternational, in this chapter, I have looked at two accounts of the possibility of language alternation, one alternational and the other insertional. The alternational model we have looked at accounts for the possibility of language alternation in terms of equivalence between the languages involved, while the insertional model accounts for the same possibility in terms of the dominance of one language, the Matrix Language, over the other, the Embedded Language. In the chapter, we have also seen that none of these models is perfect. What we retain, however, is that, despite their shortcomings, grammatical models of language alternation can be read as accounts of order in talk in two languages. In Chapter 4, a case study is proposed in which I show how some of the ideas, concepts and methodologies developed in the models can be used fruitfully to account for a specific issue of order in talk in two languages.

# 4
# Using the Models: Class Agreement in Kinyarwanda–French Language Alternation

## 4.1. Introduction

The aim of grammatical accounts of language alternation, as we have seen, is to demonstrate how speakers achieve a sense of structural uniformity despite diversity, how they use linguistic resources available to maintain a sense of order. In Chapter 3, I have reviewed two models which have been proposed as accounts of order in talk in two languages. In concluding the discussion, I suggested that one of the weaknesses of the models, the Matrix Language Frame Model in particular, is that, drawing on the assumption that the sentence is the highest unit of grammar, these models fail to capture regularities across data sets. It was also suggested that the notion of Matrix Language might not be as useful a concept as it is said to be, since each CP must be examined indifferently in order to determine exactly what its Matrix is. In this chapter, drawing on my corpus of Kinyarwanda–French bilingual conversations, I propose a case study through which I indicate how these issues might begin to be addressed.

The particular issue of order I want to focus on in this case study is class agreement in Kinyarwanda–French language alternation. This issue arises as follows. As we already know, Kinyarwanda is a class language. This means that, in Kinyarwanda, every noun belongs to a particular noun class, and verbs and adjectives agree in class with the noun-subject in the case of verbs and the noun they modify in the case of adjectives. French, on the other hand, is not a class language. Therefore, the question that arises is whether class agreement is a significant aspect of talk organisation in Kinyarwanda–French bilingual conversation. It is whether class agreement contributes to a sense of structural uniformity in this type of talk. In other words, it is whether, while using Kinyarwanda–French language alternation, participants orient to class agreement. There is overwhelming evidence that the answer to these questions has to be 'Yes'. We have seen how, in Example 3.2 in Chapter 3, class agreement is achieved by assigning the phrase '*la notion de langue*' to a particular noun class for the purpose of agreement between the verb and its subject. Likewise, in Example 3.11 in Chapter 3, it is clear that the phrase '*des institutions d'enseignement supérieur*' has been assigned to a particular class for the purpose of agreement between this head NP and its modifying adjective phrase (nyinshi cyane). From this general observation and as the notion of class agreement applies to Kinyarwanda only, one may globally say that Kinyarwanda is the Matrix Language, but this will only be a very general statement.

Since there is evidence that class agreement is a significant aspect of the organisation of Kinyarwanda–French bilingual conversations, the next question to ask is how it is organised, what its structure is. We know that, in Kinyarwanda, there are 16 classes of nouns and therefore 16 possibilities of realising agreement. Are all these realised in Kinyarwanda–French language alternation? Also, as indicated above, agreement affects both verbs and adjectives. Is it the same in Kinyarwanda–French bilingual conversations? Finally, Kinyarwanda nouns can be involved in agreement relationships with French verbs and adjectives just as French nouns can be involved in agreement relationship with Kinyarwanda verbs and adjectives. An account of the structure of agreement in Kinyarwanda–French bilingual conversation should address all these questions and dimensions. Answers to all these questions will allow me to confirm the general statement above regarding the matrix language and whether the matrix frame should, as Myers-Scotton points out (see Chapter 3), not be equated with a natural language.

In developing this account, we will also have to keep in mind the issue of bare forms. As we have seen, according to Myers-Scotton, a bare form is an EL content morpheme which, although it 'does occur in the constituent slot projected by the ML, [...] lacks the ML system morphemes to make it completely well formed according to the ML morphosyntax (Myers-Scotton and Jake, 1995/2000: 293). Consider Example 3.6 in Chapter 3, reproduced below as 4.1 for convenience:

*Example 4.1*

1. A: ubungubu ujya ahantu bashaka kukw*embrouilla* no kuguturutumbya bakavuga ngo uri *génocidaire*
2. B: ngo uri umu*génocidaire*

1. A: now if you go somewhere and that they wanted to mistreat you, they say you are a genocider
2. B: say you are a genocider

In this example, the item *'génocidaire'* is a bare form for it lacks the Kinyarwanda system morphemes while *'umugénocidaire'* is not for it has relevant Kinyarwanda system morphemes (u- &- mu-) attached to the EL content morpheme. The relevance of this notion of bare form for our discussion is twofold. First, a French bare form may occur because an adjective or verb which should receive an outsider late system morpheme in order to show class agreement does not have any. In this case, we will say that, in Kinyarwanda-French language alternation, the element or category of elements does not participate in agreement, even though, in Kinyarwanda, it does. Alternatively, a French bare form may appear in a position which commands agreement. In this case, the issue is, how is agreement achieved? Does the fact that a noun is bare mean it is classless?

### 4.2. Grammatical agreement in Kinyarwanda and in French

One of the most noticeable aspect of Kinyarwanda, and many other Bantu languages, is its noun morphology. A typical noun in Kinyarwanda comprises three morphemes: a 'pre-prefix', the function of which is to categorise the word as a 'noun', a 'classifier prefix' or 'class morpheme' and a 'stem'. Thus the following nouns are analysable as:

| UMUNTU (Person): | U- | MU- | NTU |
|---|---|---|---|
| | Pre-prefix | CL. Morpheme | Stem |
| ABANA (Children): | A- | BA- | ANA[1] |
| | Pre-prefix | CL. Morpheme | Stem |

Altogether, in Kinyarwanda, there are 16 classes as in Table 4.1.

As Table 4.1 indicates, in Kinyarwanda, class agreement must obtain between a noun and adjectives either in an NP or in complement constructions as in:

– Umuntu mugufi (a short person): u- MU-ntu (person) + MU-gufi (short) (CL1)
– Ikibo ni kini (the basket is big): i-KI-bo (basket) + ni (is) + KI-nini (big) (CL7)

Table 4.1  Noun classes in Kinyarwanda (adapted from Kimenyi, 1980)

| Class | Noun | Adjective | Subject | Object | Example |
|---|---|---|---|---|---|
| CL1  | Mu- | MU- | A-  | -MU- | UMUNTU (person) |
| CL2  | BA- | BA- | BA- | -BA- | ABANTU (persons) |
| CL3  | MU- | MU- | U-  | -WU- | UMUTI (medicine) |
| CL4  | MI- | MI- | I-  | -YI- | IMITI (medicines) |
| CL5  | RI- | RI- | RI- | -RI- | IRYINYO (tooth) |
| CL6  | MA- | MA- | A-  | -YA- | AMATA (milk) |
| CL7  | KI- | KI- | KI- | -KI- | IKIGORI (maize) |
| CL8  | BI- | BI- | BI- | -BI- | IBITI (trees.) |
| CL9  | N-  | N-  | YA- | -I-  | INKA (cow) |
| CL10 | N-  | N-  | ZI- | -ZI- | INKA (cows) |
| CL11 | RU- | RU- | RU- | -RU- | URUVU (chameleon) |
| CL12 | KA- | KA- | KA- | -KA- | AKAGURU (leg) |
| CL13 | TU- | TU- | TU- | -TU- | UTUGABO (small men) |
| CL14 | BU- | BU- | BU- | -BU- | UBUKWE (ceremonies) |
| CL15 | KU- | KU- | KU- | -KU- | UKURI (truth) |
| CL16 | HA- | HA- | HA- | -HA- | AHANTU (somewhere) |

Agreement must obtain between the noun and the subject morpheme. In Kinyarwanda, every conjugated verb takes a subject morpheme which refers back to the actual subject as in:

- Ubukwe burashoje (the ceremonies are finished): u-BU-kwe (ceremonies)+BU-rashoje (are finished) (CL14)
- Umugezi utemba (a river which flows): u-MU-gezi (river) + U- temba (flows) (CL3)

Class agreement must also obtain in the case of a pronominal object as in:

- Inkweto yazitaye (he lost the shoes): i-N-kweto (shoes) + ya- ZI- taye (lost them) (CL10)
- Yamusomye (she kissed him): ya- MU- somye (CL1)

Because every noun belongs to a particular class, other types of grammatical agreement such as number and gender are inexistent in Kinyarwanda. On the other hand, French is not a class language. However, it marks grammatical agreement at the level of number and gender as in:

- *Un homme joyeux* (a happy man) vs. *Une femme joyeuse* (a happy woman), with gender agreement obtaining between the noun and its determiner (un vs. une) and its modifier adjective (joyeux vs. joyeuse),

or as in:

- *Un bon garcon* (a nice boy) vs. *de bons garcons*, with number agreement obtaining between the noun and its modifier (bon vs. bons).

Furthermore, in French, although there is agreement between the verb and its subject, it is only agreement in number (singular vs plural) as in:

- *Les hommes chantent* (the men sing) vs. *les femmes chantent* (the women sing), where plural is indicated by –ent and no gender is indicated.

An exception to this occurs in the case of perfect tenses which involve the use of participles. In this case, gender agreement, in addition to number agreement, may also be necessary as in:

- *Les hommes que j'ai vus* (the men I have seen) vs. les *femmes que j'ai vues* (the women I have seen)

Finally, in French, unlike in Kinyarwanda, pronominal objects show gender and number agreement with the noun they replace, but, more importantly, they are not affixed to the verb.

- *Je les ai vus* (I saw them), where 'les' is the object pronoun showing number agreement with the noun it replaces.

It is because of differences such as these that the issue of agreement in Kinyarwanda–French language alternation can be seen as that of order. As the two systems are significantly different, language alternation is 'impossible in principle' (Muysken, 1995: 195–196). The issue therefore is, how is agreement achieved in language alternation? That is, how is structural uniformity achieved despite diversity?

## 4.3. Class agreement in Kinyarwanda–French language alternation[2]

### 4.3.1. French adjectives and verbs in agreement-governed position

In examining the structure of agreement in Kinyarwanda–French language alternation, views must be taken from two angles. French items must be examined from the position where they are governed for agreement purposes (adjectives, verb, and object) and from the position where they have to govern agreement (nouns). A first general observation regarding the structure of agreement in Kinyarwanda–French language alternation is that, unlike their Kinyarwanda counterparts, French adjectives do not take class agreement. That is to say, class agreement is not oriented to as a significant aspect of talk organisation at this level. That is to say again, in Kinyarwanda–French language alternation, French origin adjectives in an agreement-governed position remain bare. An example is the adjective *'privées'* in 'amashuri hano ni *privées'* in Example 4.2.

*Example 4.2*

A: noneho rero nka bariya b'impunzi ukuntu bigenda (.) babagira ba- a- **amashuri hano ni *privées*** (.) ni *privées* mbega (.) kuburyo rero kugirango aze muri iyi *université* agomba kwishyura

A: then refugees like him the way the deal with them (.) they do they – schools here are private (.) they are private (.) so for him to be able to attend this university he must pay

If the syntactic slot occupied by *'privées'* had been filled by a Kinyarwanda adjective, a morpheme indicating CL6 would have been used to mark agreement with the noun 'a-ma-shuri' (school) (e.g. a-ma-shuri ma – kuru = high school). In the example, no class marker is used. A second example is *'pure'* in the NP 'ikinyarwanda *pure'* (pure Kinyarwanda), as jointly produced by participants in the following exchange:

*Example 4.3*

A: ibintu byo mu Rutonde bavuga ngo bakore **ikinyarwanda** (.) kitagize
B: [ *pure*
C: [ *pure*
A: Hmm ibyo narabirwanyaga *dès le début*

A: like the business of Urutonde where they wanted to create kinyanrwanda (.) which is
B: [pure
C: [pure
A: hmm I was against it from the beginning

Here again, if a Kinyarwanda adjective replaced the French item *'pure'*, a CL7 system morpheme would have to be used to show agreement with the noun 'Kinyarwanda'. A final example I can give is the following:

*Example 4.4*

A: iNairobi Kenya Kenya (.) ifite bya *universités* (.) ifite *universités* zirenga eshanu (.) **izo ni *publiques***

A: Nairobi Kenya Kenya (.) has many universities (.) has more than five universities (.) those are public

The interesting clause is 'izo ni *publiques*'. As the z- in the demonstrative 'izo' (those) indicates, the noun governing agreement belongs to CL10, in this case *universités* (see below). The adjective *'publiques'* has not taken any class morpheme while, if it were Kinyarwanda, it would. It is along these lines that the use of the bare form *'génocidaire'* in Example 4.1 can be understood.

To be sure, in Kinyarwanda–French language alternation, French adjectives are bare forms only to the extent that they do not show class morphemes to mark agreement with the head noun. Otherwise, more like in Fongbe–French language alternation (Meechan and Poplack, 1995), they follow the grammar of French and agree in number and gender with the French equivalent of the head noun. For example, the sentence 'umugore we ni *jalouse*' (his wife is jealous), where gender agreement is realised, would be preferred to 'umugore we ni *jaloux*' (her husband is jealous), where gender agreement is not indicated. A similar strategy has been observed by Fuller and Lehnert (2000) in their work on gender assignment in German–English bilingual data. It is for this reason that, in transcribing Example 4.2 above, I have marked the adjective *'privées'* for gender and number and, in Example 4.4, I have marked *'publiques'* for number.

From the discussion above, three points can be made. First, the fact that, in Kinyarwanda–French language alternation, French origin adjectives are bare forms does not mean alternation is random. Rather, the absence of class agreement itself is systematic. That is to say, structural uniformity at this level means absence of class agreement. Secondly, it is important to note that, given this regularity, Myers-Scotton's suggestion that bare forms can be accounted for in terms of functional motivation is difficult to maintain, as this is clearly a general regularity. Finally, the case of adjectives demonstrates that, in language alternation, the grammatical frame, that is the matrix frame, need not correspond to a natural language. As we have seen, Kinyarwanda can globally be said to be the Matrix Language in the data at hand. However, at the level of French origin adjectives, the system of Kinyarwanda does not apply.

As for French verbs, following a subject in Kinyarwanda, they always show class agreement with the subject. That is, at this level, uniformity means marking conjugated verbs for class agreement with their subjects. An example of a conjugated verb form is the item 'iraba*soutena*' used twice in Example 4.5.

*Example 4.5*

A: Noneho MRND **iraba*soutena*** ((laughter)). ni nabwo X yajyaga muri ntuza, zaa, zaa, mmm, zaa *manifestations* zaa MRND n'iki, MRND **iraba*soutena*** igira gute, bakora *de de de nouvelles elections et de nouveaux candidates*

A: MRND supported them ((laughter)). This is the time X went to MRND's meetings etc. MRND supported them, and they organised new elections with new candidates

This verb form 'iraba*soutena*' is analysable as below where the class marker i- (CL9) refers back to the subject, namely MRND.

I–        RABASOUTENA
SUBJ CL9

Also consider the verb form 'ba*nomma*' (they appointed) in the clause 'ba*nomma* Agathe Uwiringiyiman' in Example 4.6. The morpheme ba- indicates that the real subject of the verb belongs to CL2.

*Example 4.6*

A: yeee.
B: *bon*, noneho nibwo hajemo iriya *période* rero- hazamo kujijinganya (.) ba*nomma* X.
A: nabwo bamaze kujijinganya

A: yes
B: yes. then came that period- they hesitated (.) they appointed X
A: even then after hesitation

70   Talk in Two Languages

Finally consider the verb form 'bamu*souten*nye' in Example 4.7. At the level of class agreement, the form is analysable as BA- MU- *souten*nye, where BA- indicates agreement with the subject (CL2) and MU-indicates class agreement (CL1) at the level of the object. This analysis, especially regarding the subject, is confirmed by that of the verb form 'bagabanye' (reduce) in the same sentence, analysable as 'BA-gabanye' and where BA- refers to the same subject as in 'bamusoutennye'.

*Example 4.7*

A: ariko mbere yari yaramwemeye
B: *puisque* **bamu*souten*nye** bashaka kugirango **bagabanye** *la, la, la force du MDR.*
C: aaah

A: while before they had support him
B: since they had supported him only in order to weaken MDR
A: aaah

Briefly, French verbs, unlike French adjectives, when they appear in an agreement-governed position, always show relevant class agreement. That is to say, they always appear as Embedded EL constituents. That is to say again, at this level, structural uniformity is ensured through embedding. Finally, note that, at this level, the grammatical matrix in language alternation and the natural language coincide.

### 4.3.2. French nouns in agreement-commanding position

Let us now look at the issue from the other end, that of the noun. As we have said, in Kinyarwanda, the noun is referred to for agreement by adjectives and conjugated verb forms. In Kinyarwanda, there are 16 classes of nouns while in French, there are no classes. French is not a class language. The issues therefore are as follows: when used in Kinyarwanda–French language alternation, do French nouns enter the class system? And if they do, what classes do they fit into? And, in the case of bare French nouns, how is agreement achieved?

Observation of the data reveals a relatively rigorous system. At the level of singly occurring nouns, those which should be taking early class morphemes, there seems to be a distinction between nouns with the marker [+HUMAN] and nouns with the marker [–HUMAN]. On the whole, French origin nouns with the marker [–HUMAN] appear as bare forms. That is, they do not take any class marker morpheme.

This is illustrated by the nouns *'municipalité'* and *'bourse'* in Example 4.8. Further examples of this phenomenon are *'période'* in Example 4.6 and *'universités'* in the clause 'ifite *universités* zirenga eshanu' in Example 4.4.

*Example 4.8*

1. A: ni nka **municipalité**
2. B: nka **municipalité** *c'est ça* (.) **municipalité** ya hano ni yo yamuhaye **bourse**

1. A: it's like a municipality
2. B: like a municipality that's right (.) it's the local municipality that gave him a grant

For the purpose of agreement, however, these bare forms actually command CL9 for the singular and CL10 for the plural. For example, in Example 4.8 above, *'municipalité'* selects the class morpheme Ya- in 'ya hano', 'yo' and 'yamuhaye'. Likewise, in the clause 'ifite *universités* zirenga eshanu' in Example 4.4, *'universités'* selects zi- (CL10) in the verb form 'zi-renga'. Also consider Example 4.9.

*Example 4.9*

A: *Donc* ubwo euh **côté** ya X iba *très faible* kuburyo ntiyashoboraga gukoresha meeting. Ntibishoboka.

A: So euh X's side became so weak that they could not hold a rally (political). It was not possible.

The French noun *'côté'* commands class 9 in 'ya', 'i-ba' and 'nti-ya-shoboraga'.

I have said above that French origin nouns with the feature [-HUMAN] generally appear as bare forms. However, for reasons I am not yet in a position to clarify, when in plural, such nouns may some times appear with a token class marker (CL10). This occurs, for example, in the phrase 'zaa, mmm, za *manifestations* za MRND' in Example 4.5, where the class marker (CL10) is pre-positioned to the French noun 'manifestations' and dictates agreement at the level of the relational item 'za' in 'za MRND'. A similar process of token class marker assignment can be found in the phrase 'za *accords*' in Example 4.10.

*Example 4.10*

A: aaah!? Kuberako ariwe wari gusinya **za** ***accords***.
B: *puisque* niwe wari gusinya **za** ***accords*** (. ) *le risque etait que* azitangaho *comme candidat,* yamu, ya ntuza.
A: mmmm

A: since he was the one who was going to sign the agreement
B: since he was the one who was going to sign the agreement, chances were that he was going to put himself forward as the candidate for the, the thing
A: mmm

A related phenomenon is worth mentioning here. In Kinyarwanda, classes are grammatical categories, but they also, some of them at least, have some semantic meanings. For example, CL7 and CL8 can be assigned to convey negative connotations (singular and plural respectively) and CL12 and CL13 can be assigned to convey positive connotations. The same process of class attribution is found in Kinyarwanda–French language alternation, leading to the situation where a class morpheme is attached to a French noun. For example, in Example 4.4, the phrase 'bya *universités*' in the clause 'ifite bya *universités*' appears. Once a specific class has been attributed in this fashion, it relevantly conditions agreement.

As for the category of nouns with the feature [+HUMAN], a distinction is made between nouns which are used as titles and those which are used as common nouns. Titles, always in the singular because they refer to one person, are bare. Consider Example 4.11. However, where relevant, such bare forms select CL1 for agreement as in the NP 'Secrétaire w'ishyaka' in Example 4.11, where the relational element 'wa' looks back to 'Secrétaire' for class agreement.

*Example 4.11*

1. A: Batoramo na X.
2. (.)
3. A: Uramuzi?
4. B: Wigishaga I Nyakinama?
5. A: hmm,
6. B: *mais comment laaa*?
7. A: Niwe wari **Secrétaire waa- w'ishyaka**.
8. B: Yagiye muri *aile* ya Y?
9. A: Yeep

1. A: they voted for X
2. (.)
3. A: do you know him?
4. B: the one who used to teach at Nyakinama?
5. A: hmm
6. B: how is that?
7. A: he was the Party Secretary
8. B: He joined Y's faction?
9. A: yeep

Likewise, in Example 4.12, the bare form vice-president commands CL1 agreement at the level of the verb 'a-kava' in the clause 'vice-président akava muri ayo mashyaka abiri'

Example 4.12

1. A: Yari FPR *je crois. Puisque le,le*,ntuza- MRND yatangaga *Président de la République,* MDR igatanga *Premier Ministre,* FPR igatanga ntuzaa,
2. B: *Parlement.*
3. A: *L'Assemblée.* Eeeh, noneho [*Vice-Pésident*
4. B:                                              [*Vice-Président*
5. A: **Vice-Président akava muri ayo mashyaka abiri**

1. A: It was RPF I think. Since the something- MRND provided the President of the Republic, MDR provided the Prime Minister, RPF provided something
2. B: Parliament
3. A: Assembly. Euh then the Vice-president
4. B: Vice-President
5. A: The Vice-Present would come from those parties

On the other hand, if a noun refers to a general category, it is always integrated, that is, it takes Kinyarwanda class morphemes, either CL1 [mu-] for the singular or CL2 [ba-] for the plural. An example of CL1 is 'umu*génocidaire*' in Example 4.12, which is analysable as

| U- | MU- | GÉNOCIDAIRE |
|---|---|---|
| PRE-PREF | CL1- | genocider |

Another example is the word 'umu*licencié*' (somebody with a first degree), in Example 4.13 from a conversation recorded in Rwanda in

1987 (Gafaranga, 1987b). Also interesting in the example is the contrast between this word and the bare form (adjective) 'spécialisé'.

*Example 4.13*

A: wenda wowe ibyo bintu ushobora kuba ubizi uri umu*licencié* =
B: hmm
A: = ariko ukaba ubizi *d'une façon générale* ariko we akaba ari *specialisé* muri byo

A: As someone with a first degree you may know those things, but you will only have a general knowledge of them while he knows them as a specialist.

The word 'umu*licencié*' is analysable as:

| U- | MU- | *LICENCIÉ* |
|---|---|---|
| PRE-PREF | CL1 | first degree |

Also consider 'umu*candidat*' in Example 4.14 below

*Example 4.14*

A: Noneho X ati *bon, je suis candidat.* Haza n'undi **mucandidat we n'undi, wari umuhutu witwagaaa** (. ) euh ni inde ra? *D'ailleurs je l'ai oublié.* Baratora.

A: then X said okay I am candidate. Another candidate also came forward, one, who was a hutu whose name was [...] euh what's his name? I have forgotten it. They proceeded to vote.

The noun 'umu*candidat*' is analysable as

| U- | MU- | *candidat* |
|---|---|---|
| PRE-PREF. | CL1 | candidate |

As can be seen from the verb forms 'wari' and 'witwaga', agreement with these nouns is realised by means of CL1 outsider late system morphemes.

An example of CL2 is 'aba*jeunes*' in 'ba*recrut*a aba*jeunes* ibihumbi bitatu' in Example 4.15.

*Example 4.15*

1. A: Ba-bata- bataye ubutaka bwabo (.) bazarwana (.) [*avec*
2. B: [*pour reconquérir leurs terres*
3. A: *voilà* (.) ubwo ba ba ba*recruta* aba*jeunes* ibihumbi bitatu

1. A: those who lost their land (.) they will fight [with
2. B: [to recover their land
3. A: that's it (.) they then recruited three thousand youths

The item 'aba*jeunes*' is analysable as

| A- | BA- | *JEUNES* |
|---|---|---|
| PRE-PREF | CL2 | youth |

In this case, if agreement is required, it will be realised by means of CL2 system morphemes.

Briefly, two points must be retained from the discussion above. First, the discussion shows that, at the level of singly occurring French origin nouns, class agreement in Kinyarwanda–French language alternation is not random. A very strict system is used. Speakers make a distinction between nouns with the feature [–HUMAN] and those with the feature [+HUMAN], adopting bare forms for the first category. When the feature [+HUMAN] obtains, they further make the distinction between nouns used as titles and those used as common nouns. In the first case, nouns remain bare, while, in the second, they take CL1 or CL2 early system morphemes. Once these decisions have been made, speakers realise agreement assigning CL9 and CL10 for agreement with nouns in the category [–HUMAN] and CL1 and CL2 for agreement with nouns in the category [+HUMAN]. Clearly, this actual matrix differs from Kinyarwanda in at least two very significant respects, namely the fact that not all French origin nouns take class morphemes and the fact that, at the level of agreement-governed items, the number of possible classes is reduced from 16 to just 4. Secondly, the discussion shows that the issue of bare forms itself is not random. A very strict system exists which allows to predict which items will appear as bare forms and which will not. Here again, an explanation of bare forms in terms of functional motivation would appear to be unwarranted. Rather, one is dealing with a general regularity.

### 4.3.3. Class agreement and multi-word fragments

In Kinyarwanda–French language alternation, the issue of class agreement is not limited to singly occurring elements. It extends to multi-word fragments as well. Two key concepts we have encountered in our discussion of the models need to be kept in mind here, namely the notion of 'internal EL island' from the MLF model and that of 'constituent insertion' from Poplack. Regarding the notion of 'constituent insertion', we have said that it is problematic because it represents a significant departure from the spirit of the model which, as we have seen, is alternational rather than insertional. As for the notion of 'internal EL island', the issue was felt to be that of what counts as a relevant structure with respect to which 'peripherality/internality' is identified. It is also important to realise that both models point out the similarity between these multi-word fragments and singly occurring nouns (borrowings in Poplack, bare forms in Myers-Scotton). It is from this mention of similarities between multi-word fragments and singly occurring nouns that we can begin to understand the issue of class agreement where such constructions are involved.

The issue multi-word fragments raise is as follows: how is class agreement achieved between a French island and a Kinyarwanda item where it is relevant? More specifically, if an island is in an agreement-commanding position, what class does it command? Consider the sentence 'tout le village irabimenya' in Example 4.16. Like a singly occurring bare form, the NP 'tout le village' has been analysed as belonging to CL9 and made to command the outsider late morpheme i- in 'irabimenya'.

*Example 4.16*

1. A: n'iyo akoroye
2. B: hmm
3. A: **tout le village irabimenya**
4. C: oui (unclear)

 

1. A: when he coughs
2. B: hmm
3. A: the whole village notices it
4. C: *yes* (unclear)

Also note how the constituent '*la procédure électorale*' is made to call for CL9 in the verb group 'yari i-tararangira' in Example 4.17.

*Example 4.17*

1. A: *Puisque* **le la procédure électorale** yari itararangira. Hari harimo *des reclamations* n'iki, *bien, partout Bon* baba bamushyizeho.
2. B: Aaah?

1. A: since the election process had not been completed yet. There were still claims and things all over the place. So they appointed him
2. B: Is it so?

On the other hand, consider Example 4.18. In the example, the NP '*des des des institutions d'enseignement supérieur*' (many higher education institutions) calls for CL10 for the purpose of agreement as revealed in the outsider late system morpheme ni- of 'ni-inshi cyane'.

*Example 4.18*

A: *ils ont* **des des des institutions d'enseignement supérieur** nyinshi cyane (.) bafite abanyeshuri barenga *cinquante mille*

A: they have many higher education institutions (.) they have more than fifty thousand students

The use of CL10 is also found in Example 4.19, where agreement is marked between the phrase '*les événements*' and the verb form '*nzumva*'. The morpheme z- (object) refers back to the NP.

*Example 4.19*

A: buretse nkubwire rero ukuntu **les événements** nzumva (.) uko nabyumvaga ni uko *Gouvernement* ya ntuza yaa, ya X yagombaga kurangira *le cinq Avril*.

A: let me tell you how I understand the events (.) the way I understood it is that the government of somebody of, of X had to fold on the fifth of April

Briefly, just like nouns with the feature [–HUMAN], islands with the same feature call for classes 9 (singular) and 10 (plural) for agreement purposes.

On the other hand, NP islands with the marker [+HUMAN] call for class 1 and 2 for agreement purposes. Consider the following:

*Example 4.20*

A: Hanyuma kuri iyi ngiyi bikagaragara ko *à un certain moment, l'individu* aba *obligé d'expliquer*.

A: On this it becomes clear that, at some point, the individual has to explain

In the clause '*l'individu* aba *obligé d'expliquer*', the French fragment '*l'individu*' commands CL1 at the level of the verb 'aba', analysable as A-ba. Note in passing the bare form in the participle '*obligé*'. Also consider Example 4.21.

*Example 4.21*

A: *Bon. à la limite* njyewe ngera aho nkavuga nti *finalement, est ce que l'a- euh, les arguments que ce soit* **des extremistes ba** abatusti cyangwa **ba** abahutu ntizigera hamwe *finalement*, kuko **les extremistes ba** abahutu **bo baravuga** bati FPR ni abatutsi

A: okay. At the end of the day I think that at the end, the arguments by extremists whether Tutsi or Hutu have the same results for Hutu extremists say: RPF are Tutsis

In this example, the relating elements 'ba' in the phrases 'ba abahutu' and 'ba abatutsi' look back to the French island '*des (de les) extremistes*'. Likewise, the island '*les extremistes*' commands agreement for the verb forms 'baravuga' and 'bati'. In all of these cases, CL2 marker ba- is used. Incidentally, in the same example, note how the island '*les arguments*' calls for CL10 agreement in the verb form 'nti-**zi**-gera'.

An even more interesting situation is found in Example 4.22. The verb 'baravuga' in the clause 'nawe *avec sa faction* baravuga bati' is analysable as BA-ra-vuga (CL2). The subject of this verb is 'nawe *avec sa faction*'. At the level of this subject there is a potential clash as 'nawe' (and he) has the feature [+HUMAN]+[SINGULAR] and therefore, if it were alone, would call for A- (CL1). On the other hand, the French multi-word fragment '*sa faction*' has the feature [−HUMAN]+[INGULAR] and, alone, would call for I- (CL9). [SINGULAR]+[SINGULAR] presumably gives [PLURAL], but what does [+HUMAN]+[−HUMAN] give? This clash is neutralised by adopting [HUMAN], hence the morpheme BA- in the verb form.

*Example 4.22*

A: X nawe ati *non, ca ne peux pas marcher comme ca* (.) **Nawe avec sa faction** baravuga bati *pour commencer*, bariya bantu b'abadepite, bariya batowe, ntuza ariya matora yabo turayanuye *puisque ils se sont méconduits (-) à l'égard du parti.*

A: X said No, it cannot be like that (.) Him along with is faction they said to start with, these people, these MPs, those who've just been elected, we invalidate those elections (.) because they have misbehaved (.) towards the party.

## 4.4. Conclusion

At the start of this chapter, we noted that the issue of class agreement in Kinyarwanda–French language alternation can be viewed as that of order. And this is so because the two languages involved are significantly different. More specifically, while Kinyarwanda is a class language, French is not. I therefore wondered how speakers involved in language alternation maintain a sense of structural uniformity, given these differences. Observation of the data revealed a very systematic pattern for class agreement in Kinyarwanda–French language alternation. In Kinyarwanda–French language alternation, French adjectives, unlike their Kinyarwanda counterparts, do not take outsider late system morphemes. That is to say, they are consistently bare. French verbs, on the other hand, consistently agree with their subjects taking relevant outsider late system morphemes. French nouns with the feature [–HUMAN] are always bare. However, for the purpose of class agreement, they are assigned to class 9, if singular, and class 10, if plural. As for nouns with the marker [+HUMAN], they are bare if used as titles and they take class 1 (singular) and class 2 (plural) early system morphemes if they are used as common nouns. If agreement is required, corresponding outside late system morphemes are assigned. The same pattern is used in the case of French internal islands. French islands with the feature [–HUMAN] take classes 9 and 10 respectively and those with the feature [+HUMAN] take classes 1 and 2. Briefly then, in Kinyarwanda–French language alternation, class agreement is very structured, and it is through adhering to this structure that participants in

Kinyarwanda–French bilingual conversation maintain as sense of structural uniformity, that is a sense of order.

This investigation of class agreement in Kinyarwnda–French language alternation sheds some light on some of the central concepts in grammatical models of language alternation. First, as Myers-Scotton has pointed out, the notion of Matrix Language should not be equated with a particular natural language. The study of class agreement in Kinyarwanda–French language alternation confirms this view. As we have seen, the notion of class agreement applies to Kinyarwanda only. Therefore, the fact that Kinyarwanda–French language alternation shows class agreement can be used as evidence that, in the data, Kinyarwanda is the Matrix Language. However, this generalisation should not be taken to mean that the actual grammatical frame of utterances is that of Kinyarwanda. Observation of the data revealed that there are points where the grammar of Kinyarwanda is significantly departed from. For example, in Kinyarwanda–French language alternation, French origin adjectives do not agree with the noun they modify. Likewise, as we have seen, as regards French nouns, the system of Kinyarwanda–French language alternation is significantly simplified, with 4 classes rather than 16.

Secondly, this case study sheds light on the notion of bare form as used in the MLF model. As we have seen, Myers-Scotton suggests that the use of bare forms responds to a functional motivation. As we have seen in Chapter 1, Section 1.2, any idea of functional motivation assumes deviance from the norm. The data examined in this case study does not support the view that bare forms are deviant. Both in the case of French origin adjectives and in the case of French origin nouns with the marker [–HUMAN], the data reveals regularities which go beyond mere deviance. In fact, there does not appear to be any other norm against which deviance would be seen. For example, there are no cases of embedded French origin adjectives to function as the norm against which to view bare forms as deviating from. Likewise, in the case of French origin nouns, even if there are nouns which are embedded, these cannot be used as the norm as analysis reveals that they actually belong to a different category.

Both Poplack and Myers-Scotton's distinguish between singly occurring elements and longer stretches. In the latter case, they also make a distinction between constituent insertion and code-switching in the case of Poplack and between internal and peripheral EL islands in the case of Myers-Scotton. This discussion of class agreement in Kinyarwanda–French language alternation supports these distinctions, but it also specifies them. One of the problems with the notion of 'constituent insertion' is that it is identified only with reference to the order of elements in the sentence. The discussion of class agreement shows that the order of elements is not necessarily the only defining criteria. As for the notion of 'internal island', it was found to be problematic, for Myers-Scotton defines it with reference to the Argument-Predicate structure. The discussion of class agreement in Kinyarwanda–French language alternation shows that the Argument-Predicate might not be the only point of reference with respect to which centrality/peripherality of elements is defined. Rather, investigation of class agreement in Kinyarwanda–French language alternation suggests that these notions must be defined with respect to specific aspects of talk organisation.

Some general comments regarding the nature of studies of language alternation can be proposed by way of a conclusion. First, the case study confirms that, at the grammatical level, language alternation is indeed an issue of order. For example, since 'the grammar of a language is [...] a system *où tout se tient'*, Kinyarwanda–French bilingual talk is 'impossible in principle', as one of the two languages is a class language while the other is not. Secondly, the case study highlights the need for language alternation to be approached from the perspective Lerner (1991) refers to as 'interactionally relevant grammar'. The case study has been conducted, not with a view to describe the grammar of language alternation as an abstract system in the minds of speakers, but rather with a view to describe the grammar speakers actually use to realise class agreement as an observable aspect of talk organisation. At the end of the discussion, it is obvious that the grammar relevant for this aspect of talk organisation is neither that of French nor that of Kinyarwanda, but rather an adhoc, and yet systematic, combination of the two. Whether this 'third grammar' is referred to as the Matrix Language or not is not very important. In fact, that the structure of class agreement in Kinyarwanda–French alternation is different from the grammars of the two languages used should not be surprising because, as many researchers have argued before (e.g. Gumperz, 1982; Alvarez-Caccamo, 1998; Gafaranga and Torras, 2001; Myers-Scotton, 2002), the code that bilingual participants use in actual interaction need not correspond to language A or language B. Thirdly, the need for analysis to focus on specific aspects of order in talk in two languages has been highlighted. More often than not, studies of language alternation follow a pattern more or less like this: a theory is put forward, counter-examples are found and the theory is rejected en bloc. In my view, this is an unhealthy approach as no theory is ever a 100 percent adequate. To assess the value of existing theories of language alternation, we should adopt an attitude Conversation Analysts refer to as a specimen perspective (Ten Have, 1999). That is to say, we should identify significant aspects of talk organisation and investigate them fully in terms of the theory or theories we are interested in. A theory will then be rejected with reference to specific aspects of talk organisation and may be retained for some other aspects. Fourth and following from the above, the issue of language pairs comes up. Some language pairs offer opportunities which are not available if different pairs are considered and indeed, much too often, general theoretical claims have been formulated while they may actually better be seen as language specific. For example, the issue of class agreement is by no means universal. It is an issue only if one or both languages involved is a class language. It follows therefore that a theory might be useful as an account of specific aspects of order in specific language pairs and less so as an account of other specific aspects of order in the same or in different language pairs. In short, through the general review of the models conducted in Chapter 3 and the particular case study I have conducted in Chapter 4, I hope it is clear that, at the grammatical level, language alternation is an orderly phenomenon and that its orderliness is accountable.

## Notes

1. Co-occurrence of two A's results in elongation.
2. Also see Myers-Scotton (2002: 129–131) for a brief discussion of class agreement in language alternation involving Bantu languages in general.

# 5
# Interactional Order in Talk in Two Languages: Identity-Related Accounts

## 5.1. Introduction

As we have seen in Chapter 3, from a grammatical point of view, language alternation is an issue of order because, in principle, it runs against the Structural Uniformity Principle. Likewise, at the level of interaction, a general principle is at the basis of the view that language alternation is an issue of order. Provisionally, let me call this principle 'One-Situation–One-Language Principle'. Elsewhere, I have referred to this principle as the norm of 'language separateness' (Gafaranga, 2000a). Like the Structural Uniformity Principle, in monolingual contexts, the One-Situation–One-Language Principle might not be of any particular interest because, presumably, every interaction takes place in one language. However, in bilingual contexts, the principle gains paramount importance. It is such a principle that would have motivated Weinreich (1953) to formulate the now famous statement that

> the ideal bilingual switches languages according to appropriate changes in the speech situation and not in an unchanged speech situation and certainly not in the same sentence. (1952: 73)

Examples such as the following instance of 'medium repair' (Gafaranga, 2000b) can be used as evidence of participants' own orientation to the One-Situation–One-Language Principle. Ongoing interaction is conducted in Catalan. At some point, CU6 misses a word in this language. Although she knows the word in another language (Castilian) and that, apparently, both participants speak and understand both languages, she cannot just use the Castilian word. An account (highlighted) for why she is about to engage in talk in two languages must be provided.

*Example 5.1*

CU6: allò que se'n diu que se'n diu espera't t'ho **haig de dir en castellà perquè no sé com es diu en català**
(talk omitted)
Own: digues
CU6: **codillos**
OWN: si (.) **codillos**

CU6: that you call which you call **hang on I've got to tell you in Castilian because I don't know how it is called in Catalan**
(talk omitted)
OWN: say it
CU6: shanks
OWN: ye (.) shanks

In the last two chapters, we have seen that Weinreich's statement that bilingual speakers never use two languages within the same sentence is not true. Bilingual speakers often switch languages within the same sentence but, when they do, switching is accountably orderly. As I show in this chapter, the first part of the statement is not true either. Bilingual speakers often switch languages within the same situation. The issue therefore is, is language alternation within the same situation random or is it orderly and, in the latter case, how can that orderliness be accounted for?

As we saw in Chapter 3, the territory of the study of language alternation can be represented by the flow chart in Table 3.1, which, expanded to cover the detail of the node 'grammatical perspective', looks as in Table 5.1. In this representation, accounts of the 'interactional order' of language alternation all come under the node 'sociofunctional perspective'. In turn, as the representation shows, this node divides into identity-related and organisational explanations. In this chapter, I will focus on the two terminal nodes under identity-related explanation. These correspond to the Interactional Sociolinguistics perspective as developed by Gumperz (Blom and Gumperz, 1972; Gumperz, 1982) and the 'Markedness Model' as developed by Myers-Scotton (1983, 1988, 1993b). As it will become clear, my claim is that the so-called 'identity-related models' of language alternation, at

*Table 5.1* Studies of language alternation (ii)

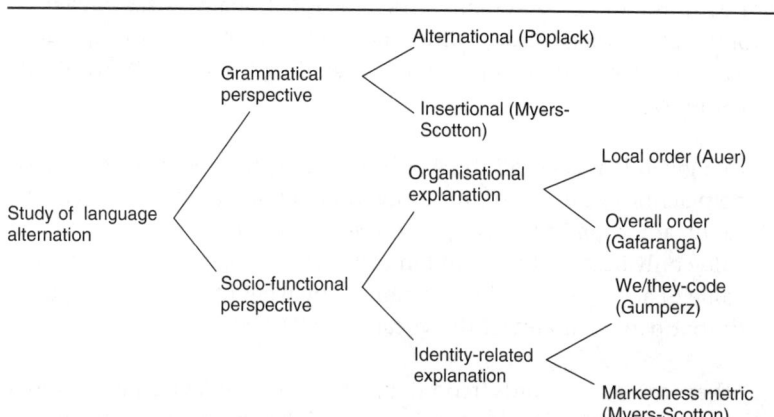

least the two I will review in this chapter, explain language alternation in terms of the One-Situation–One-Language Principle. That is, they view language alternation against the backdrop of language sparateness in terms of appropriate situations of use. In order to contextualise these two models of language alternation, it is necessary first to stablish the existence of the principle of language separateness as a research framework. I will do this by reviewing briefly a model which explains language choice, in monolingual as well as in bilingual contexts, in terms of the One-Situation–One-Language Principle. This is the model of 'diglossia'.

## 5.2. Diglossia: language alternation and/in the Sociology of Language

The Sociology of Language, an approach mostly associated with Fishman (see below), is based on a structuralist/functionalist view of language in society. A structure, by definition, is an orderly arrangement of things. The two defining elements of a structure are its components or units and the relationship among/between them. In this sense, a structure is different from a random pile of the same or different elements. Also in a structure, elements relate to one another in a particular way; typically, they do not overlap. In a structure, as de Saussure says, 'What characterises each (element) most exactly is being whatever the others are not' (1995: 115). Functionalism, on the other hand, is the view that elements either have a distinct role/function to play in the system or they do not exist as part of the system. Structural/functionalist ideas have been adopted in a variety of disciplines, but they are nowhere as explicit as in Sassurian Linguistics. For example, regarding the values of words, de Saussure writes,

> In a given language, all the words which express neighbouring ideas help define one another's meaning. Each set of synonyms like *redouter* (to dread), *craindre* (to fear), *avoir peur* (to be afraid) has its particular value only because they stand in contrast with one another.... So the value of any given word is determined by what other words there are in that particular area of the vocabulary. (1995: 114)

In other words, the words 'redouter', 'craindre' and 'avoir peur' form a structure and each of them remains part of that structure for as long as it has a function to play, that is, for as long as its value does not coincide with that of another. Likewise, regarding the sounds of a language, he writes,

> Each language constructs its words out of some fixed number of phonetic units, each one clearly distinct from the others. What characterises those units is not, as might be thought, the specific positive properties of each; but simply the fact that they cannot be mistaken for one another. Speech sounds are first and foremost entities which are contrastive, relative and negative. (1995: 117)

An even more readily understandable example of a structure is what we have seen in relation with French origin nouns in Kinyarwanda–French language alternation. As we have seen, for the purpose of class agreement, French origin nouns divide into those with the feature [+HUMAN] and those with the feature [–HUMAN]. The possibility for the same noun to have both features is inexistent.

As regards language choice, structuralist/functionalist ideas led to the model of diglossia. According to Ferguson (1959)[1] diglossia is

> ...a relatively stable language situation in which, in addition to the primary dialects of the language (which may include a standard or regional standards), there is a very highly codified (often grammatically more complex) superposed variety, the vehicle of a large and respected body of written literature, either of an earlier period or in another speech community, which is learned largely by formal

education and is used for most written and formal spoken purposes but is not used by any section of the community for ordinary conversation. (1959/2000: 75)

According to Ferguson, in those communities where diglossia obtains, language varieties can be seen as forming a structure. There are two (or more) varieties (units) of the language. Furthermore, these varieties are differentiated from each other at different levels (acquisition, standardisation, prestige, literary heritage, grammar, etc.). However, the level of functional differentiation seems to be the most important of all. These varieties stand in a functional relationship vis-à-vis each other, for each has a 'definite role to play' (2000: 65). One is used in very specific domains and the other is used in very specific other domains, with little overlap. Depending on the nature of the domains in which each variety is used, one is referred to as the 'High' (H) variety and the other as the 'Low' (L) variety. Ferguson visualised this functional differentiation of language varieties in diglossia as in Table 5.2 (2000: 68).

It is important to stress that Ferguson intended his model to apply only to communities he considered to be very specific cases of monolingualism, for he saw diglossia as 'a particular kind of standardization' (2000: 65). The communities Ferguson investigated are the following: the Arab world (colloquial Arabic vs classical Arabic), German speaking Switzerland (Swiss German vs Standard German), Haiti (Haitian Creole vs French) and Greece (Katharévusa vs Dhimotiki). Of course, one may question the assumption that all these situations are similar.

*Table 5.2* Functional differentiation of language varieties in diglossia

|  | H | L |
|---|---|---|
| Sermon in church and mosque | x |  |
| Instructions to servants, waiters, workmen |  | x |
| Personal letter |  | x |
| Speech in parliament | x |  |
| University lecture | x |  |
| Conversation with family, friends and colleagues |  | x |
| News broadcast | x |  |
| Radio 'soap opera' |  | x |
| Newspaper editorial, news story, caption on picture | x |  |
| Caption on political cartoon |  | x |
| Poetry | x |  |
| Folk literature |  | x |

For example, we now know that Haitian Creole and French are two different languages, but, then, they were not considered to be. One may also wonder how stable the situation has to be and for how long. In this respect, Ferguson (2000: 70) cites three factors which may lead to a different sociolinguistic structure. They are as follows:

(i) more widespread literacy
(ii) broader communication among different segments of the population
(iii) desire for political sovereignty

Although, as I have said above, Ferguson intended his model to describe very specific cases of monolingualism, it attracted attention from a variety of researchers, including those with interest in bilingualism. Top among the latter was the sociolinguist Fishman (1967)[2]. Up until the early 1960s, research in bilingualism had mainly focused on the psycholinguistic dimension. Departing from this tradition, Fishman felt that there was a need to reconcile psychological and sociological accounts of bilingualism in one framework and the notion of diglossia offered itself as capable of realising that connection (2000: 81). Thus, he kept the term 'bilingualism' for the psychological dimension (competence in two or more languages) and adopted diglossia to designate the patterned use of two or more languages. Building on Ferguson's ideas and those of other researchers who had followed in Ferguson's tradition, he saw diglossia as a universal phenomenon.

> diglossia exists not only in multilingual societies which recognise several languages and not only in societies that utilise vernacular and classical varieties, but also in societies which employ separate dialects, registers, or **functionally differentiated language varieties** of whatever kind. (Fishman, 2000: 82) (my emphasis)

In working out the different possibilities in which bilingualism could relate to diglossia, Fishman came up with four possibilities as shown in Table 5.3 (2000: 82).

According to Fishman, situations of 'neither diglossia nor bilingualism' are those where people have access to one variety and use it all the time. Such situations were felt to be extremely rare. Situations of 'diglossia without bilingualism' are very common and are observed every time when people have access to different varieties of the same language (hence 'No bilingualism') and functionally differentiate among them.

Table 5.3  Diglossia and Bilingualism

|  |  | Diglossia | |
|---|---|---|---|
|  |  | + | − |
| Bilingualism | + | 1. Both diglossia and bilingualism | 2. Bilingualism without diglossia |
|  | − | 3. Diglossia without bilingualism | 4. Neither diglossia nor bilingualism |

More important for us are the quadrants 1 and 2 in the above representation for, in both cases, bilingualism is involved. Situations of 'both diglossia and bilingualism' are those in which people have access to two languages and differentiate between them functionally. Such situations require 'very widespread (if not all-pervasive) bilingualism' (2000: 82). On the other hand, situations of 'bilingualism without diglossia' are those in which people have access to two or more languages, but do not differentiate between/among them functionally. In Fishman's own words, these are situations where 'bilinguals of similar cultural extraction [...] function without the benefit of a well-understood and widely accepted social consensus as to which language is to be used between which interlocutors, for communication concerning what topics or for what purposes' (2000: 85). Of these two, only the situation of bilingualism with diglossia should be regarded as normal since '[...] bilingualism without diglossia tends to be transitional both in terms of the linguistic repertoire of speech communities as well as in terms of the speech varieties involved per se' (2000: 87). And, Fishman explains this situation in structural/functionalist terms as follows:

> Without separate though complementary norms and values to establish and maintain functional separation of the speech varieties, that language or variety which is fortunate enough to be associated with the predominant drift of social forces tends to displace the other(s). (2000: 87)

Two comments need to be made regarding Fishman's model. First, it is important to stress that the model confirms and reinforces the One-Situation–One-Language Principle. And it does so in two ways. First, it sees bilingualism with diglossia as the norm. Secondly, it views the absence of diglossia against this norm as the backdrop and as accountable by reference to it. The second comment that can be made is in relation with the claim that diglossia is a stabilising factor. The model claims that stability obtains where there is bilingualism with diglossia.

> A speech community maintains its sociolinguistic pattern as long as the functional differentiation of the varieties in its linguistic repertoire is systematically maintained. As long as each variety is associated with a **separate class of situations** there is good reason and established means for retaining them all, each in its place:... (1972a: 51) (my emphasis)

A number of studies, including Gal (1979) and Eckert (1980), have shown not only that language shift takes place despite diglossia, but also that diglossia is in fact 'a force of language shift' (Eckert, 1980: 1053).

However, despite these shortcomings in Fishman's extension of the model of diglossia, other researchers have adopted it and looked at specific contexts, leading to different local variants (for a general review, see Fasold, 1984). Of these new versions of diglossia, I can only mention one, for it is particularly relevant for our discussion of the models of language alternation. This is the model originally called 'triglossia' by Mkilifi (1978) and later on aptly termed 'double overlapping diglossia' by Fasold (1984). According to Mkilifi, in Tanzania, two overlapping diglossia can be observed: one involving English (H) and Swahili (L) and one involving Swahili (H) and local languages (L).

The model of diglossia, as briefly sketched above, has important implications in terms of conceptualising language alternation. First, under diglossia, language alternation as normative linguistic behaviour is denied. The norm is for the languages to be kept separate in terms of the domains in which they can be used. That is, the norm is one-situation–one-language. Language alternation runs counter this norm and this is precisely the reason why it must be seen as an issue of order. However, that language alternation runs counter the principle of one-situation–one-language does not mean that it never occurs. All it means is that, when it does occur, language alternation is accountable by reference to the norm. In turn, two possibilities can be thought of. In the first case, language alternation, occurring in the context of bilingualism without diglossia, is evidence of change in progress. In this case, language alternation can be characterised as repairable deviance.

> Under circumstances such as these (of bilingualism without diglossia) no well-established, socially recognised and protected functional differentiation of languages obtains [...]. (Members) are particularly

inclined to use their mother tongue and the other tongue for intragroup communication in a **seemingly random fashion**. (2000: 86) (my emphasis)

The second possibility, occurring in the context of bilingualism with diglossia, is functional deviance, also known as 'metaphorical code-switching' (Blom and Gumperz, 1972, also see below). In this respect, Fishman writes,

> Once established, [...] bilingualism under circumstances of diglossia becomes an ingredient in [...] metaphorical switching patterns available for the purposes of intra-communal communicative appropriateness. (1972a: 97–98)

To summarise, the model of diglossia as developed by scholars such as Ferguson and Fishman has established the principle of language separateness as a scheme of interpretation for language choice. Under diglossia, language alternation can be seen as an issue of order because it runs counter to the principle of one-situation–one-language. According to this principle, the norm is for languages to be kept separate in terms of the situations in which they are appropriately used. Because of this norm of language separateness, language alternation can be seen as impossible in principle. However, that it is impossible in principle does not mean it never occurs. Models of diglossia, as any other normative framework, allow for language alternation to occur either in the form of repairable deviance or in that of functional deviance. The two models of language alternation I review in the next sections can be seen as a continuation of the diglossic view of language in society. They too are irrevocably based in the structural/functionalist mode of thinking about language in society.

## 5.3. We-/they-codes: language alternation and/in Interactional Sociolinguistics

### 5.3.1. Interactional Sociolinguistics

The perspective of Interactional Sociolinguistics was pioneered by Gumperz. The object of Sociolinguistics, as practiced by Labov (1972) and his followers, is to account for the orderliness of linguistic variability by reference to social structures such as gender, class, ethnicity and so on. For this reason, Labovian Sociolinguistics is also known as Variationist Sociolinguistics. Gumperz's approach is also called Sociolinguistics, for it too is interested in linguistic variability. However, Gumperz's interest is not in relating linguistic variation to social variation, but rather in examining how linguistic variation, among other things, is used as a resource by actual speakers in actual face-to-face interaction, hence the term 'interactional'. Gumperz's stated his main concern as in the following:

> There is a need for a social theory which accounts for the **communicative functions of linguistic variability** and for its relation to speakers' goals without reference to untestable functionalist assumptions about conformity or non-conformance to closed systems of norms. (1982: 93) (my emphasis).

In other words, Gumperz was interested, not necessarily in the structure of language in society, as was Fishman and Labov, but in actual face-to-face communication.

It is important to highlight the view that language variability can be seen as a resource that speakers use in actual interaction. The following example from Holmes (1999: 133) illustrates a rather common use of language variation in actual interaction, namely language variation as indexical of the speaker's identity. In the example, the listener uses language variation to tell aspects of the speaker's identity including regional origin (Scotland), gender (woman) and education (well-educated).

*Example 5.2*

Telephone rings

    Pat: Hello.
    Caller: Hello, is Mark there?
    Pat: Yes, just hold on a minute.
Pat(to Mark) **There is a rather well-educated young lady from Scotland on the phone for you**

In the example above, we can see that aspects of language variation have been used as resources because the situation required that use to be reported. In most situations, however, no need to report such uses is felt. Rather, listeners draw 'inferences' and base their own actions upon them in the hope that, through their own subsequent actions, interlocutors will confirm or reject those inferences. Conversation Analysts refer to this process, whereby understandings are negotiated through the chaining of actions as 'sequentiality'. Thus, according to Gumperz, 'communication is a social activity requiring the coordinated efforts of two or more individuals. Mere talk to produce sentences, no matter how well formed or elegant the outcome is, does not by itself constitute communication' (1982: 1). Central to this sense of communication as a coordinated activity is obviously the negotiation of meanings between participants. And this is so because actual meanings do not necessarily reside in linguistic forms. Indeed, Gumperz himself said that he was interested in 'conversational inference' and 'situated interpretation' rather in 'referential meaning' (1977).

The following example vividly depicts the kind of problems that Interactional Sociolinguistics should help solve.

> We can begin to see why individuals who speak English well and have no difficulty in producing grammatical English sentences may nevertheless differ significantly in what they perceive as meaningful discourse cues. Accordingly, their assumption about what information is to be conveyed, how it is to be ordered and put into words and their ability to fill in the unverbalized information they need to make sense of what transpires may also vary. This may lead to misunderstandings [...] (1982: 172)

That is to say, Interactional Sociolinguistics should account for the fact that people may fail to understand each other even when they share a common language, defined as a lexico-grammatical system. Conversely therefore, it should also explicate how participants in interaction manage to communicate successfully. Gumperz answers both questions saying that successful communication, just like the lack of it, is a matter of 'contextualization cues'. According to Gumperz, contextualisation cues are 'surface features of message form which [...] speakers (use to) signal and listeners (to) interpret what the activity is, how semantic content is to be understood and how each sentence relates to what precedes or follows' (1982: 131). Such cues may be phonetic, syntactic, lexical or stylistic variables. They may consist of formulaic routines, formulaic expressions, discourse routines such as openings and closings, speech delivery features such as prosody (loudness, tempo, stress, intonation, silence, laughter, backchannels) and even of language alternation (Gumperz, 1982: 129). For Gumperz, contextualisation cues are conventional in the sense that their meanings and their uses can vary from culture to culture. Thus, when these cues are shared by all participants, 'interpretive processes are taken for granted and tend to go unnoticed. However, when (they are not shared), interpretation may differ and misunderstanding may occur' (1982: 132).

### 5.3.2. Language alternation in Interactional Sociolinguistics

How does language alternation fit into this analysis of face-to-face communication as developed by Gumperz? In the above, we have seen that Gumperz explicitly states that language alternation itself works as a contextualisation cue. Elsewhere he writes,

> Code switching signals contextual information equivalent to what in monolingual settings is conveyed through prosody or other syntactic or lexical processes. It generates the presuppositions in terms of which the content of what is said is decoded. (1982: 98)

Gumperz defines his scheme for interpreting language alternation as follows. In bilingual communities, languages form a structure and are functionally differentiated. The following description of language choice in the Norwegian village of Hemnes that Blom and Gumperz (1972)[3] studied is very much in line with Ferguson and Fishman's model of diglossia (see above). In the village, two varieties are used, namely a local dialect and a standard form of Norwegian. Blom and Gumperz described the situation as in the following:

> Casual observations and recording of free speech among locals in homes, workshops, and the various public meeting places [...] show that **only** the dialect is used there. However, statuses defined with respect to the superimposed national Norwegian system elicit the standard. Examples of these are church services, presentation of text material in school, reports and announcements [...] at public meetings. Similarly, meetings with tourists or other strangers elicit the standard at least until the participants' identity becomes more clearly known. (2000: 125-126) (my emphasis).

Fishman would have said that Hemnes is a case of diglossia without bilingualism.

As regards bilingual contexts and in line with the above, Gumperz proposes the following structure:

> The tendency is for the ethnically specific, minority language to be regarded as the 'we code' and become associated with in-group and

informal activities, and for the majority language to serve as the 'they-code' associated with more formal, stiffer and less personal outgroup relations. (1982: 66)

That is to say, in bilingual communities, languages form a structure and are functionally differentiated. One is the 'we-code' while the other is the 'they-code'. On the other hand, because of this association, language varieties and situations in which they are used, identities they are associated with, social values they communicate become co-selective. Fishman terms this co-selectivity 'domain congruency' (Fishman, 1972b).

The following example taken from Myers-Scotton's (1993b: 88) study of language choice in East Africa can be used by way of exemplifying Gumperz's ideas. The sociolinguistic context of the example is Kenyan Bilingualism, a situation which can be described as 'double-overlapping diglossia' (Fasold, 1984 – see above), with English and Swahili as the H's and they-codes and the various local languages as the L languages and we-codes. In the specific example, the languages involved are Swahili (H) and Luya (L). Talk takes place at the entrance of the IBM Nairobi office. The visitor (V), from the Luyia area of western Kenya, approaches and addresses the security guard (G). Luya is italicised; otherwise Swahili is used.

*Example 5.3*

1. G: Unataka kumuwona nani?
2. V1: Ningependa kumuwona Solomon I.
3. G: Unamujua kweli? Tunaye Solomon A –Nadhani ndio yule.
4. V1: Yule anayetoka Tiriki – yaani Luyia.
5. G: *Solomon menyu wakhumanya vulahi?*
6. V1: *yivi mulole umuvolere ndi Shen L. –venyanga khukhulola.*
7. G: *Yikhala yalia ulindi.*
Another visitor (V2) comes.
8. V2: Bwana K – yuko hapa?
9. G: Ndio yuko – anafanya kazi saa hii (talk goes on in Swahili).

1. G: Whom do you want to see?
2. V1: I would like to see Solomon I.
3. G: Do you really know him? We have a Solomon A- I think that's the one [you mean].
4. V1: That one who comes from Tiriki – that is, a Luyia person.

5. G:  *Will Solomon know you?*
6. V1: *You see him and tell him Shem L- wants to see you.*
7. G:  *sit here and wait.*
Another visitor (V2) comes.
8. V2: *Is Mr K- here?*
9. G:  *Yes, he's here – he is doing something right now* (talk goes on in Swahili).

(Original transcription slightly modified)

At the beginning of the interaction, participants do not know each other and normatively choose Swahili, the they-code, as the 'medium' of their interaction (Gafaranga and Torras, 2001, also see Chapter 6). In the course of the interaction, they recognise each other as coming from the same region of Kenya where Luya is used. This recognition triggers the shift from speaking Swahili to using Luya, the we-code. Later on, when another visitor comes, talk goes back to Swahili. That is, in this interaction, participants themselves are using the structure we-/they-code to conduct their talk in an orderly manner.

Thus, in Gumperz, as in Ferguson and Fishman, the norm is one-situation–one-language. However, here too, the fact that the norm of language separateness obtains does not mean that language alternation never occurs. Rather, it means that, when it does occur, language alternation is interpreted in terms of the norm of one-situation–one-language. To be sure, Gumperz's model allows for two types of language alternation: 'situational code-switching' and 'metaphorical code-switching'. In situational code-switching, language alternation occurs because of or as a way of negotiating 'appropriate changes in the speech situation' (Weinreich, 1953: 73). Consider Example 5.3 again. By switching from Swahili to Luya, the guard is proposing a renegotiation of the speech situation from *doing being* strangers to *doing being* members of the 'local team'. That is, as soon as the guard realises that his interlocutor and he himself come from the same language background, the situation changes and, as a result, the appropriate language has to be selected. Even more subtle cases of language choice such as the following can be seen as instances of situational code-switching. The example comes from a study of bilingual service encounters in Barcelona. The languages involved are English (Italics) and Castilian (Bold).

*Example 5.4* (translation in brackets)

AAA: *hello*
BBB: *hello* (.) [eh:

CCC: [dues de negra no (two of stout right)
BBB: **quires pewueña o grande** (would you like it small or large)
CCC: **grande** (large)
BBB: **grande** (large)
AAA: mmm mmm
BBB: *eh: one big (.) one half pint (.) for me (.) [one half pint for me*
AAA:                                                        *[one half pint for you*
BBB: *and one pint for him*

As the transcript shows, talk to the bar attendant is conducted in English while customers use Spanish between themselves. In short, in the case of situational code-switching, language alternation is orderly, for it conforms to the principle of one-situation–one-language.

The second possibility of language alternation Gumperz's framework allows is metaphorical code-switching. Just like situational code-switching, metaphorical code-switching draws on the co-selectivity between language varieties and social situations. However, the two are different in the sense that situational code-switching consists of a direct application of the norm while metaphorical code-switching works through 'violation of co-occurrence expectations' (Gumperz, 1982: 98). That is to say, metaphorical code-switching is orderly because it is an instance of deviance from the norm of one-situation–one-language. As we have seen, deviance from the norm is either functional or repairable. As the name suggests, metaphorical code-switching is functional. It is used when the speaker wants to convey a meaning beyond what s/he says. It is in this sense that, according to Gumperz, metaphorical code-switching has a semantic value, is directional.

> The semantic effect of metaphorical code switching depends on the existence of a regular relationship between variables and social situations [...]. The context in which one of a set of alternates is regularly used becomes part of its meaning so that when this form is then employed in a context where it is not normal, it brings in some of the flavour of this original setting (Blom and Gumperz, 2000: 127).

Remember that Fishman himself had identified this possibility.

Consider Example 5.5. The conversation was recorded by Gal (1979) during her study of language shift in Oberwart. The languages involved are Hungarian (plain characters) and German (bold). The general sociolinguistic situation is such that German is H while Hungarian is L. In the example, a grandfather asks his two grandchildren to stop what they are doing and come to him. Initially, he uses Hungarian. But as the children resist his order, he ups the stakes by switching to German, thus drawing on the force of the language to reinforce his order. In this case, the switch to German is clearly directional.

*Example 5.5*

Grandfather: *Szo! Ide dzsüni! (pause) jeszt jerámunyi*
(Well, come here! Out all this away)

*mind e kettüötök, no hát akkor! (pause)*
(both of you, well now)

**kum her**! *(pause) Nëm koapsz vacsorát*
(**Come here**!) you don't get supper

However, Gumperz is careful to point out that the directionality of metaphorical code-switching does not always obtain. 'In many cases [...] it is the choice of code itself in a particular conversational context which forces interpretation' (1982: 83). The following two examples from my corpus of Kinyarwanda–French language alternation jointly support this. In Example 5.6, A is saying that he is doing research on French lexical competence among Rwandan secondary school children. He stresses that he has limited himself to the first years, reiterating the French phrase 'premières années' in Kinyarwanda as 'imyaka ya mbere'.

*Example 5.6*

1. A: hee (.) *donc* nkora muri *lexicologie* (.) *plus précisément muri competence lexicale* muri *école secondaire*
2. B: umh
3. A: (unclear) *je me suis limité aux* **premières années** (.) **imyaka ya mbere**
4. B: umh
5. A: kuko nkeka *hypothèse* yanjye ni uko iyo abana bavuye muri *primaire* nta gifaransa baba bazi

1. A: yes (.) so my work is lexicology (.) precisely on lexical competence at secondary school level
2. B: umh

3. A: I have limited myself to the first years (.) first years
4. B: umh
5. A: for my hypothesis is that when children graduate from primary school they do not know French

On the other hand, consider Example 5.7. The topic of the conversation is how difficult it used to be to travel around in Rwanda. To illustrate this, B says that he used to walk for two-and-a-half days to go to the secondary school he attended. By way of stressing the amount of time the walking used to take, he reiterates the Kinyarwanda phrase 'iminsi ibiri n'igice' using the French equivalent 'deux jours et demi'.

*Example 5.7*

1. A: mpa dusangire
2. B: kuko twe twakoreshaga iminsi **ibiri hafi n'igice** (.) *deux jours et demi*
3. C: eh nzi nzi abantu bavaga iwacu kakajya wiga (.) iZaza (.) n'amaguru
4. A: umh
5. C: bakoreshagaa icy (.) icyumweru cyose
6. A: icyumweru

1. A: let's share
2. B: as for us we used to walk for about two days and a half (.) two days and a half
3. C: eh I know people from my village who used to go to school (.) in Zaza (.) on foot
4. A: umh
5. B: they would walk for a whole week
6. A: a week

Clearly, in cases like these, it is doubtful whether one would still be justified to speak of metaphorical code-switching as, in order to serve a given function, language alternation need not follow any specific direction. Briefly, the orderliness of this type of language alternation is left unaccounted for.

Also, there is the issue of whether language alternation is always functional. As we have seen, Sankoff (1972) and Kachru (1978) do not think it is. Two types of non-functional language alternation need to be distinguished. The first type of non-functional language alternation consists of instances which participants themselves orient to as repairable. Consider the following instance (from Auer, 1988/2000: 178) of what Auer (1984) refers as participant-related transfer (see below). In the example, while speaking Italian, Alfredo misses the *mot juste*, uses German (Fehler) and goes on to repair it (errori).

*Example 5.8*

Al: arOpë – guarda le: – *Fehler*- alOrë i = errori
((lento))
e tutto sbal' c'i vonno lovare ventic'inkwe
((hesitating))
*Anschläge*- c'ai:/-

Al: and then – she has a look at the – MISTAKEs – I mean the mistakes- and (for) every mistake they take away 25 TOUCHES-which is/-

Also consider the following instance of 'medium repair' (Gafaranga, 2000b) from my Kinyarwanda–French bilingual conversations. In turn 3, A misses the *mot juste*, interrupts the flow of his talk to signal that he is moving into another language (see 'babyita'), and then uses an English expression ('local government'). In turn 4, B shows agreement and, using a 'continuer' (Schegloff, 1982), encourages A to keep talking. In turn 5, A corrects the English expression he has used and changes it from 'local government' to 'local authority' before trying a translation ('ni nka'). In turn 6, B provides the repair (translation) and, in turn 7 A confirms it and talks on. That is, in the example, participants themselves have oriented to the alternation towards English as a repairable problem.

*Example 5.9*

1. A: noneho rero nka bariya b' impunzi ukuntu bigenda (.) babagira ba- a a amashuri hano ni *privées quoi* (.) ni *privées* mbega (.) kuburyo rero kugirango aze muri iyi *université* agomba kwishyura
2. B: umh
3. A: *mais comme* nta mafaranga afite ay- yatse *bourse le*- babyita **local government**
4. B: umh
5. A: **local authority** *donc* ni nkaaa
6. B: ni nka **municipalité**
7. A: ni nka **municipalité** *c'est ça* (.) *municipalité* yahano niyo yamuhaye *bourse*

1. A: refugees like him are- schools here are *private* (.) they are *private* so that he must pay to study at this *university*
2. B: umh
3. A: *but as* he doesn't have money he has had to apply for a *grant* from the- they call it **local government**
4. B: umh
5. A: **local authority** well it's likeee
6. B: it's like a **municipality**
7. A: that's right it's like a **municipality** (.) he got a *grant* from the local *municipality*

Given the importance of repairable deviance in any account of order, the fact that Gumperz is silent on this type of language alternation must be seen as a shortcoming on the part of his model as an account of order in talk in two languages.

Secondly, there is the type of non-functional language alternation which Gumperz himself recognises and refers to as 'conversational code-switching'. The use of French and Kinyarwanda in Example 5.9 is a good example. In the example, speakers are alternating so frequently between French and Kinyarwanda that it would be impossible to attempt a functional explanation for every instance. According to Gumperz, this type of non-functional language alternation obtains in contexts where 'individuals live in situations of rapid transition, where traditional inter-group barriers are breaking down and norms of interaction are changing [...] (It) occurs in conditions of change where speakers' ethnic identities and social background are not matters of common agreement' (1982: 64). As we have seen, Fishman refers to this type of language alternation as occurring under bilingualism without diglossia. If this argument was accepted, this type of language alternation too would have to be seen as repairable deviance. The problem is that, unlike in the case of the use of English, in the case of the use of French and Kinyarwanda in Example 5.9, nothing indicates that participants themselves perceive the alternate use of these two languages as requiring any repair.

Briefly, Gumperz's model of language alternation is based on a structural/functionalist mode of thinking about language in society. The specific version of language separateness it adopts is the distinction between what he calls the we-code and what he calls the they-code. On the basis of this structure, Gumperz can easily account for the orderliness of two types of language alternation, namely situational code-switching and metaphorical code-switching. Situational code-switching is normative, for it does not violate the principle of one-situation–one language.

On the other hand, metaphorical code-switching is also orderly because it is a case of functional deviance from the norm of language separateness. However, the orderliness of other types of language alternation is not so easily explained in Gumperz's model. On one hand, as if to try and preserve the structure we-/they-code at all costs, Gumperz evokes the very same structure by way of explaining language alternation which is neither situational nor metaphorical. Referring to this type of language alternation as conversational code-switching, he says that it is indicative of ongoing changes in the sociolinguistic structure. That is, this type of language alternation is viewed as repairable deviance; repair is actually to have taken place when a new sociolinguistic structure has been achieved. On the other hand, there are instances which are oriented to by participants themselves as repairable. Presumably, this could also be viewed as repairable deviance in the model. However, if this happened, there would be a need to distinguish between the two types of repairable deviance, for this second type can occur even in the case of normative monolingual talk. Finally, there are instances which, although functional, cannot be accounted for in terms of the structure we-/they-code. Because of these difficulties, in the next section, I examine the markedness model as an alternative identity-related account of the orderliness of language alternation.

## 5.4. Markedness: a rational choice model of language alternation

### 5.4.1. Language choice as a rational act

The Markedness Model of Codeswitching was developed by Myers-Scotton and associates in a series of publications (Myers-Scotton, 1983, 1988, 1993b, 1998b, 1999; Myers-Scotton and Bolanyai, 2001). Although it shows influence from a variety of sources including the Cooperative Principle (Grice, 1975) and Relevance (Sperber and Wilson, 1995), the Markedness Model was mostly inspired by Elster's (1979, 1989) Rational Choice model. This influence can be seen in the kind of general questions the model asks. These questions are set out in Myers-Scotton and Bolonyai (2001: 1) as follows:

> What is the engine that drives speakers to select one linguistic variety over another? Why speak English rather than Spanish while discussing a deadline with a fellow worker if you're both Chicanas in Los Angeles? Why switch to an approximation of a 'good ole boy'

Carolina accent when asking your car mechanic for advice in urban South Carolina?

In other words, what is the 'motivation' for language choice? Regarding language alternation, the question is, 'what motivates speakers to switch languages within a single conversation?' (Scotton and Bolanyai, 2001: 6).

Referring to Elster (1979, 1989), Myers-Scotton and Bolonyai answer the questions above as follows:

> we argue that talk follows principles of **rational behavior**. These principles hold that choices in specific interactions are best explained as cognitively based calculations that depend on the actor's estimation of what action offers him/her the greatest utility. (2001: 2) (my emphasis)

Elsewhere, Myers-Scotton writes,

> The decision to engage in codeswitching is a prime example of an intentional, if often unconscious, social message in a bilingual community. To switch codes is a calculation that the anticipated interpersonal rewards codeswitching will yield are greater than those that initiating or maintaining a monolingual discourse pattern can confer. That actors consider the costs and rewards associated with alternative choices and then act to optimise their returns is the premise of rational actor models. (1999: 1259–1260)

Early on, Myers-Scotton had stated that 'a major motivation for using one variety rather than another as a medium of interaction is the extent to which this choice minimises costs and maximises rewards for the speaker' (1993b: 100).

It is important to note that the object of the Markedness Model is 'the why' of language alternation (Wei, 1998). As we have seen above, it is, 'what motivates speakers to switch languages within the same conversation?'. As we have already seen, a systematic account of order in social action starts by identifying the norm and describing normative conduct. Then, in the light of the identified norm, deviance is noticed and accounted for either as functional (why) or as repairable. That is to say, in a systematic account of order in social action, the 'why' question arises only after the norm has been identified and only in the case of deviance from it. That is to say again, the Markedness Model, by concerning itself only with 'the why' of language alternation, starts from the unstated assumption that language alternation is deviant, in which case it must specify what it deviates from (what the norm is). More specifically, because it focuses only on the 'social motivation for codeswitching' (Myers-Scotton, 1993b), the Markedness Model skips the important question of 'how' language alternation is possible in the first place. However, even though the Markedness Model does not directly address the issue of the possibility of language alternation, reading between the lines, it is possible to detect the view of order that underlies it. It is this view that I want to make explicit in this section.

### 5.4.2. The markedness model

#### 5.4.2.1. *Some premises*

Myers-Scotton's starting point is the view that, in bilingual societies, language varieties form a structure and that they entertain functional relationships between/among them. Speaking of the notion of 'markedness', Myers-Scotton echoes de Saussure's statement about the sounds of a language (see above):

> Using the concept of markedness implies that code choice is viewed as a **system of oppositions**. This follows the fact that markedness is a property of oppositions. (1993b: 81–82) (my emphasis)

That is, the premise for the Markedness Model is a structural view of language in society. Indeed, on many occasions, in her monograph, Myers-Scotton (1993b) acknowledges the similarity between her approach and diglossia models, which she also refers to as the 'allocational paradigm'. For example, speaking of her initial observation of language choice in Nairobi, she writes,

> My problem was that I was viewing the Nairobi community as at least reminiscent of diglossic communities, and certainly within a cognitive framework based on a combination of the domain and binary-choice models in the 'allocational paradigm'. But many students' field notes included more than just conversations to which one linguistic variety was allocated, the prediction of the domain and binary-choice models. They also reported interactions conducted in two languages without a change in participants, locale, or even topic. (1993b: 49)

In other words, Myers-Scotton's aim was not to question structuralism as such, but rather using 'many of the premises of the allocational paradigm ... (as) a foundation-stone of the markedness model' (1993b: 92), to account, not only for the use of either of the bilingual's languages, but also for the possibility of using 'two languages without a change in participants, locale or even topic' (1993b: 49).

Myers-Scotton formulated her version of the sociolinguistic structure in bilingual communities as in the following:

> This model assumes that all linguistic code choices are indexical of a set of rights and obligations holding between participants in the conversational exchange. That is, any code choice points to a particular interpersonal balance, and it is partly because of their indexical qualities that different languages, dialects and styles are maintained in a community. (1988: 152)

The similarity between Myers-Scotton's and Fishman's views, especially regarding the retention of language varieties, is explicit enough. According to both scholars, language varieties are maintained only if they each have a specific role to play. Each language indexes a different 'rights and obligations set'.

Regarding the 'indexicality' of linguistic choices, Example 5.3 can be looked at again by way of an example. As we have seen, as soon as the guard realised that he and the visitor come from the same ethnic background, he switched to the shared regional language. In other words, there seems to be an unstated, although oriented to, rule that people from the same language background speak the shared regional language even when they have access to other languages as well. Thus, region of origin and the use of the local language become co-selective. Also consider Example 5.10 from the same Nairobi corpus (Myers-Scotton, 1988: 167–168):

*Example 5.10*

Passenger: (Lwidakho) (speaking in a loud voice and addressing the conductor) Mwana weru, vugula khasimoni khonyene
*(Dear brother, take only fifty cents)*
(laughter from conductor and other passengers)
Passenger: (Lwidakho) Shuli mwana wera mbaa
*(aren't you my brother?)*

Conductor: (Swahili) Apana. mimi si ndugu wako. Kama ungekuwa ndugu wangu ninjekujua kwa jina... lakini sikujui wala sikufahamu
(*No, I am not your brother. If you were my brother. I would know you by name. But I don't know you or understand you*)
Passenger: (Swahili) Nisaidie tu bwana .. Maisha ya Nairobi imeshinda kwa sababu bei ya kila kitu imeongezwa .. mimi ninakti Kariobang'i pahali ninapolipa pesa nying sana kwa nauli ya basi
(*Just help me mister. The cost of living in Nairobi has defeated me – the price of everything has gone up – I live at Kariobang'i – the fare to get there is very high*)
Conductor: (Swahili) Nimecukua peni nane pekee yake
(*I have only taken eighty cents*)
Passenger: (English, Swahili) Thank you very much. Nimeshukuru sana kw huruma ya huyu ndugu wango.
(*I am very thankful for the pity of this one, my brother.*)

In the example, the main task at hand is the negotiation of a favour, namely a reduced bus fare. It would not be very wrong to speak of corruption here. One of the 'felicity conditions' (Searle, 1969) for such an act is social closeness between the participants. The closer the participants, the higher the likelihood of success. In the example, the passenger shows orientation to this in two ways. First, he claims that the driver is his 'brother'. In the African context, the term 'brother' essentially means 'friend' and not necessarily somebody related to the speaker by blood relationships. The right to ask for a favour and the obligation to do favours is part and parcel of being friends. It is in Sacks' (1972) terms a 'category-bound' attribute. Secondly, the conductor chooses to use Lwidakho, a local language in this public setting, as if to tell the conductor that he is not any 'brother' (friend), but somebody from the same ethnic background. Whatever the result of the negotiation has been, it is clear that, in the example, participants themselves are using the social indexicality of languages to go about talking as practical social action.

A pre-requisite for Myers-Scotton's sociolinguistic structure is the notion of 'conventionalised exchange' or 'interaction type'. According to her,

> A conventionalized exchange is any interaction for which speech community members have a sense of 'script'. They have this sense because such exchanges are frequent in the community to the extent that at least their medium is routinized. That is the variety used

or even specific phonological or syntactic patterns or lexical items employed are predictable. (1988: 152) (my emphasis)

Here again, the similarity between this and Fishman's notion of domain congruency is obvious. The 'routinized', that is predictable, medium of a particular conventionalised exchange is said to be the 'unmarked choice' for that interaction type.

Also important in Myers-Scotton's framework is the notion of 'markedness metric/evaluator'. This is an innate and universal ability that people have to evaluate choices as marked or as unmarked for specific interaction types. In this respect, Myers-Scotton writes,

> The markedness model [...] depends on the addition of a speaker's 'markedness metric' to an enlarged conception of linguistic competence. This metric is part of the innate cognitive faculty of all humans. It enables speakers to assess all code choices as more or less unmarked or marked for the exchange type in which they occur. (1993b: 79–80)

This innate universal ability is then adjusted to specific situations through 'experience with language in actual use' (1999: 1261). This mature context-specific evaluator then 'enables speakers to sense the degree to which alternative linguistic choices are unmarked or marked for a given interaction type' (1999: 1261).

Thus, given the social context and the information from the markedness evaluator, speakers as rational actors make the most 'optimal' choice based on available evidence. This optimal choice may or may not be the most desirable for the speaker (1999: 1263). And they do so confident that their choices will be recognised and correctly interpreted by interlocutors because they operate in a 'normative framework' (1999). Speaking of this normative framework, Myers-Scotton writes,

> I argue that it would not be possible for a speaker to assume that his or her messages, whether the choice is unmarked or marked, have communicative intentions (i.e. as unmarked or marked) unless an underlying normative framework existed, with readings of markedness for the potential code choices. That is, the normative framework is necessary for speakers to be able to interpret code choices. (1993b: 109)

As we have already seen, according to Garfinkel (1967), a norm is a scheme of interpretation and it is because social action takes place within a normative framework that 'reciprocity of perspectives' is possible between participants.

### 5.4.2.2. Types of language choices

As for the choices themselves, they fall into two categories. Language choices are either unmarked or marked. An unmarked choice is one which, in a particular interaction type, corresponds to the 'script' and a marked choice is one which deviates from the script. In other words, the unmarked choice is 'the linguistic variety which is most expected, while the marked choice is most unusual' (1993b: 89), is 'a break from the communicative norm' (Givon, 1979, cited in Myers-Scotton 1993b: 89). In turn, under the category of unmarked choice, different possibilities can be observed. First, bilingual speakers may choose to conduct their conversation monolingually. With reference to the principle of one-situation–one-language, such a practice is obviously normative. Alternatively, they may start in one language and, as new information about the situation becomes available, switch to the other language, thus producing the pattern of language choice Myers-scotton refers to as 'sequential unmarked codeswitching'. Myers-Scotton herself recognises the similarity between this pattern and Gumperz' pattern of situational code-switching. Here again, participant's behaviour is normative, for, at any one time, the principle of one-situation–one-language is adhered to. An example of such a pattern is Example 5.3, reproduced below as Example 5.11 for convenience.

*Example 5.11*

1. G:   Unataka kumuwona nani?
2. V1:  Ningependa kumwona Solomon I.
3. G:   Unamujua kweli? Tunaye Solomon A –Nadhani ndio yule.
4. V1:  Yule anayetoka Tiriki – yaani Luyia.
5. G:   *Solomon menyu wakhumanya vulahi?*
6. V1:  *yivi mulole umuvolere ndi Shen L. –venyanga khukhulola.*
7. G:   *Yikhala yalia ulindi.*
Another visitor (V2) comes.
8. V2:  Bwana K – yuko hapa?
9. G:   Ndio yuko – anafanya kazi saa hii (talk goes on in Swahili).

1. G:   Whom do you want to see?
2. V1:  I would like to see Solomon I.
3. G:   Do you really know him? We have a Solomon A- I think that's the one [you mean].

4. V1: That one who comes from Tiriki – that is, a Luyia person.
5. G: *Will Solomon know you?*
6. V1: *You see him and tell him Shem L- wants to see you.*
7. G: *sit here and wait.*
Another visitor (V2) comes.
8. V2: Is Mr K- here?
9. G: Yes, he's here – he is doing something right now (talk goes on in Swahili).

(Original transcription slightly modified)

As the transcript shows, having selected to use Swahili as the medium because interaction takes place between strangers, participants switched to Luya as soon as information became available that they were from the same language group.

Thirdly, the optimal choice may turn out to be the alternate use of two languages or 'codeswitching itself as the unmarked choice'. This type of language choice deserves some further comments. As we have seen, in Fishman and in Gumperz, there is a type of language alternation which is seemingly random, for it is not functional. We have also seen that both Fishman and Gumperz explain it in terms of ongoing changes in the sociolinguistic structure. As we have seen, other researchers refer to it as code-mixing (Kachru, 1978; Auer, 1999). It would seem that it is this type of language alternation that Myers-Scotton refers to as code-switching itself as an unmarked choice. Myers-Scotton explains this type of language choice as in the following:

> The motivation for such switching is the same as that for choosing a single linguistic variety which is an unmarked choice: any variety is indexical of the speaker's position in the rights and obligations balance. When the speaker wishes **more than one social identity to be salient** in the current exchange, and each identity is encoded in the particular speech community by a different linguistic variety, then those two or more codes constitute the unmarked choice. (1988: 162) (my emphasis)

That is, unlike Fishman and Gumperz, Myers-Scotton does not see this type of language alternation as a case of repairable deviance. Rather, by saying that it is an unmarked choice, she suggests that it must be seen as normative choice.

However, the details of Myers-Scotton's argument regarding the orderliness of this type of talk are problematic. As implied in the quotation above, Myers-Scotton's view is that code-switching as an unmarked choice is arrived at through a simple mathematical rule of addition. Language A indexes the rights and obligations set A, and language B indexes the rights and obligations set B. Therefore, language alternation A and B is used when both sets of rights and obligations are salient. Elsewhere, I have argued that there is a need to demonstrate that these sets of rights and obligations are interactionally relevant (Gafaranga, 2001b, 2005). But there is another difficulty as well. As Myers-Scotton herself notes, this type of language alternation is not found in all bilingual communities (1993b: 119–125). It is community-specific, rather than the result of simple mathematical addition. Therefore, for the view that language alternation itself can be an unmarked choice, that it can be an instance of normative action, to be sustainable, the sociolinguistic structure itself must be re-adjusted. This type of language alternation itself must be seen as a variety in its own right which is recognised as such in the specific community. Such is indeed the view held by Herbert (2001: 239–346) who maintains that 'the label "unmarked choice" seems misleading' and suggests to use the term 'code switching as a linguistic variety' instead. Thus, the sociolinguistic structure underlying the possibility of code-switching as an unmarked choice must be seen as including language alternation A and B in addition to languages A and B, rather than as consisting of language A and language B only. Only then will language alternation itself be said to have a social value which can be recognised by the community-specific markedness evaluator as marked or unmarked for specific conventionalised exchanges. Without this recognition, it would be impossible to choose this particular form of speech as an unmarked choice. In turn, in order to reflect this new reality, the general principle of one-situation–one-language itself needs to be re-adjusted. The underlying principle with reference to which language alternation is seen as an issue of order would have to be not one-situation–one-language, but rather 'one-situation–one-variety', where variety may, but need not, consist of one language. Under this version of the principle, language alternation itself as an unmarked choice would indeed be normative conduct.

It is precisely because language alternation as unmarked choice is normative conduct that, as Myers-Scotton stresses, in code-switching as an unmarked choice, 'each switch need have no special significance; rather it is the overall pattern of using two varieties which carries social meaning' (1988: 162). Here is an example:

*Example 5.12*

A: Ariko njye nkeka ko *hypothèse de base* umuntu yashyiramo ni uko ikiri *important* ari *l' interlocuteur-* ni uko *les* euh, *les* euh, *les* euh, *comment dire, les- donc* ikiri *important pour les gens qui parlent* ni uko *interlocuteur* yumva icyo ushaka kuvuga.

A: As for me I think that the hypothesis could be that the important thing is the interlocutor – is that the euh- the euh- the euh- how how can I put it- the well- what's important for speakers is that the interlocutor understands what they want to say.

In a situation where participants constantly alternate between their two languages as in this example, it would be futile to try and assign functional meaning to every switch. To be sure, if each instance of switch carried a separate functional load, interaction would be impossible. As Garfinkel (1967) has indicated, if the norm is constantly disrupted, interaction becomes impossible. Rather, according to Myers-Scotton, it is the fact of using two languages in this fashion which globally carries meaning.

As I have indicated above, according to the Markedness Model of Codeswitching, choices may be unmarked, but they may also be marked. In turn, there are two types of marked choices. The first type is when the speaker switches from one language to the other by way of negotiating a different rights and obligations set, or more commonly a change in the speech situation. If the negotiation succeeds, the new language becomes the unmarked choice for the new situation. Also note that, in terms of order, this is normative conduct as only one language is used at anyone time. An example of such marked switching is the following from Myers-Scotton (1988/2000: 160) herself. Talk takes place in a Nairobi hotel where a young man is begging a young woman for a dance. Talk goes on in Swahili until the young woman gets annoyed and explicitly rejects the young man's solicitations. This shift of attitudes corresponds to the shift from Swahili to English.

*Example 5.13*

*He (Swahili)*: Nisaidie na dance, tafadhali.
          (please give me a dance.)
*She (Swahili)*: Nimechoka. Pengine nyimbo ifuatayo.
          (I'm tired. Maybe a following song.)
*He (Swahili)*: Hii ndio nyimbo ninayopenda.

(This is the song which I like.)
*She (Swahili)*: Nimechoka!
(I'm tired!)
*He (Swahili)*: Tafadhali.
(Please.)
*She (interrupting) (English)* : Ah, stop bugging me.
*He (English)*: I'm sorry. I didn't mean to bug you, but I can't help it if I like this song.
*She (English)*: OK, then, in that case, we can dance.

Also consider Example 5.14 from a service encounter in Barcelona. Talk takes place at a chamber of commerce. Z has called to report that a cheque he should have received has not reached him yet. The interaction is conducted in English until turn 10. In this turn, the interpersonal relationship between participants changes. Z calls for a proper professional relationship and, retrospectively, accuses B to have been unprofessional up to this point. This change of interpersonal relationship coincides with language alternation from English to Castilian.

*Example 5.14*

1. B: uh: well uh: ((laughs)) m- my news is that the cheque uh has been sent- I: suppose er: last week or:
2. Z: OK but Ok but I wa- I was told that it had been sent
3. B: yeah
4. Z; er: I was told this er: four weeks ago
5. B: four weeks ago
6. Z: yeah- obviously you tell me now that it was sent last week
7. B: yeah
8. Z: then obviously – the first message- wasn't correct
9. B: well no no actually I don't know exactly the date when this has been sent – but well er: – the ne- – er [what they know is ]
10. Z: [no no no OK OK ] let's OK- **vamos a ser professionales**
                                        (*let's be professional*)
11. B: yeah
12. Z: **y: necesito:**
   (*and I need*)
13. B: **Sí** (*yeah*)
14. Z: **una carta:**
   (*a letter*)
15. B: **Sí** (*yeah*)

According to Myers-Scotton, the crucial difference between sequential unmarked code-switching and this type of marked code-switching is that, in sequential unmarked code-switching, new information about the context becomes available independently of the speaker while, in the case of marked code-switching, the speaker himself/herself initiates to renegotiate the context. As we have seen, in Gumperz' framework, both types of language alternation come under situational code-switching. Furthermore, the similarity between the two must be recognised, for, with reference to the principle of one-situation–one-variety, both are instances of normative language choice. In marked code-switching, as in sequential unmarked code-switching, only one variety is used at any one time.

The second possibility of marked switching is when speakers momentarily use language B in a discourse in language A. According to Myers-Scotton, such switchings, unlike the pattern of code-switching itself as an unmarked choice, are functional.

> There are many variants of switching as a marked choice, with many of them relatively brief in duration – only a word or two. Yet, the same motivation characterizes such momentary switches as longer ones: a bid to dis-identify with the unmarked rights and obligations balance for the exchange. (1988: 169–170)

Clearly, this type of switching would constitute deviance from the norm of one-situation–one-variety. That is there would be order here too. This parallels Gumperz' category of metaphorical code-switching. However, the issue is whether all such momentary switches are functional or whether some of them are instances of repairable deviance. Consider Example 5.15. In the example, the relevant alternation is that involving Swahili (fukuza munyarwanda). In this case, alternation is clearly functional, for it corresponds to a specific conversational function, namely direct speech reporting (see Chapter 7).

*Example 5.15*

1. A: ubu rero ab (.) buretse (.) abazayuruwa bagiye gutangira ngo (.) *fukuza munyarwanda* (.) [( )
2. B:                    [ *avec raison (.)[ puisque* turi imbwa
3. A:                                [( ) ((laughter)) ariko
4. C: *avec raison* (.) none se none wanzanira ibibazo iwanjye

1. A: now Zairians Zair (.) wait a minute (.) Zairians are going to start saying **kick out Rwandan** (.) [( )
2. B: [*rightly so (.) [as* we do not deserve any respect
3. A: [( ) ((laughter)) but
4. C: *rightly so* (.) if you bring problems to my door

By contrast, consider the choice of English in Example 5.9. As we have seen, in this particular case, deviance is repairable and indeed has been repaired by replacing 'local authority' by 'municipalité'. The issue is also, in the case of functional deviance, whether functionality can always be explained with reference to the social values associated with the languages in the community. This is the problem of the directionality of language alternation as we have discussed it in the context of Gumperz's framework. As we have seen, functional language alternation need not be directional.

To summarise, Myers-Scotton's model of language alternation, like Gumperz', can be read as an account of order in talk in two languages. In the Markedness Model, the norm remains that of one-situation–one-language. However, the model goes a step further compared to previous ones and focuses on those situations where it is impossible to interpret every instance of alternation in functional terms and proposes to see this alternation itself as normative conduct. However, as we have indicated above, this proposal runs against a difficulty at the level of the underlying norm of language separateness. The possibility of language alternation itself as the unmarked choice can be envisioned only if the norm ceases to be that of one-situation–one-language and becomes that of one-situation–one-variety, where variety need not consist of one language. Of course, Myers-Scotton did not phrase her model in these terms, but, as we have seen, other authors are willing to entertain this possibility.

## 5.5. Conclusion

This chapter has concerned itself with accounts of the orderliness of language alternation which have been developed from an identity-related position. Identity-related accounts of language alternation, as I have indicated in this chapter, all share the same scheme of interpretation, namely the norm of one-situation–one-language, a norm which was first established by diglossia studies such as Ferguson (1959) and Fishman (1967). Using this norm as the backdrop, the models I have surveyed in this chapter can easily account for the orderliness of two types of language alternation, namely language alternation which corresponds to changes in the speech situation and momentary shifts which convey information metaphorically. With reference to the scheme of interpretation, the first possibility can be seen as normative language choice, while the second can be seen as functional deviance. In the models, an attempt is also made to account for the orderliness of frequent language alternation in which no particular functional motivation can be attached to specific instances. As we have seen, two of the models see language alternation as a case of repairable deviance, while the third one claims that language alternation itself is normative language choice. However, each of these views is problematic. For example, the view that language alternation is a type of deviance which will be repaired some time in the future (when the sociolinguistic structure has stabilised) fails to account for the possibility of language alternation in the here and now. On the other hand, the view that language alternation itself can be seen as normative language choice is problematic because, for this to be possible, the underlying scheme of interpretation must be adjusted. The norm must cease to be that of one-situation–one-language and become that of one-situation–one-variety, where variety need not consist of one language. Finally, there are two types of language alternation which are not accounted for by these models, namely momentary departures into another language which are oriented to by participants themselves as repairable deviance and momentary language alternation which, although functional, cannot be explained by reference to the values of the languages involved in the relevant community. In the next chapter, I look at models of language alternation which have been developed from an organisational perspective and see how they handle these problematic cases, in addition to the less problematic ones whose orderliness we have already been able to account for.

## Notes

1. Quotes from this paper will come from its reprint in Li Wei (2000).
2. Quotes to come from the reprint in Li Wei (2000)
3. Ibid.

# 6
# Interactional Order in Talk in Two Languages: Organisational Explanation

## 6.1. Introduction

In Chapter 3, we saw that, at the grammatical level, language alternation can be seen as an issue of order because it runs counter to the Uniform Structure Principle. In Chapter 5, we saw that, under identity-related perspectives, language alternation is an issue of order for it runs counter to the One-Situation–One-Language Principle. Therefore, at the organisational level, for language alternation to be seen as an issue of order, there must be an organisational principle counter to which language alternation can be seen as running. In the literature, two related and yet different principles have been proposed. These are the 'Preference for Same Language Talk' as adopted by Auer (1984, 1988, 1995) and the 'Preference for Same Medium Talk' as adopted by Gafaranga (1998, 1999, 2000b, 2005) and Gafaranga and Torras (2001, 2002). These two principles correspond to the two approaches to language alternation which, in Table 5.1, are listed under the node 'organisational explanation'. It is to these approaches that I now turn.

The two organisational perspectives on language alternation share the same theoretical background, namely Ethnomethodology and Conversation Analysis (CA). In Section 1.2, I have briefly sketched these two approaches and shown how they view order in social action and in talk in particular. To recall, Ethnomethodology is 'the study of the production of social order' (Livingston, 1987: 18). Its aim is to uncover the orderliness of social action by inspecting the methods participants themselves (ethnos) have used in accomplishing that very same action. As we have seen, from this perspective, order is the very possibility of social action. Without order, social action is impossible. As for CA, it aims to account for the orderliness of talk itself as practical social action. Some of the key features of CA are as follows: (i) the view of talk as an activity in its own right, (ii) an emic perspective whereby talk organisation is seen from participants' own perspective, (iii) sequential analysis and so on. (see Psathas (1995), Hutchby and Wooffit (1998) and Ten Have (1999) for some introductory texts). For the purpose of this chapter, in the following section, I will only focus on the notion of 'preference' as an aspect of talk organisation as it is central to the two models of language alternation I will be reviewing in this chapter.

## 6.2. The notion of 'preference' in Conversation Analysis

One of the key concepts in CA is the notion of *preference*. Detailed accounts of preference can be found in Pomerantz (1984), Heritage (1984), Bilmes (1988), Schegloff (1988) and so on. To understand this notion, we need to refer back to the notion of norm as used in Ethnomethodology and its relationship with the social actor on the one hand and with social action on the other. According to Ethnomethodology, although norms are central for the orderliness of social action, they do not dictate action, that is they do not tell people what to do. Actors are not mere *judgemental dopes* (Heritage, 1984: 110–115) whose role is only to apply norms. Rather, a norm must be seen as a scheme of interpretation, as an interpretive base (Heritage, 1984). In actual situations, even the most norm-regulated ones, there are always alternative options for actors to choose from. A typical example that is recurrent in the literature is that of a greeting situation. It is relatively easy to understand that, in most societies, there is a norm that can be put in many words as 'if greeted, return the greeting'. However, in actual situations, after a greeting, people sometimes return the greeting and sometimes they do not. In this context, the norm works only as a scheme of interpretation because, after a greeting, return or non-return of the greeting is always judged with reference to the norm. Return is seen as normal and normative, while non-return is seen as deviance from the norm. That is to say, when greeted, people do not have to return the greeting, but they must be aware that, whatever they choose to do, their action will be assessed by interlocutors with reference to the norm. This is an issue of social accountability. It is precisely this aspect of norms which accounts for the orderliness of social action.

In CA, the notion of 'preference' is very close to that of norm in Ethnomethodology. In conversation, each act always comes either before or after another act. This is so because talk is time-linear and is organised sequentially. However, some acts are more bound to one another than others. Consider Example 6.1. Talk takes place in an Irish pub in Barcelona and customer BBB is trying to order a drink of whisky (Lagavulin).

*Example 6.1*

1. AAA: hola!
   (hi)
2. BBB: *erm are you Scottish?*
3. AAA: *no (.) I'm Irish.*
4. BBB: *oh well.*
5. AAA: *near enough.*
6. BBB: *erm (.) I'll have (.) a Lagavulin.*
7. AAA: *a which?*
8. BBB: *Lagavulin.*

In this example, talk in turn 2 is more related to talk in turn 3 than it is to talk in turn 1. Likewise, talk in turn 6 is not directly related to talk in turn 5. In fact, the example could be divided into sequences such that turn 1 could be called the greeting sequence, talk from turn 2 through to turn 5 could be set apart as the identification sequence and turn 6 onwards as the order sequence. The issue of act relatedness could then be pursued within each sequence. For example, in the identification sequence, turn 2 and 3 are closely related. Turn 2 is a question and turn 3 is its answer. Turn 3 depends on turn 2. Turn 2 makes turn 3 relevant. The relationship between these two is such that, if turn 3 was not present, its absence would be noticeable. Such is indeed the case after turn 1 in the example. Turn 1 is a greeting and, as such, it makes relevant a return-greeting. Because a return-greeting is relevant, its absence is visible. In CA, such closely bound pairs of acts have been referred to as 'adjacency pair' (Schegloff and Sacks, 1973). Other examples of adjacency pairs, in addition to question–answer and greeting–greeting, are request–granting, invitation–acceptance and so on. Note that, in each case, an alternative 'second part' of the pair is possible. A greeting may or may not be returned, a request may or may not be granted and an invitation may or may not be accepted and so on. That is, as active actors, when faced with a 'first pair part' of an adjacency pair, speakers have to choose between available options and that is precisely why they are not mere judgemental dopes. However, in each case, options do not have the same status. One is expected and normative and the other is unexpected and deviant. The default identifications above represent normative cases and the list of alternative second pair parts represents deviant cases. In CA, normative second pair parts are referred to as 'preferred', while deviant second pair parts are referred to as 'dispreferred'.

Preferred and dispreferred actions are also different structurally. Dispreferred actions are physically marked while preferred actions are not. In this respect, Levinson writes,

> Preference is a structural notion that corresponds closely to the linguistic concept of markedness. In essence, preferred seconds are unmarked – they occur as structurally simpler turns; in contrast dispreferred seconds are marked by various kinds of structural complexity. Thus dispreferred seconds are typically delivered: (a) after some significant delay; (b) with some preface marking their dispreferred status; (c) with some account of why the preferred second cannot be performed. (1983: 307)

For example, in Example 6.2 (from Cameron, 2001: 96), two interlocutors (Julia and Anita) have reacted differently to Daphne's suggestion. Julia has accepted the suggestion while Anita has rejected it. Observation of the details of talk in the light of Levinson's description of preference makes it clear that Julia's response (acceptance) is preferred while Anita's (rejection) is dispreferred. In the example, 'dispreference markers' include the preface 'well', the pause (.) and the account 'I've stopped ... to the ocean' in Anita's talk.

*Example 6.2*

Daphne: I was thinking we could have fish
Julia: Fine
Anita: well actually (.) I've stopped eating fish now because of you know the damage it does to the ocean

Because of these structural differences, it becomes possible to talk of preference in structural terms, that is, without reference to intentions, desires, volitions and so on. That is, it becomes possible to tell preference only on the basis of these structural features of talk.

## 6.3. Local order in bilingual conversation

### 6.3.1. Some premises

The organisational explanation of language alternation, that is the conversation analytic perspective, was pioneered by Peter Auer in a series of publications (1984, 1988, 1995, 1998, 2000, etc). Auer is explicit about CA influence on his work, for he entitles one of his publications 'A conversation analytic approach to code-switching and transfer' (1988). This influence is also explicit in some of his significant statements. For example, he states his view of bilingualism in terms of activities as in the following:

> *I propose then to examine bilingualism primarily as a set of complex linguistic activities* [...]. From such a perspective, bilingualism is a predicate ascribed to and by participants on the basis of their visible, inspectable behaviour. [...] We need a model of bilingual conversation which provides a coherent and functionally motivated picture of *bilingualism as a set of linguistic activities*. (1988/2000: 167) (my emphasis)

In line with this, Auer and other researchers who adopt a CA perspective refer to language alternation in terms of 'language choice acts'.

Announcing his research agenda, Auer states the following where he commits himself to an 'emic perspective':

> the procedures we aim to describe are supposed to be those used by participants in actual interaction, i.e. [...] they are supposed to be interactionally relevant and 'real', not just as a scientific construct designed to 'fit the data'. So there is a need for an analytic interest in *members' methods* (or procedures), as opposed to an interest in external procedures derived from a scientific theory. In short, our purpose is to analyze *members' procedures to arrive at local interpretations of language alternation*. (1984: 3) (original emphasis)

In this citation, expressions such as 'members' methods', 'members' procedures', 'interactionally relevant' all reveal influence from both Ethnomethodology and CA. Finally, Auer argued for a 'sequential analysis' of language alternation saying:

> any theory of conversational code alternation is bound to fail if it does not take into account that the meaning of code-alternation depends

in many ways on its 'sequential environment'. This is given, in the first place by the conversational turn immediately preceding it, to which code-alternation may respond in various ways. (1995: 116)

A key concept in Auer's model of language alternation is that of 'turn constructional unit' (TCU). The term 'turn-constructional unit' was introduced in the CA literature by Sacks *et al.* (1978) in their seminal description of the turn-taking system. They wrote,

There are various unit-types with which a speaker may set out to construct a turn. Unit-types of English include sentential, clausal, phrasal, and lexical constructions. Instances of the unit-types so usable allow a projection of the unit-type under way, and, what, roughly, it will take for an instance of that unit-type to be completed. (1978: 12)

Anything that can constitute material for a complete turn is a TCU. The original interest in TCUs was that they help account for the orderliness of turn-taking in conversation. According to Sacks *et al.*, at the end of each TCU, change of speakership may, but need not, be effected. If change of speakership takes place at the end of a TCU, talk goes on smoothly for the principle of 'one speaker at a time' is observed. However, if a speaker takes a turn in the course of an ongoing TCU, a feeling of interruption follows, overlapping talk occurs and overlapped talk may be recycled. Consider Example 6.3 from Coates (1998: 243). In the transcript, Coates uses the sign (/) to indicate a complete TCU.

*Example 6.3*

1. C: I mean I think it really depends on the ATTitude of the
2. B: [yeah/
3. C: survivors who are [THERE/. I- if they want the person
4. A: I don't think it depends on that Cathy/
5. C: to [go/ .then the person should go/
6. E: [mhm/
7. A: I think it depends on [um-
8. C: [Oh I do/ if one of mine died/
9. E: and. er I mean- my- . if it were- whichever one
10. E: it were the other one would expect me to go/

In the example, a number of observable organisational features of talk can be accounted for by reference to the concept of TCU. First, a small overlap occurs between turn 2 (B) and turn 3 (C). Such small overlaps are very recurrent in conversation (see also turn 6), and they can be explained in terms of yet another aspect of TCU. Although, as we said above, normative turn transition takes place at the end of TCU, speakers often anticipate and start a turn slightly before the actual end of previous speaker's TCU. Secondly, substantial overlapping talk occurs between turn 4 (A) and turn 5 (C). As the transcription clearly indicates, C's TCU ended with 'go', leading E to take the turn anticipatively (6). Exactly for the same reason as E, A takes the turn. Unfortunately, as Sacks *et al.* (1978) show, at the end of a TCU, current speaker need not relinquish their right to a turn. They can keep talking. Thus, A and C overlap because they made two different decisions. Finally, an interesting phenomenon occurs between turn 7 and turn 8. As the transcript shows, A's talk in turn 7 is not a complete TCU. Therefore, by taking the turn at this point, C is demonstrably interrupting. Briefly, the use of TCU is a participant's own method for turn-taking. In conversation, participants use TCUs to take turns in an orderly manner.

Coates' transcript above reveals yet another aspect of TCUs. It is almost impossible to define a TCU purely in structural terms. Turn constructional units may consist of whole sentences, of fragments and even of simple minimal responses such as 'yeah'. As a result of this, it is currently agreed that TCUs should be viewed as units of action.

> It is the ability to 'do' something, be it proposing, requesting, accepting, showing surprise, or whatever, that makes a sound or string sounds into a TCU. (Ten Have, 1999: 112)

Thus, in Example 6.3, 'yeah' in turn 2 is a complete TCU because it does the job of a continuer (Schegloff, 1982) (agreeing and encouraging co-participant to keep talking). Likewise, 'oh I do' in turn 8 is a TCU even though it does not actually constitute a full turn. The item is enough to express disagreement with A. Therefore, right after it, change of speakership could have been effected. On the other hand, the item 'it depends on um-' is not a complete TCU, even though right after it, there has been change of speakership, because it does not do exactly what it was meant to do.

Although Sacks *et al.* (1978) predicted that orderly turn transition takes place at the end of a TCU, later research, especially by Lerner (1991), introduced some reservation. Lerner demonstrated that it is possible for a speaker to join in another speaker's interactional space without interrupting. This is the case in what he refers to as a 'compound TCU'. This is a TCU which is jointly produced by two speakers. Consider Example 6.4. In the example, participants are saying that in Europe, unlike in Rwanda, it would be expensive to have a houseboy/maid. As the transcript shows, participant B completes participant A's TCU to show understanding and agreement.

*Example 6.4*

1. A: ba- u- ushatse umuntu ugutekera-
2. B:                              wamuhemba
3. A: wamuhemba (.) ibihumbi mirongo mirongo euh itanu itandatu

1. A: if you got somebody to cook for you-
2. B:                              you'd pay them
3. A: you'd pay them (.) fifty to sixty thousand

In this respect, Example 6.5 is even more interesting for it involves language alternation. Like in the above, B completes A's TCU although he does it in what appears to be a different language.

*Example 6.5*

1. A: izo *bus* zagarutse-
2. B:                *vides*
3. A: *vides*

1. A: those buses came back
2. B:                empty
3. A: empty

### 6.3.2. Preference for same language talk

Drawing on the concept of preference and that of TCU, Auer is able to formulate his scheme of interpretation for language alternation, namely the preference for same language talk (1984: 23). According to this principle, once a TCU has occurred in a particular language, bilingual participants have to decide whether to keep talk going in the same language or in a different language. That is to say, bilingual participants monitor each other's TCUs, not only to be able to take turns in an orderly manner, but also to choose language in an orderly manner. In this perspective, as Auer says, 'code-switching [...] is conceptualised as divergence from the language of the prior turn or turn constructional unit' (2000: 137). Of the two options available to bilingual participants, according to Auer, the preferred choice is to keep talk going in the same language. A typical example of language alternation corresponding to the end of a TCU is in the case of inter-turn language alternation. In this case, next speaker takes the turn in accordance with the turn-taking system and at the same time switches to another language. Consider the following piece of talk taken from the transcript of a service encounter in Barcelona. Talk takes place at a town hall office between an enquirer (EN) and a receptionist (REC). The languages involved are Catalan (bold) and Castilian (plain).

*Example 6.6*   (English translation in brackets)

1. EN:   hola
         (hi)
2. REC:  **Déu vos guard**
         (God you guard -hello)
3. EN:   **Déu vos guard** ((laughs)) queremos saber-
         (Hello          (((laughs)) we'd like to know-)
4. REC:                                        **Déu vos guard**
                                               (Hello)
5. EN:   Bueno no sé si lo digo bien ((laughs))
         (Well I don't know if I said it correctement ((laughs)))

In turn 2, REC normatively takes the turn to return a greeting and, at the same time, switches from Spanish to Catalan. However, as we have seen, the end of a TCU does not necessarily correspond to change of speakership. Therefore, the second possibility is for language alternation to correspond to a new TCU within the same speaker's turn. In the example above, this possibility is observed in EN's talk in turn 3.

Alternatively, language alternation takes place within the same TCU. In turn, two possibilities can be observed. In the first case, the TCU is produced by the same speaker. Consider Example 6.7. Participants are talking about the difficulties Rwandan politicians experienced in appointing a transitional government before the genocide. In the transcript, TCUs are indicated by (/).

*Example 6.7*

1. A:  gu- gushyiraho *premier ministre* uzasinya *les accords*/.
2. B:  Yeee./

3. A: *Bon.*/ noneho nibwo hajemo iriya *période* rero./ hazamo kujijinganya/ (.) ba*noma* X./
4. B: Nabwo bamaze kujijinganya/

1. A: to appoint the Prime Minister who would sign the peace agreements
2. B: Yeeeee
3. A: okay. That's how that period came about. They hesitated (.) appointed X
4. B: even then after hesitations

As the transcript shows, in this case, unlike in Example 6.6, language alternation in turn 1 and turn 3 occurs within the same TCUs by the same speaker. Conversely, language alternation can occur within a jointly produced TCU, each speaker's contribution adopting a different language. Example 6.5 is a case in point.

Thus, it is because, in Auer, language alternation is discussed with reference to turns and TCUs that his model can be said to be based on the local level of talk organisation, as an account of the local order in bilingual conversation. Auer himself states this position saying:

> I want to argue that rather than dealing with language choice on the macroscopic level of the base language of a whole episode or a major part of it, and rather than separating code-choice (of the base language) and code-switching (below it), we should look at language choice **on a turn-by-turn basis level** in order to do justice to bilingual participants' conversational practices. This means describing and explaining patterns of conversational code choice *on a local basis*, i.e. by analysing speakers' language choices for one particular turn or turn constructional unit with reference to language choices directly or indirectly preceding it, as well as in the consequences for language choice in the turns to follow. (2000: 137) (my emphasis)

Two implications follow from the view that, in conversation, there is a preference for same language talk. First of all, the implication is that language alternation is a dispreferred occurrence. As such, it should be accompanied by dispreference markers. Auer seems to point to this possibility when he says that language alternation, as a contextualisation cue, tends to co-occur with other contextualisation cues (1995: 124).

Consider the following instance from Milroy and Wei (1995: 148). The languages involved are Cantonese (plain) and English (italics).

*Example 6.8*

1. A: Oy-m-oy faan a? A ying a?
   (want or not rice?)
2. B: [No response]
3. A: Chaaufaan a.Oy-m-oy?
   (Fried rice. Want or not?)
4. B: (0.2) *I'll have some shrimps.*
5. A: mu-ye? (.) Chaaufaan a.
   (What? Fried rice)
6. B: Hai a
   (OK)

In the example, a mother (A) has offered rice to her daughter (B). B accomplishes the dispreferred act of rejecting the offer. She marks this dispreferred act by delaying it (no response in turn 2 and 0.2 pause in turn 4). She also offers an account by stating an alternative choice (*I'll have some shrimps*). At the same time as rejecting the offer, B accomplishes the dispreferred act of shifting from Chinese to English. In other words, language alternation is one of the devices that B uses to mark dispreference as Milroy and Wei rightly argue. That is, language alternation co-occurs with these other ways of marking dispreference. This analysis is further supported by the fact that, when B eventually accepts the offer, that is accomplishes a preferred act, she aligns with A at the level of language choice (turn 6). Again, this is in line with Heritage (1984), who maintains that preference in conversation can be explained in terms of affiliative acts.

In the above, language alternation corresponds to a TCU for it takes place across turns. However, as we have seen, such need not be the case. Language alternation may occur within TCUs. Consider Example 6.9. Here, three languages are involved: English (plain), French (bold) and Catalan (underlined). In the following, I will only focus on the switch from English to French.

*Example 6.9*

1. STU: I'm sorry it's not your fault right
2. SEC: no [ uh no that's you you you
3. STU: [I'm erm I offended you
4. SEC: mmm (.) **LE LE DROIT LE** (to RES) el dret

5. RES: the right.
6. SEC: the right (.) you have the right to protest eh OK

4. SEC: mmm (.) the the right the (to RES) the right

SEC encounters a problem of the *mot juste* in the middle of a TCU. To solve this problem, she switches from English to French. Before she actually switches, she uses a variety of ways to signal dispreferrence, including repetition 'you you you', use the speech marker 'mmm' and the small pause (.). Briefly, there seems to be evidence that language alternation, in some cases at least, is structurally marked as a dispreferred occurrence. However, I am not aware of any systematic study of this aspect of bilingual conversation and, therefore, I will not pursue it any further.

The second implication from the view that, in conversation, there is a preference for same language talk is that language alternation is an instance of deviance from this preference. In other words, according to this view, it is against the background of this preference for same language talk that language alternation can be identified and interpreted. The preference for same language talk, 'as long as it exists, is an important resource for generating meaning via language use and has to be treated accordingly' (Auer, 1984: 24). Take Example 6.9. In the example, as revealed in turn 5, RES has interpreted the difficulty SEC was having as that of finding the *mot juste*. How did she come to this interpretation? Through the repetition of 'you' in turn 2, the delaying 'mmm' and the pause, it is obvious to everybody that SEC is word-searching. This search leads to the French item 'le droit' and the Catalan word 'el dret'. The question therefore is, why did RES go on to give the English equivalent in turn 5? The answer to this question is obviously that either of these two, although it is semantically correct, deviates from the preference for same language talk. The ongoing TCU 'you have the right' is in English. That is, using the preference for same language talk as the backdrop, RES identified the two non-English items as deviant and therefore as requiring an explanation. The explanation for deviance she came up with, given available evidence (dispreference markers), is that this was repairable deviance. Also consider Example 6.1, reproduced as Example 6.10 for convenience.

*Example 6.10*

1. AAA: hola!
   (hi)
2. BBB: *erm are you Scottich?*

3. AAA: *no (.) I'm Irish.*
4. BBB: *oh well.*
5. AAA: *near enough.*
6. BBB: *erm (.) I'll have (.) a Lagavulin.*
7. AAA: *a which?*
8. BBB: *Lagavulin.*

In turn 1, the bar attendant used Spanish. In his own turn, the customer deviated from the preference for same language talk and used English. In turn, the bar attendant interpreted this deviance from the norm as functional, as an indirect way of inviting her to adopt English as the medium of their interaction (see language negotiation sequence below). That is, there is some evidence that, in bilingual conversation, participants do indeed use the preference for same language talk as a scheme of interpretation.

### 6.3.3. Language preference

A final premise of Auer's approach to language alternation is the notion of 'language preference' (not to be confused with preference for same language talk). According to Auer, language preference 'should not be taken to imply any kind of psychological concept [...]. What the term refers to are rather the interactional processes of displaying and ascribing predicates to individuals' (1998: 8). The term preference 'must not be understood as a psychological disposition of the speaker, but rather in the more technical, conversation-analytic sense of an interactionally visible structure' (1995: 125). Auer identifies two types of language preferences. Preference can be related to participants' linguistic competence, but it may also be related to external ideological factors. He writes,

> By preference-related switching, a speaker may simply want to avoid the language in which he or she feels insecure and speak the one in which he or she has greater competence. Yet preference-related switching may also be due to a deliberate decision based on political considerations. (1995: 125)

Consider Example 6.11 from Codó (1998). Talk takes place in an English pub in Barcelona. Right after the exchange of greetings, the customer (BBB) interrupts the flow of the service encounter and requests to use English. The reason for this is that BBB does not feel confident enough to carry out the whole interaction in Catalan. In other words, switching away from Catalan to English tells co-participant and analysts something about BBB's linguistic competence.

*Example 6.11*

AAA: hola.
     'hi'
BBB: hola (.) *can I order in English* (.) *yeah*
     'hi'
AAA: Sí
     'yes'
BBB: *uh: I'd like to have a pint of blonde beer*
AAA: mmm mmm

Likewise, consider Example 6.9. As we have seen, SEC switches to French because she is experiencing difficulties in English. Therefore, the switch tells us something, not only about SEC's competence in English, but also something about her competence in French.

Conversely, consider Example 6.12. Talk takes place in an English pub in Barcelona. The bar attendant is from the United Kingdom while customers are Catalan. After greeting the bar attendant, BBB and CCC realise that they have not sorted out their order. Therefore, they engage in an insertion/aside sequence. In turn 3, CCC uses Catalan, but, in turn 4, BBB uses Spanish. For the rest of the sequence, Spanish is adopted. Because participants are fluent in both Catalan and Spanish, the Switch from Catalan to Spanish cannot be explained in terms of participants' linguistic competence. Rather, it must be understood in terms of ideological considerations, in terms of the wider politics of language in Catalonia.

*Example 6.12*

1. AAA: hello.
2. BBB : hello (.) [eh: [(unclear)
3. CCC:         [dues [de negra no?
           (two of stout right)
4. BBB: **quieres peqeña o grande**.
           (would you like it small or large)
5. CCC: **grande**
           (large)
6. AAA: mmm mmm
7. BBB: eh: *one big (.) one half pint (.) for me (.) [one half pint for me*
8. AAA:                              *[one half pint for you*

Likewise, in Example 6.9, the switch to Catalan after the use of French is not due to any lack of linguistic competence in French on the part of RES (personal knowledge). Rather, it is because both RES and SEC are Catalans. Therefore, this is a case of preference due to external factors.

This notion of language preference is particularly interesting because it allows Auer to explain language alternation phenomena known in the literature as 'language negotiation sequences' (Auer, 1995; Codó, 1998; Torras, 1998). In Myers-Scotton (see Chapter 5), these phenomena are referred to as 'codeswitching as an exploratory choice'. According to Auer, a language negotiation sequence 'begins with a disagreement between two or more parties about which language to use for interaction, and ends as soon as one of them "gives in" to the other preferred language' (1984: 20–21). In Example 6.11, for example, participants started at diverging positions as to which language should be used. As the transcript shows, the bar attendant implicitly suggested to use Catalan, but the customer requested and obtained the use of English. Likewise, in Example 6.10, AAA offers to use Catalan (or Spanish as 'hola' is ambiguous). In turns 2 through to turn 5, participants negotiate to use English. Finally, in Example 6.12, in the insertion sequence, one customer offered to use Catalan and the other offered to use Spanish and the first gave in. A dramatic instance of language negotiation is Example 6.13 below from Heller (1982). Interaction takes place at a hospital reception in Montreal, Canada. In the example, participants are alternating between French and English by way of testing which of the two languages the interlocutor would like to see adopted for the interaction.

*Example 6.13*

1. Clerk: *Central Booking, may I help you?*
2. Patient: Oui, Allo?
3. Clerk: Bureau de rendez-vous, est-ce que je peux vous aider? *May I help you*
4. Patient: [French]
5. Clerk: [French]
6. Patient: [English]
7. Clerk: [English]
8. Patient: [French]
9. Clerk: [French]
10. Patient: Etes-vous française ou anglaise? (are you French or English?)

11. Clerk: n'importe, je ne suis ni l'une ni l'autre ... (it doesn't matter, I'm neither one nor the other ... )
12. Patient: Mais ... (But ... )
13. Clerk: Ça ne fait rien (It doesn't matter)
14. Patient: [French] [Conversation goes on in French]

As these examples show, language negotiation can be accomplished explicitly (e.g. Example 6.11), but it may also be implicit (e.g. all the others).

### 6.3.4. Categories of code alternation

Auer's scheme of interpretation allows him to identify two types of language alternation and two dimensions along which each of the two can vary. The four possibilities can be represented in a quadrant as in Table 6.1 below from Gafaranga (2007: 299).

As the above representation shows, the first axis of variation is whether language alternation is discourse-related or whether it is participant-related. Along this axis, language alternation is said to generate meanings of either of two types: it can generate meanings regarding the organisation of talk (*discourse-related*) and it can generate meanings about participants (*participant-related*). As Auer says, faced with language alternation, participants ask themselves:

> Is the language alternation in question providing cues for the organisation of the on-going interaction [...], or about attributes of the participants? (1984: 12)

An example of 'discourse-related code alternation' is Example 6.12. As we have seen, in this example, language alternation occurs at the same time as participants are moving from the main sequence to the insertion sequence. Other discourse-related functions that language alternation has been observed to serve are preference marking, repair and

*Table 6.1* Categories of code alternation

|  | Code-switching | Transfer |
|---|---|---|
| Discourse-relatedness | X | X |
| Participant-relatedness | X | X |

presequences (Milroy and Wei, 1995; Shin and Milroy, 2000), but are also included functions such as marking quotation (see Chapter 7) and reiteration for emphasis (see Gumperz, 1982 for a list of such functions). As for participant-related language alternation, it is found in Examples 6.9, 6.11 and 6.12. In all three examples, there is an issue of participants' language preference. In all three, language alternation tells something about participants.

According to Auer, when faced with language alternation, bilingual participants ask themselves whether it tells them something about the organisation of the conversation or whether it is a hint to the attributes of the participants. Additionally, Auer says, participants ask themselves the question:

> is language alternation in question tied to a particular conversational structure (for instance a word, a sentence, or a larger unit) or is it tied to a particular point in the conversation? (1984: 12)

If alternation is analysable in terms of a particular point in the conversation, it is said to be 'code-switching' and if it is analysable as 'tied to a particular conversational structure', it is called 'transfer'. In other words, code-switching is a point of departure into another 'language-of-interaction' (see below) while transfer is the use of an identifiable stretch of talk (e.g. a specific expression) in another language. An example of transfer can be found in Example 6.9. In the example, by using French, SEC is not inviting STU to switch to this language. She is simply indicating that she has a specific problem with a specific linguistic item. This is precisely how other participants, including RES, have analysed the situation. In Example 6.13, on the other hand, by switching from one language to the other, interlocutors are hoping that co-participants will follow them and adopt the switched-to language as the new medium. In other words, Example 6.13 is a case of code-switching while Example 6.9 is a case of transfer, although both are participant-related. Likewise, in Examples 6.6 and 6.12, language alternation is code-switching, for it corresponds to a point of departure into the medium of the insertion sequences.

As for an example of discourse-related transfer, consider the following exchange between an Irish bar attendant and a Dutch customer in Barcelona. Before the exchange, AAA has identified herself as Irish. When BBB identified himself as Dutch, the following talk ensues. In the example, by using Spanish in turn 3, AAA is not negotiating to have it adopted as the new medium. Rather, she is trying to find out the cause of the misunderstanding by pronouncing 'Ireland' and 'Holland' as the Spanish would pronounce it to see if that could be the reason for the confusion.

*Example 6.14*

AAA: whenever I say Ireland in Spanish they all think I say Holland ((laughs))
BBB: Ireland?
AAA: yeah (.) **Irlanda Holanda**
BBB: oh it's quite different
AAA: yeah

To summarise, in Auer's model, the norm, expressed as the preference for same language talk, is the use of one language. Consequently, language alternation, whether in the form of code-switching or in the form of transfer, is orderly because it is a case of deviance from this norm. To be sure, language alternation is a case of functional deviance, for it always tells something either about the organisation of talk or about the speaker. However, the model must face at least three problems. First, as Auer himself says, he wanted to develop an account of language alternation which does 'justice to bilingual participants' conversational practices' (2000: 137). However, his categories of language alternation, especially transfer, fall short of this stated target. As we have seen, transfer divides into participant-related transfer and discourse-related transfer. However, this view ignores important differences between the two types. As Auer's own discussion (1984: 55–60) shows, participant-related transfer is always oriented to by participants themselves as repairable, while discourse-related transfer never is. To refer to both cases as transfer blurs this important distinction.

Secondly, Auer proposes a turn-by-turn/TCU-by-TCU analysis because the meaning of language alternation depends on its sequential environment, which 'is given in the first place by the conversational turn immediately preceding it, to which code-alternation may respond in various ways' (1995: 116). Behind this is obviously the view that language alternation is alternational (see Chapter 2). That is, the turn/TCU must be seen as the unit of analysis, language choice in one TCU being interpreted against the choice in the immediately preceding TCU. While such a sequential analysis is quite possible and indeed commendable in the case of 'prototypical codeswitching' (1999: 131), it is not clear how sequential analysis can be used to describe language alternation which occurs within the same TCU, either by the same speaker or by two speakers.

Thirdly, although, as we have seen, Auer explicitly states that his model of language alternation is based on the local order of talk; throughout his work, there is a tension between the local explanation of language alternation and the one which is based on the overall order of talk. This is particularly true when he introduces the notion of 'language-of-interaction'. For example, regarding language negotiation sequences, Auer writes,

> It (a language negotiation sequence) begins with a disagreement between two or more parties about which language to use for interaction, and ends as soon as one of them 'gives in' to the other preferred language. (1984: 20–21)

In other words, participants choose a language for the interaction and not necessarily for individual TCUs. Indeed, as I will argue in Section 6.4, language negotiation sequences would be meaningless if language choice acts were accountable only at the level of individual turns and TCUs. Elsewhere, he says,

> In many communities, there is a preference for same language talk; code-switching (discourse- or participant-related) runs counter to this preference – which, of course, only heightens its signalling value– whereas transfer is neutral vis-à-vis questions of negotiating the *language-of-interaction*. (1984: 29–30)

In this case, participants are said to orient, not to the language of the preceding TCU, but rather to the language-of-interaction. Orientation to the language-of-interaction is said to be at the basis of the difference between code-switching and transfer, the two main types of language alternation. Auer distinguishes code-switching from language mixing by reference to the language-of-interaction.

> if more than one participant frequently switches languages within turns [...], it becomes less and less relevant to speak of a *language-of-interaction* forming the background against which language alternation, must be seen. (1984: 84)

Finally, in his discussion of the difference between code-switching and language mixing, Auer writes,

Prototypical code-switching can be portrayed as follows: (a) it occurs in a sociolinguistic contexts in which speakers orient towards a preference for one language at a time; that is, it is usually possible to identify the *language-of-interaction* which is valid at a given moment and until code-switching occurs; (b) through its departure from this established *language-of-interaction*, code-switching signals otherness of the upcoming contextual frame and thereby achieves a change of footing. (1999: 311–312)

In this case, preference for same language talk is equated with preference for the same language-of-interaction. Of course, if speakers maintain the same language TCU after TCU, and turn after turn, one may speak of a language-of-interaction. The issue here is that of the unit of analysis. Is it the TCU (more like the sentence in grammar) or is it a whole conversational episode (a whole conversation why not)? That is, is language alternation an issue of the local order or is it an issue of the overall order in talk in two languages? In the following section, I turn to a model of language alternation which sees language alternation precisely as an aspect of the overall order in talk in two languages.

## 6.4. Overall order in bilingual conversation

### 6.4.1. Overall order in talk-in-interaction

As we have noted above, Auer's model of language alternation is based on the view that conversation is locally managed. While it is true that many aspects of conversational organisation can be explained locally, there are others for which reference must be made to the overall organisation. Here are three examples of overall organisation. As amply discussed in Schegloff and Sacks (1973) and Levinson (1983), an everyday telephone conversation has the structure:

a. Opening
b. First topic (+optional other topics)
c. Closing

On the other hand, an emergency call, as described by Whalen and Zimmerman (1990), has the structure:

a. Opening/identification/acknowledgement
b. Request
c. Interrogative series

d. Response
e. Closing

Finally a doctor–patient consultation, according to Ten Have (1989), is structured as:

a. Opening
b. Complaint
c. Examination
d. Diagnosis
e. Treatment or advice
f. Closing

The point about these overall structures of talk-in-interaction is that participants use them as schemes of interpretation. Consider Example 6.15 (from Button, 1991: 267). In the example, after the opening episode, two topics are introduced, but they are clearly oriented to as different in terms of their status. One is the first topic, the object of the call, even though it will be dealt with second, and the other is not.

*Example 6.15*

1. E: Ha'lo.
2. J: Hi Elsie, John here
3. E: Ah:: (0.2.) so how are you.
4. J: Fine, thanks = LOOK I rang to see if you could tell me how to run that fuckin program::me, = but furst do you know what's the matter with Colin.
5. E: Why?

Also consider the following from Whalen *et al.* (1988: 344). In this emergency call, after the identification/acknowledgement in turn 1, the caller was expected to proceed to the 'request' phase. Therefore, the Desk interpreted the silence in turns 2 and 3 specifically as an official absence of a request and went on to explicitly call for one (what's the problem?). Also note that, once this problem is solved, the generic structure of an emergency call is observed.

*Example 6.16*

1. Desk: Mid-city Emergency
2.

3.
4. Desk: Hello? What's thuh problem?
5. Caller: We have an unconscious, uh: diabetic
6. Desk: Are they insiduv a building?
7. Caller: Yes they are:
8. Desk: what building is it?
9. Caller: It's thuh adult bookstore?
10. Desk: We'll get somebody there right away...

Finally consider Example 6.17 from Gafaranga and Britten (2005: 81). P is a regular user of the GP surgery and, previously, he has been consulting about heart problems. On this occasion, he has come for a different complaint. As argued in Heath (1981), Gafaranga and Britten (2005) and Robinson (2006), the complaint section normally starts with a *'first concern elicitor'* of the type 'what can I do for you?' or 'how are you?'. In turn, this opening is locally organised as an 'adjacency pair' (Schegloff and Sacks, 1973) such that 'what can I do for you?' is used for new consultations and 'how are you?' is used when the consultation is viewed as a follow-up consultation. An important characteristic of adjacency pairs is that a first pair part is always required while a second pair part may be absent. In this example, no concern elicitor, that is no first pair part of the adjacency pair, was used. Rather, P anticipated and moved straight into presenting his problem, a second pair part. Clearly, the orderliness of P's action, that is its possibility, cannot be accounted for by reference to the local order (adjacency pairs) for, in adjacency pairs, a first pair part must always be present. Rather, it must be explained with reference to the overall structure of doctor–patient consultation, which provides for a specific slot for patient's complaint. Thus, using the structure as a scheme of interpretation, P was able to move into presenting his complaint even without any elicitor from D, confident that D, himself using the same overall structure, will see exactly what P is doing.

*Example 6.17*

1. Doctor: Come in
((Door opens))
2. Doctor: Hello Mr G
3. Patient: Hello
4. Doctor: Come and sit yourself down
((Door closes))

5. Patient: Nothing to do with the heart this time
6. Doctor: Is it not? ((laughs))
7. Patient: Lower back
8. Doctor: Sit yourself down
9. Patient: Okay
10. Doctor: What's been the trouble?

Gafaranga (1998, 1999, 2000b, 2005), Gafaranga and Torras (2001, 2002), Torras and Gafaranga (2002) and Torras (1998, 2002, 2005) (hereafter referred to simply as Gafaranga) have drawn on this fact that talk-in-interaction has a significant overall organisation and developed an alternative organisational account of language alternation.

### 6.4.2. Preference for same medium

An important premise in this alternative model is the notion of 'medium'. One of the most recurrent issues in studies of language alternation is known as that of the 'base language' or, to use Auer's terminology, that of the language-of-interaction. This issue is felt to be important because, without a clearly defined base language, it is impossible to know, in an example of talk where two languages are used, what elements of which language to interpret. Any analysis is inevitably selective. For example, in Example 6.16, we were able to focus on the silences in turns 2 and 3 only because we knew what the norm is, namely the overall structure of emergency calls. Likewise, in Example 6.17, we were able to focus on patient's actions, especially in turn 5, by referring to the norm in doctor–patient interaction. Without any point of reference, no analysis could have been possible, for nothing could have been noticed as interesting. Therefore, in studies of language alternation, the need for a base language is felt because the base language, if clearly identified, works as such a point of reference against which instances of language choice are identified as deserving the researcher's attention. In other words, the base language works as a norm, a scheme of interpretation. The question therefore becomes, how should the base language be identified?

In one of the most explicit discussions of this issue currently available, Auer (2000) considers all possibilities (quantification, language proficiency, situational factors, etc.) and concludes that there are no objective criteria for determining the base language from the outside, as it were. Obviously, where language alternation is relatively rare, as in Examples 6.9 and 6.14, the problem does not really arise. In these examples, we intuitively know that English is the base language because the other language occurs only once. Therefore, analysis targets the language which is least represented. In other cases, however, it is not obvious which language should be used as the norm against which occurrences of the other are seen. Here is an example:

*Example 6.18*

A: X nawe ati *non (.) ça ne peut pas marcher comme ça (.)* Nawe *avec sa faction* baravuga bati *pour commencer* bariya bantu b'aba*dépités*- bariya batowe- ntuza- ariya matora yabo turay*anuy*e *(annuler) (.) puisque ils se sont méconduits (.) à l'égard du parti* ((laughter))

A: then X said no (.) it can't work like that (.) then he and his faction said to start with the so-called MP's- those who've been elected- something- those elections we declare them invalid (.) because they have misbehaved (.) towards to party

In a piece of talk like this, even if all researchers agreed on what to count (which is not likely), it is not obvious that they would end with any significant difference between the two languages. In terms of competence, participants are all educated and very proficient in both French and Kinyarwanda. In terms of situations, among these educated Rwandese, it is rather rare for them to use either French or Kinyarwanda separately (see Section 1.5 I.5) when talking among themselves. In other words, there is no a priori reason to think that one language and which one is the base language.

Because of difficulties such as those illustrated by the example above, Auer initiates an interesting re-specification of the problem saying that 'determining the base language of an interaction [...] is a matter of permanent concern for bilingual participants themselves who usually deal with it as part of the background business of making the conversation work' (2000: 130). That is, both analysts and participants themselves need the base language. Analysts need to determine the base language in order to carry out their analyses of language alternation in an accountably orderly manner, and participants need to establish the base language for their interaction in order to go about talking in an orderly manner. Evidence that, in talk-in-interaction, participants themselves feel the need to establish the base language for their interaction can be found in language negotiation sequences. As it has been well documented, language negotiation sequences occur very early on in the interaction and it is my contention that this sequential placement is significant. Here is an example from Codó (1998). Talk takes place in a tourist office in Barcelona.

*Example 6.19*

1. ENQ: Hola.
    'Hello'
2. AS1: hola
    'hello'
3. ENQ: **hablas ingles?**
    'do you speak English?'
4. AS1: *yes*
5. ENQ: *uh I'd like to know some addresses like International House*

Our focus is on turn 3. To understand what is going on in this example, we need to refer first of all to the overall structure of service encounters as described by Ventola (1987). This structure comprises the following phases:

a. Offer of service
b. Request for service
c. Transaction
d. Salutation

As Torras (2005) notes, in service encounters, the greeting sequence is optional. Also, because this is face-to-face interaction, participants have adopted the default identities of 'service provider' and 'service seeker'. This default definition of the situation explains the lack of any explicit service offer. Therefore, after the exchange of greetings, we could have expected to see the service request. In the example, it is delayed until turn 5. In between, an adjacency pair is inserted during which participants ascertain that they both speak English. The relevance of this sequence, which disrupts the normative structure, is that it allows participants to choose English as the base language for the ensuing interaction.

The second piece of literature we need to refer to is Schegloff (1968, 1979). Schegloff has demonstrated that one of the functions of the opening sequence in talk-in-interaction is to allow participants to achieve alignment between them, which alignment will characterise the ensuing interaction. One level where participants must achieve alignment is language choice. It is in that sense that, as I have stated elsewhere, language choice is 'a significant aspect of talk organisation' (1999). Just like participants must establish alignment at the level of their identities very early on in the interaction, so too must they align with each other at the level of language choice. In most cases, alignment at the level of language choice is accomplished implicitly, without any explicit negotiation. In Example 6.15, for example, the issue of language choice is settled at the same time as participants recognise each other as Elsie and John. Also consider Example 6.20 from Myers-Scotton (1993b: 88). As we have seen, talk takes place at an IBM office in Nairobi between the guard and two visitors. The languages involved are Swahili (plain) and Lwidhako (italics)

*Example 6.20*

1. G:   Unataka kumuwona nani?
2. V1:  Ningependa kumwona Solomon I.
3. G:   Unamujua kweli? Tunaye Solomon A –Nadhani ndio yule.
4. V1:  Yule anayetoka Tiriki – yaani Luyia.
5. G:   *Solomon menyu wakhumanya vulahi?*
6. V1:  *yivi mulole umuvolere ndi Shen L. –venyanga khukhulola.*
7. G:   *Yikhala yalia ulindi.*
Another visitor (V2) comes.
8. V2:  Bwana K – yuko hapa?
9. G:   Ndio yuko – anafanya kazi saa hii (talk goes on in Swahili).

1. G:   Whom do you want to see?
2. V1:  I would like to see Solomon I.
3. G:   Do you really know him? We have a Solomon A- I think that's the one [you mean].
4. V1:  That one who comes from Tiriki – that is, a Luyia person.

5. G:   *Will Solomon know you*
6. V1:  *You see him and tell him Shem L- wants to see you.*
7. G:   *sit here and wait.*
Another visitor (V2) comes.
8. V2:  Is Mr K- here?
9. G:   Yes, he's here – he is doing something right now (talk goes on in Swahili).
(Transcription slightly amended)

Given the relevant sociolinguistic context, at the same time as participants recognise each other as Guard and Visitor, Swahili is adopted. And as soon as they recognise each other as coming from the same region of Kenya, the local language is adopted. Thus, as Auer says, language negotiation sequences, especially of the explicit type as in Example 6.19, come about because alignment at the level of language choice is lacking (1984: 20–21). Briefly, as the base language is a permanent issue for participants and as they solve it in the interaction itself, one can inspect the interaction and witness the base language, as it has been decided by participants themselves.

But how do we observe interaction in order to tell the base language as it has been told by participants themselves? What do we look for? That is to say, what is the methodology for telling the base language? The most obvious method for telling the medium is by observing language negotiation sequences during which participants settle it. In Example 6.19, for example, we can easily see that the base language for the encounter is English, as participants' negotiation led to the choice of this language (see turn 4 and 5). The same procedure can be applied in Examples 6.12 and 6.13 if the reader wants to refer back to these examples. However, this methodology might be limited since, as Auer says, participants usually settle the issue of the base language implicitly 'as part of the background business of making the conversation work' (2000: 130). For example, in Examples 6.16, 6.17, no need to explicitly negotiate to use English was felt. The choice of English as the language of interaction was arrived at as part and parcel of the process of the job of achieving alignment that participants accomplish in the opening sequence. That is, as a method for settling the base language issue, language negotiation sequences are the exception rather than the norm. Therefore, other ways of witnessing the base language must be found.

Since the base language is a norm, we can also tell it by looking at how participants have used it to go about the business of talking. According to Ethnomethodology, one of the most reliable methods for telling the norm is to do 'deviant case analysis' (Heritage, 1988). As we have seen, if an act deviates from the norm, participants orient to it either as functional deviance or as repairable deviance. Particularly useful in this respect is repairable deviance. By repairing an act, participants reveal what they themselves hold the norm to be. Consider Example 6.9 again. In the example, three languages have been used, namely English, French and Catalan. Of the three, only English is not repaired. And the repair for the other two takes the direction of English. Therefore, through this repair work, we can see that English is the base language for the interaction. Here is another example. Like in Example 6.9, talk takes place at a University campus in Barcelona. A student has reported to the office to enquire about his registration.

*Example 6.21*

SEC: matriculated (.) and after this eh it has to wait (.) four five six *jours* eh- six –
STU: days?
SEC: days (.) after being matriculated

Here again, through the repair of the French word and only this, we can easily see that English is the base language.

So far I have been speaking of the base language and, if I stopped here, it would still be possible to speak of the preference for same language talk. That is, the only specification I have so far added to Auer is that language choice is an aspect, not of the local order, but rather of the overall order in talk organisation. In fact, the story does not end here. Consider Example 6.22. Participants are talking about the possibility for a refugee to study in British universities.

*Example 6.22*

1. A: noneho rero nka bariya b' impunzi ukuntu bigenda (.) babagira ba (.) a a amashuri hano ni *privé quoi* (.) ni *privé* mbega (.) kuburyo rero kugirango aze muri iyi *université* agomba kwishyura
2. B: umh
3. A: *mais comme* nta mafaranga afite ay yatse *bourse le* (.) babyita **local government**
4. B: umh
5. A: **local authority** *donc* ni nkaaa
6. B: ni nka ***municipalité***
7. A: ni nka ***municipalité*** *c'est ça* (.) *municipalité* yahano niyo yamuhaye *bourse*

1. A: refugees like him are (.) schools here are *private* (.) they are *private* so that he
must pay to study at this *university*
2. B: umh
3. A: *but as* he doesn't have money he has had to apply for a *grant* from the (.) they call it **local government**

4. B: umh
5. A: **local authority** well it's likeee
6. B: it's like a *municipality*
7. A: that's right it's like a *municipality* (.) he got a *grant* from the local *municipality*

The similarity between Example 6.22 on the one hand and Examples 6.9 and 6.21 on the other is obvious. In all three cases, there is repair of language choice. In Example 6.22, the choice of English, unlike that of French and Kinyarwanda, is repaired. Since, in Example 6.21, the fact that French is repaired reveals the base language, so should the fact that English is repaired in Example 6.22. Whatever is not repaired should be seen as the norm. Here is another example. Participant A, who lives in Germany, is narrating a situation which happened to his family when their last child was born.

*Example 6.23*

1. A: kw*enregistra* umwan n'ibiki (.) byose kugirango *donc* (.) abone amafaranga- *donc* kugirango (unclear) (.) *bon* ((laughter)) njya muri ntuza- muri za *ministères*- murii (.) **Sozialamt** (.) *donc* ni kimwe-
2. B:            *ministères des affaires sociales*
3. A: oya (.) ni *service en fait* ntabwo ari *ministère*

1. A: registering the child and so on (.) all that so (.) she receives the money (.) well so that (unclear) so I went to something- to the ministry departments (.) to the (.) Social welfare office (.) well it's like-
2. B:                             Ministry of Social Affairs
3. A: no (.) in fact it's an office it's not a ministry

Like in Example 6.22, in Example 6.23, although three languages (Kinyarwanda, French and German) are used, only German is repaired. Therefore, only German is seen as deviant and, by implication, whatever is not German must be seen as normative.

In order to capture the similarity between Examples 6.9 and 6.21 on the one hand and Examples 6.22 and 6.23 on the other, that is in order to account for the work participants have accomplished in all four instances using one framework, it is necessary to suspend the notion of 'language'. As I have argued elsewhere, 'speakers don't speak a language' (Gafaranga and Torras, 1998). Rather, they use a 'code', which may or may not be monolingual (see Gafaranga and Torras, 2001). In other words, the issue is not that of the base language, but rather that of the 'base code'. Thus, in all four examples, repair reveals the base code. The only difference is that, in Examples 6.9 and 6.21 the code is monolingual, while in Examples 6.22 and 6.23, it is bilingual. And this is consistent with observations by Gumperz (1982) who says that, in actual interaction, participants' 'own code' may be different from the grammarian's notion of language as well as observations by Alvarez-Caccamo (1998) who argues that the notion of communicative code and that of language are different. Crucially, Alvarez-Caccamo argues that, in actual interaction, participants draw on a variety of codes and that the linguistic code is only one of them. To highlight the specificity of this linguistic code and its independence from the notion of language, I use the term 'medium'. Thus, the organisational principle against which language alternation can be seen can be phrased as 'preference for same medium talk'.

### 6.4.3. Categories of language alternation

The view that language alternation is an aspect of the overall order in talk in two languages together with the preference for same medium talk captures various uses of language alternation as in Table 6.2 (Gafaranga and Torras, 2002: 19).

In the representation, the first terminal node is 'language alternation itself as the medium'. This corresponds to the normative use of two languages in the same conversation. As we have seen, Auer speaks of the 'new code'. However, in Auer, the orderliness of this type of talk was left unaccounted for, because his organising principle is that of preference for same language talk. Under this principle, it is impossible for

*Table 6.2* Categories of language alternation

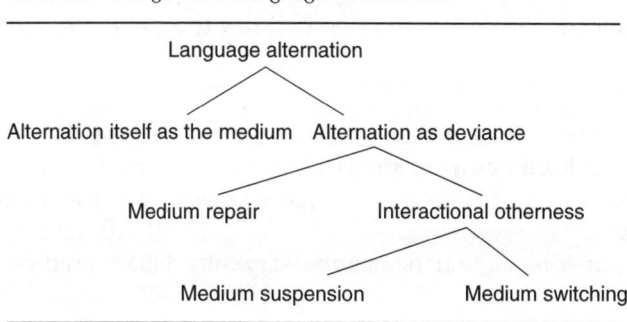

language alternation itself to occur as the preferred choice. Correspondence may also be found with Myers-Scotton's category of code-switching itself as an unmarked choice, but it is important to note that the two are arrived at from two different perspectives. Illustrative examples of this type of talk are the use of French and Kinyarwanda in Examples 6.18, 6.22 and 6.23.

While language alternation may be used as the norm, it may also be an instance of deviance from the medium. Under language alternation as deviance, the first terminal node is 'medium repair'. This is when alternation is oriented to as repairable deviance from the medium, whether the medium is monolingual or whether it is bilingual. Auer, as we have seen, discussed only repairs that take place in an otherwise monolingual context and, even then, under the heading of transfer and on a par with functional deviance. As we have seen above, this category of language alternation is crucial, for analysts can use it to tell the medium as participants themselves view it. For some examples of this phenomenon, look at Examples 6.9, 6.21, 6.22 and 6.23.

Deviance from the medium may be repairable, but it may also be functional. In the representation above, functional deviance comes under the node 'interactional otherness'. Two terminal nodes are found here, namely 'medium suspension' and 'medium switching'. Medium suspension consists of momentary deviance from the medium which is not repaired. And, as it is not repaired, such a departure must be concluded to be functional. Auer's category of discourse-related transfer must be seen as only one case of medium suspension, namely suspension of a monolingual medium (see Examples 6.14 and 6.15). But a bilingual medium too may be suspended. Here is an example. To recall, talk took place in October 1996, right after the Rwandan army had invaded Eastern Congo (former Zaire), where many Rwandans lived in refugee camps. In the example, participants are saying that Zairians will blame this invasion on Rwandan refugees and threaten to throw them out of the country.

*Example 6.24*

1. A: ubu rero ab (.) buretse (.) abazayuruwa bagiye gutangira ngo (.) **fukuza munyarwanda** (.) [( )
2. B:                                  [ *avec raison (.)[ puisque* turi imbwa
3. A:                                            [( ) ((laughter)) ariko
4. C: *avec raison* (.) none se none wanzanira ibibazo iwanjye

1. A: now Zairians Zair (.) wait a minute (.) Zairians are going to start saying **kick out Rwandan** (.) [( )
2. B: [*rightly so (.) [as* we do not deserve any respect
3. A: [( ) ((laughter)) but
4. C: *rightly so* (.) if you bring problems to my door

In the example, A suspended the bilingual medium they had adopted (French and Kinyarwanda) and used Swahili (highlighted) to do the specific activity of direct speech reporting. As switching is meant to accomplish a specific interactional task, it is not repaired (see Chapter 7).

The second node under interactional otherness is medium switching. Medium switching occurs when participants stop using one medium and negotiate to use a different one for whatever reason. That is, it occurs when a new alignment at the level of language choice is established. Correspondences can be established with the category of code-switching in Auer's framework, with that of sequential unmarked code-switching in the Markedness Model and with situational code-switching in Gumperz's framework. Many examples of this type of language alternation have already been discussed, but refer to Examples 6.12 and 6.20 in this chapter. It is important to stress that this type of language alternation consists of a renegotiation (implicit or explicit) of the medium. Consider Example 6.12 reproduced as Example 6.25 for convenience. In turn 3, CCC offers to use Catalan (italics) for the insertion sequence. In 4, BBB does no take up the proposed medium and makes a counter proposal, namely to use Spanish (bold). Subsequently, CCC 'gives in' and Spanish is established as the medium for the sequence.

*Example 6.25*

1. AAA: hello.
2. BBB: hello (.) [eh: [(unclear)
3. CCC: [*dues [de negra no?*
   (two of stout right)
4. BBB: **quieres peqeña o grande.** (would you like it small or large)
5. CCC: **grande**
   (large)
6. AAA: mmm mmm
7. BBB: eh: *one big (.) one half pint (.) for me (.) [one half pint for me*
8. AAA: [*one half pint for you*

As a case of renegotiating alignment, medium switching should not really be seen as deviance because deviance presupposes an already established norm. In Example 6.25, for example, to view language alternation merely as deviance would not adequately capture participant's work in turns 3 and 4. Likewise, in Example 6.20, the smoothness of talk organisation, despite language alternation, is not properly captured if language alternation is seen merely as a case of deviance.

To summarise, the overall order model of language alternation views language alternation as essentially consisting of two types. First, there is language alternation which takes place in the context of negotiating the medium. This occurs at the beginning of the interaction, but it may also occur anywhere in the course of the interaction if participants feel the need to negotiate a new alignment at the level of language choice. Traditionally, the first possibility has been called language negotiation sequence and the latter has alternatively been called situational code-switching (Gumperz), sequential unmarked code-switching (Myers-Scotton) and code-switching (Auer). In terms of order, this type of language alternation has always been seen as orderly, independently of the angle from which it was viewed. Secondly, there is language alternation which takes place in the context of an already established medium. In this case, two possibilities can be found: either language alternation itself is the medium or it is a case of deviance from the medium. In turn, if language alternation is deviance from the medium, it is either repairable deviance (medium repair) or it is functional deviance

*Table 6.3* Language alternation as an aspect of the overall order in talk in two languages

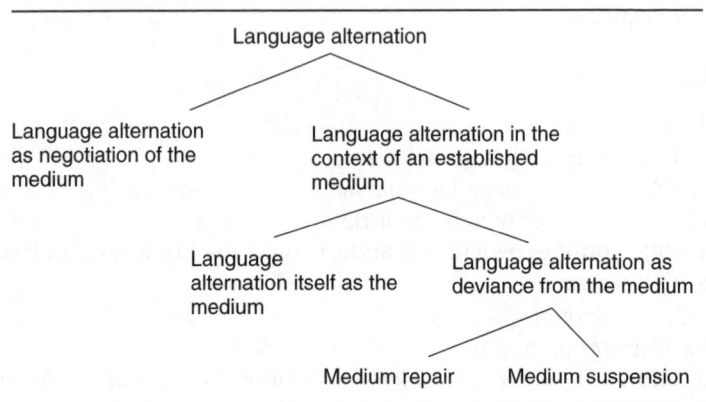

(medium suspension). That is, language alternation which takes place in the context of an already established medium is orderly either because it consists of normative conduct (language alternation itself as the medium) or because it consists of accountable deviance from the norm (medium repair vs medium suspension). Thus, Figure 6.1 can be modified and expanded as Table 6.3.

## 6.5. Conclusion

As a title by Wei (1998) suggests, studies of language alternation address two main questions: the 'why' question and the 'how' question. The identity-related approaches to language alternation I examined in Chapter 5 address the issue of order from the 'why' perspective. In this perspective, language alternation is seen as orderly from the perspective of what it does for speakers. On the other hand, the two approaches I have focused on in this chapter address the same issue of order from the 'how' perspective. Drawing on Ethnomethodology and CA, the two approaches view language choice as an activity in its own right that participants in interaction accomplish while talking. In other words, in these approaches the issue of order is addressed directly. Following on from this, they view 'language choice as a significant aspect of talk organisation' (Gafaranga, 1999) and account for the orderliness of language alternation by reference to the general organisational principle of preference. Thus, Auer speaks of the 'preference for same language talk' while Gafaranga speaks of the 'preference for same medium talk'.

At first, the difference between the two approaches may seem to be merely terminological ('language' vs 'medium'). However, close examination reveals that they are different in very important ways. As we have seen in this chapter, Auer sees language choice as an aspect of the local order in talk organisation, and his account of the orderliness of language alternation reflects this view. His units of analysis are the turn and TCU and he explains particular instances of language alternation by referring to speakers' choices in the immediately preceding turn or TCU. On the other hand, Gafaranga's view is that language choice is an aspect of the overall order in talk organisation. Rather than explaining particular instances of language alternation with reference to choices in immediately preceding turn or TCUs, my view is that language alternation should be explained with reference to the medium that participants have adopted for their interaction. Secondly, the two models differ with regard to the usefulness of the notion of 'language'. In Auer, the assumption is that people speak a language while Gafaranga's assumption is that people 'do not speak a language' (Gafaranga and Torras, 1998). Although Auer mentions the possibility of what he calls a 'new code', a strong assumption, probably due to the nature of the data he works with, remains that the notion of 'code' and that of 'language' are the same (see his use of the notion of 'language-of-interaction'). On the other hand, in his work, Gafaranga suspend the notion of 'language' in favour of that of 'medium' or the actually oriented-to linguistic code, partly because of the data he has worked with, but also partly for theoretical reasons. Thus, Gafaranga argues that, among bilingual speakers, the code or medium may be monolingual just as it may be bilingual (Gafaranga and Torras, 2001). In short, together, these two perspectives, despite their differences, show not only that language alternation in talk in two languages is an issue of order, but also that the orderliness of language alternation as practical social action is accountable. To reinforce this conclusion, in Chapter 7, I propose a case study in which a specific aspect of order in talk in two languages is investigated drawing on ideas and concepts developed in this chapter.

# 7
# Using the Models: Direct Speech Reporting in Talk in Two Languages

## 7.1. Introduction

In Chapters 5 and 6, I have surveyed the main perspectives on language alternation from a socio-functional perspective. We saw that, while some researchers account for the orderliness of language alternation in terms of its social motivation (identity-related explanation), others account for that same orderliness in terms of talk organisation (organisational explanation). Each of these accounts obviously has its own merits, but they also have their limits and, throughout the last two chapters, I have pointed out some of those advantages and weaknesses. Therefore, rather than engaging in any further theoretical discussion of the models, it is more interesting to see how the models can actually be used to address specific issues of order in talk in two languages. Thus, in this chapter, drawing on ideas and concepts developed in the preceding theoretical survey, I examine a specific issue of order in talk in two languages, namely the orderliness of language choice in the interactional site of direct speech reporting.

## 7.2. Language choice in direct speech reporting as an issue of order

Among bilingual speakers, language choice in the interactional site of direct speech reporting is an issue of order for the simple reason that, as many authors have commented (e.g. Gumperz, 1982; Auer, 1984, 1995; Alvarez-Caccamo, 1996; Alfonzetti, 1998), reporting need not adopt the same medium as the original event. An event may be reported using its original medium, just as a new medium may be adopted. Compare the following two examples. In Example 7.1, a speaker reports what some Rwandan politicians would have said and done in the period leading to the 1994 political impasse and the ensuing genocide. Given the Rwandan sociolinguistic context (see Section 1.4.), these politicians would have used Kinyarwanda–French language alternation as the medium. In reporting what they have said (highlighted), the same medium is used.

*Example 7.1*

A: X nawe ati **non, ça ne peux pas marcher comme ça** (.) Nawe *avec sa faction* baravuga bati **pour commencer, bariya bantu b'aba***depités*, **bariya batowe, ntuza ariya matora yabo turaya***nuye puisque ils se sont méconduits (.) à l'égard du parti* ((laugh))

A: X on his turn said no it can't work like that (.) he too with his group said to start with, those MPs, those elect MPs, those who have been elected, we invalidate those elections because they have misbehaved (.) towards the party ((laughter)).

On the other hand, in Example 7.2, direct speech reporting adopts a medium which could not have been used by the people quoted. In the example, participant A is telling other members what happened to his family when they came to join him in Belgium. He is saying that, on arrival at the airport, they were asked a series of questions, including whether they were planning to go back and what type of tickets they were travelling on. Presumably, these questions were asked by Belgian immigration officials. As the transcript shows, in reporting the event, A uses Kinyarwanda. Clearly, it is unlikely that these immigration officials would actually have used Kinyarwanda.

*Example 7.2*

1. A: baki- bakigera ku kibuga rero aba baje
2. B: nka wa mukobwa (X) [we rwose
3. A:                    [mbakubise mu modoka tugiye mu rugo (long talk omitted)

4. A: atubwira ibibazo bari bagize kuko barahageze bakabaza (.) ngo
   ese ngo ese muje muzasubirayo (.) ngo mufite ama*tickets*
   yahe (.) [aba barituramira nyine
5. C: [umh

1. A: when they arrived at the airport when they came
2. B: like that girl (X) [as for her
3. A: [I put them in the car to go home
(long talk omitted)
   A: he told us the problem they had had for when they arrived
   they were asked **are you going to go back** (.) **what kind of**
   ***tickets*** **do you have** (.) [these of course kept quiet
4. C: [umh

The complexity of language choice in direct speech reporting is best illustrated in Table 7.1, representing the choices I have observed in my Kinyarwanda–French corpus of bilingual conversations (Gafaranga,1998: 283).

As the table shows, in the data, an event may be reported using Kinyarwanda–French language alternation, independently of its original medium. Example 7.1 is a good example, but also consider Example 7.3. Participants are talking about Belgian bilingualism. They are saying that, in Brussels, there is a strict bilingual policy such that if a non-bilingual person is appointed to an administrative post (*bourgmestre*), important disputes follow. In order to enact those disputes in current interaction, participant A uses direct speech reporting. As the disputes are said to take

*Table 7.1* Language choice and direct speech reporting among bilingual Rwandans

| Original talk | Language alternation | Kinyarwanda | French | Other |
|---|---|---|---|---|
| **Direct speech reporting** | | | | |
| Language alternation | X | X | X | X |
| Kinyarwanda | | X | | |
| French | | | X | X |
| Other | | | | X |

Note: Top row: medium of original talk; left-hand column: medium of direct speech reporting; X: actual choice observed in the data.

place on Belgian TV, their medium must be either French or Flemish. In doing reporting, Participant A uses Kinyarwanda–French language alternation.

*Example 7.3*

1. A: si byo by' ino aha ino ahangaha (.) hari ibintu bita *les compétences linguistiques*
2. B: hmm
3. A: ibyo bya *compétence linguistiques* nibyo wumva bari gutukanaho ngoo ngo ngo **bourgmestre** ngo **utegeka aha n' aha** ngo *chez les flamands* ngo **ntabwo azi** (.) igi*flamand* ngo **avuga gake** ngo **niyo umu-** ngo **niyo umukecuru w' umu***flamand* ngo **agiye ku- kuvugana na bourgmestre** ngo **yumva ari ku- atari kucyumva** ngo **atari kumwumva** ngo *comme il faut* (.) **umh uwo mu***burgmestre* **niba baramutoraguye** (.) **niba** uretse ko bitanashoboka ngo abe ari nk'umu*wallon*

1. A: like things here (.) they have things they call *linguistic competencies*
2. B: hmm
3. A: those *linguistic competencies* you hear people quarrelling about them saying **the major** saying **who is in charge of here** saying **in a Flemish speaking area** saying **he/she doesn't know** (.) *Flemish* saying **when a** saying **when an old woman who is** *Flemish* saying **when she goes to talk to the major** saying **she finds that he/she's not understanding it** saying **he/she's understanding her** saying **as he/ she should** (.) umh if that *major* has been picked up (from the street) (.) except that it's not possible for him/her to be *Walloon*

Secondly, an event may be reported using its original medium, whatever it was. Again, Example 7.1 is a good example, but also consider Example 7.4. As we have already seen, the context of this example is the invasion of the Democratic Republic of Congo (former Zaire) by the Rwandan army in 1996. As, at the time, many Rwandan refugees were camped in Eastern Congo, participants in the conversation are saying that Zairians (Congolese) will blame the invasion of their country on these refugees and threaten to throw them out. In his contribution to the talk, participant A quotes Zairians and uses the language they plausibly could use, namely Swahili.[1]

*Example 7.4*

1. A: ubu rero ab (.) buretse (.) abazayuruwa bagiye gutangira ngo (.) ***fukuza munyarwanda*** (.) [( )
2. B: [ *avec raison (.)[ puisque* turi imbwa
3. A: [( ) ((laughter)) ariko
4. C: *avec raison* (.) none se none wanzanira ibibazo iwanjye

1. A: now Zairians Zair (.) wait a minute (.) Zairians are going to start saying ***kick out Rwandan*** (.) [( )
2. B: [*rightly so (.) [as* we do not deserve any respect
3. A: [( ) ((laughter)) but
4. C: *rightly so* (.) if you bring problems to my door

Finally, there are cases where speakers are quoted as having used French, even though they could not have. Consider Example 7.5. In the conversation, participants are talking about the racism they face in the different countries where they live. Participant A, who lives in Germany, sees racism in the kind of questions Germans ask overseas students, including himself. He quotes them as asking, among other things, 'are you studying here to go back and work in your country?'. As the transcript shows, this question uses French as its medium while its plausible original medium is German.

*Example 7.5*

1. A: ikikwereka ukuntu ari ntuza ari- badashaka abanyamahanga iwabo (.) baraza bakakubaza (.) urikwiga iki ah ngo ***c'est pour aller travailler dans ton pays***? ((laughter))
2. B: *il faut* kubasubiza uti ***oui***
3. A: reka jye ndababwira nti ubungubu nta muntu nti – jye ndababwira- jyewe ndabibabwira nti (.) *la situation* yo mu Rwanda ni *catastrophique* nta muntu ushobara gu gu gu*planifia* (.) ubu (.) aho azaba ari

1. A: what shows you that they are – that they don't want foreigners is that they come and ask you (.) what are you studying ah say ***is it to go and work in your country***? ((laughter))
2. B: *you should* tell them *yes*
3. A: no (.) I tell them today nobody- as for me I tell them- I tell them (.) *the situation* in Rwanda is *catastrophic* nobody can *plan* (.) today (.) where they will be

The issue therefore is, when does direct speech reporting adopt original medium and when does it not? If direct speech reporting deviates from original medium, what medium does it adopt? In other words, is language choice in direct speech reporting random or is it orderly and, if it is orderly, how can its orderliness be described?

Although, from very early on, the relationship between language alternation and direct speech reporting has been commented on as interesting (see Auer, 1991 for a by-no-means exhaustive list of authors who have mentioned it), no systematic account of the phenomenon has actually been proposed. For example, Gumperz (1982: 75–76), in his account of discourse strategies, only mentions quotation as a possible site for language alternation without any elaboration as to why this is so. Likewise Gal mentions language alternation in direct speech reporting, but adds that it is relatively easy to predict its medium as 'all one needs to know [...] is the language in which the original utterance was spoken' (1979: 109). Clearly, observation of actual interaction among bilingual speakers (e.g. Kinyarwanda-French bilinguals reported above) contradicts this view. A relatively more elaborate account of language alternation and direct speech reporting can be found in Auer (1984).

Auer rejects Gal's claim regarding the predictability of the medium of direct speech reporting among bilingual speakers as too simplistic, saying that 'language choice for reported speech is not determined by language choice in the reported situation' (1984: 64). Rather, language alternation must be seen as discourse-related transfer and its primary function as that of 'setting off [...] reported speech against its surrounding conversational (often narrative) context' (1995: 119), whether it reproduces the original medium or whether it does not. However, here too, a few questions are left unanswered. First, if some instances of direct speech reporting are marked (set off) by language alternation, what sets off others? Secondly, if there are different ways of marking direct speech reporting, for example voice quality, prosody, accent (Holt, 2007), what motivates the choice of language alternation? That is to say, language alternation must be understood, not in isolation, but rather relative to other ways of doing direct speech reporting.

In fact, it is doubtful whether the only role of language alternation in direct speech reporting is indeed to set off quoted material 'against surrounding conversational context'. Compare language choice in Examples 7.2, 7.4 and 7.5. In all three cases, people who are quoted could not have used Kinyarwanda–French language alternation, the medium of these conversations in the corpus. However, only in

Example 7.4 is the medium of 'original' event preserved. The difference between Example 7.4 on one hand and Examples 7.2 and 7.5 on the other seems to be that, in Example 7.4, important meanings are conveyed through language choice itself, namely that the people quoted are indeed Zairians (more on this below).

Briefly, language alternation in direct speech reporting is an issue of order, for, among bilingual speakers, it is only one of many alternative options. In doing direct speech reporting, bilingual speakers need not use language alternation. Therefore, the issue is how the orderliness of language alternation in direct speech reporting can be described. Although many researchers have noted the interest of language alternation in direct speech reporting, no satisfactory account of the phenomenon is yet available. Since, as I have just said, language alternation is only one out of many available options, its occurrence must be understood in the context of these other options. In other words, language alternation in direct speech reporting must be understood, not only against the background of a theory of language alternation as a conversation phenomenon, but also against that of a general theory of direct speech reporting in conversation. We already have available theories of language alternation (Chapters 5 and 6) and, in the account I propose below, I will particularly draw on the overall order model of language alternation. The section below brushes the broad lines of a theory of direct speech reporting in conversation I want to draw on in explaining the orderliness of language alternation in direct speech reporting. This is the *demonstration theory* as developed by Clark and Gerrig (1990).

## 7.3. Direct speech reporting as demonstration

As an aspect of language use, direct speech reporting has been studied from a variety of perspectives (linguistics, literary criticism, sociology, philosophy, etc.) and it is not my intention to review this literature here (see Holt, 1996; Thompson, 1996; Baynham, 1996; Myers, 1991; Clift and Holt, 2007). Rather, as indicated above, I intend to pick up one theory and use it as a starting point in exploring the orderliness of language alternation in direct speech reporting. Clark and Gerrig's (1990) starting point is the rejection of what they call the 'verbatim assumption', namely the assumption that direct speech reporting is a mere 'verbatim reproduction of an original utterance' (Baynham, 1996: 64). Rather, to use Tannen's words, they see direct speech reporting as 'primarily a creation of the speaker rather than the party quoted' (Tannen, 1989: 99). Indeed, in line with Clark and Gerrig, Tannen (1989) speaks of 'constructed dialogue' to highlight the nature of reported speech as a local accomplishment rather than as a verbatim reproduction of previous talk. Clark and Gerrig discuss many reasons why the verbatim assumption must be rejected, but space does not allow me to go into the detail of their argument. Three pieces of evidence, just to mention these, why direct speech reporting should be seen as a local interactional accomplishment are the fact that, sometimes, speakers report events which they themselves signal as yet to come, the fact that, sometimes, they only report 'community voices' (Thompson, 1996) rather than specific events and the fact that, in some cases, only thought rather than a previous talk is reported (Haakana, 2007). By way of an illustration, consider Example 7.4. As the transcript shows, the event reported is yet to take place. Zairians are yet to say 'kick out Rwandan'. That is there has not been any previous interaction for participants to report. Also consider Examples 7.3 and 7.5. Each of these only reports the voice of the community rather than that of specifiable individuals in actually identifiable events.[2]

Secondly, Clark and Gerrig's demonstration theory draws on Pierce's division of signs into indices, symbols and icons. Thus, their theory is based on the view that, in face-to-face communication, there are 'three fundamental methods' of conveying information: indicating, describing and demonstrating (1990: 765). To clarify the differences between these methods, Clark and Gerrig use, among other examples, the one of 'George limps'. The information that George limps can be communicated through description by uttering the sentence: 'George limps'. In this case, communication is essentially a mental activity of associating what is said and what is meant. There is no experience, direct or indirect, of the situation described. The same meaning can be communicated, through indication, by pointing at George while he is walking, such that the interlocutor actually sees George limping. Here, communication consists of 'direct perceptual experience' (1990: 767). Finally, the same meaning can be communicated, through a demonstration, by imitating some of George's body movements. In this case, the hope is that the interlocutor will be able to 'experience *what it is like* to perceive the things depicted' (p. 765) (my emphasis), what it is like to see George limping.

According to Clark and Gerrig, the two main properties of demonstrations are that they are *non-serious actions* and that they are *partial and selective*. The term 'non serious action' is borrowed from Goffman (1974) according to whom non-serious actions are 'transformations' of serious actions. Serious actions are 'real and actual' while non-serious actions are neither real nor actual and need to refer to their serious counterpart for meaning. For example, right now, I am really and actually typing on my computer. This is a serious action. Later on in the evening, I might mimic what I am doing right now, for example move my fingers, by way of telling my children what I have been doing all day. While mimicking I will not be really and actually typing on the computer. This is a non-serious action. As non-serious actions, demonstrations relate to serious actions in three ways: (i) 'demonstrations are performed as part of serious activities', that is they have a specific function to serve within the context of the serious activity. For example, in the example above, the typing demonstration would be performed as part of the telling of my day; (ii) 'Demonstrations must be distinguished from serious actions they are part of, that is their boundaries – their beginnings and ends-must be clear'; and (iii) demonstrations are either 'component parts' of the serious activity or they are 'concurrent with the serious activity' (1990: 766). For example, in the same typing example above, I might say 'I spent the day doing this' and then do the demonstration (move my fingers). In this case, the demonstration is said to be a component part of the serious activity of telling my children what I spent the day doing. Alternatively, I might say 'I spent the day typing on the computer' and, while saying this, do the demonstration. In this case, the demonstration is concurrent with the serious activity.

On the other hand, demonstrations are partial and selective in the sense that, in a demonstration, not every aspect of the depicted action is enacted. Take the serious action of typing on the computer. This action includes acts such as movement of fingers, movement of the eyes, reading of the screen, breaks to think what to do next and so on. In the non-serious action, not all of these will be enacted, and the one act which will be enacted, for example movement of fingers, might have to be exaggerated in order to actually convey the intended meaning. Following from the fact that demonstrations are partial and selective, Clark and Gerrig identify four possible aspects to every demonstration: (i) depictive aspects, (ii) supportive aspects, (iii) annotative aspects and (iv) incidental aspects. A depictive aspect is any one that has been chosen to represent the action depicted. In the typing example, the depictive aspect is the movement of fingers. Supportive aspects are those which are necessary for the depictive aspect to be possible. For instance, in the typing demonstration, for the movement of fingers to be possible as depictive of the action of typing on the computer, the arms must be in a certain position (flexed at the level of the elbow). Thirdly, annotative actions are those which 'are added as commentary on what is being demonstrated' (1990: 768). For example, while demonstrating typing, I might produce noises imitating the ones produced by hitting keys on the keyboard. Finally, incidental aspects are those which, although part of the action being demonstrated, are completely ignored in the demonstration. For example, the fact that, while actually typing, I am in a seating position might be completely ignored in the demonstration. Clearly, of the four, the most important is the depictive aspect.

Drawing on the ideas above, Clark and Gerrig argue that 'prototypical quotation is a demonstration of what a person did in saying something [...] (and that) quotations [...] display all the properties of genuine demonstrations [...]' (1990: 769). As we have seen, the first property of demonstrations is that they are non-serious actions. To see that direct speech reports are non-serious actions, consider Example 7.2. As we have seen, the reports in the example are questions as to whether A's family were planning to go back and what types of tickets they were travelling on. Clearly, in uttering these questions, A is not really and actually asking them. Likewise, in Example 7.4, A is not really and actually threatening to kick out Rwandan. In either case, A's actions are only 'patterned on' or 'transformation of' serious actions which are 'already meaningful in terms of some primary framework' (p. 770). Secondly, the quotations are performed as part of serious activities, namely the narration of what happened to A's family when they came to join him in Belgium (Example 7.1) and the narration of anticipated reaction by Zairians to the Rwandan invasion. Thirdly, in both cases, reports are clearly set off from surrounding conversational context by the use of an 'introductory component' (Holt, 2007) ('bakabaza' in Example 7.2 and 'bagiye gutangira' in Example 7.4), the use of the direct speech report marker 'ngo' in both cases and slight pauses (.) before and after the quotations. Finally, both cases are instances of concurrent demonstrations since they do not lead to any suspension of the serious activities.

The second property of demonstrations is that they are partial and selective. Regarding this property, Clark and Gerrig write,

> Face to face, people can demonstrate many things. When Alice demonstrates for Ben what George said, she can easily depict the words he uttered. But using her voice, face, arms, and body, she can also help depict George's language, dialect, drunkenness, indignation, hesitancy, arrogance, flamboyance, stuffy manner, and a variety of other things. What she chooses to depict depends on the experience she wants Ben to have. (1990: 775)

Elsewhere, they write that '[...] speakers can quote anything they can recognizably demonstrate, from intonation and dialect to non-linguistic actions of all sorts' (1990: 782). However, all these possibilities can be grouped under three general categories (p. 775):

(i) delivery: voice pitch (male, female, child), voice age (adult, child, oldster), voice quality (rapsy, nasal, slurred), speech defects lisp, stutter), emotional states (anger, sarcasm, excitement), etc.
(ii) language: language proper (English, Dutch, Japanese), dialect (British English, Bostonian English, Scottish
(iii) linguistic acts: illocutionary act (question, promise, request), propositional expression (content), locutionary act (the sentence uttered), utterance act (the utterance issued with repairs, etc.)

Thus, in Example 7.3, for example, delivery is the depictive aspect. As the transcript shows, the quotation is organised in short chunks of words with many direct speech markers (ngo) and many recycles, with the purpose of conveying specific emotional states, namely heated debate. As a result, the content of what is being said only serves as a supporting aspect. As for the medium of 'original' event (either French or Flemish), it is incidental here. Here is another example. Speaker A, a Rwandan priest, is saying that his parishioners take charge of the different aspects of life in the parish. He illustrates this using the example of the choir, saying that, on Sundays, when the clock strikes 10:30 am, the choir starts singing whether he asks them to do so or not.

*Example 7.6*

1. A: saa ine n'igice (.) mu kadomo (.) inanga ihita ivuga (.) kuko baba batangiye
2. B: ((laughter))
3. A: naba nkivugana n'umuntu *dans [le fond (unclear)*
4. B:                                              [ubwo baba batangiye
(two turns omitted)
5. A: misa itangira saa ine n'igice (.) saa ine n'igice *top* rero **umhooooooooooo** (.) *chant d'entrée*
6. B: umh
7. A: nkaba *obligé* yo kurekura uwo muntu

1. A: at half past ten (.) by the minute (.) instruments start playing (.) for they are starting
2. B: ((laughter))
3. A: whether I am still speaking to somebody *in [the back* ( unclear)
4. B: [they start

(two turns omitted)

5. A: the mass starts at half past ten (.) at half past ten *sharp* (.) **umhoooooooooo** (.) *the entry song*
6. B: umh
7. A: then I *have to* leave the person I was speaking to

This is a case of quotation as component demonstration because, during the performance of the quotation, the description is suspended and is resumed after it. In this quotation, the depictive aspect is delivery (singing) and everything else, including content and language, is incidental.

If, as indicated above, speakers can 'quote anything' (Clark and Gerrig, 1990: 775), a question arises as to how they decide what to quote and whether their choices are random or whether they are orderly. To begin to address this issue of order, we note that, as Clark and Gerrig argue, quotations are non-serious actions, consist of 'frame shift from the primary frame that we take to be immediate reality, to another frame shared for the purposes of the interaction' (Myers, 1991: 379). In other words, and in ethnomethological terms, direct speech reporting is a case of functional deviance. Two general functions are identified, namely *detachment* and *direct experience*. By detachment, Clark and Gerrig mean the fact that, in using DSR, the speaker takes 'responsibility only for *presenting* the quoted matter', the responsibility for the depicted aspects themselves remaining with the 'source speaker' (p. 792). In Goffman's (1981) words, the speaker is only an 'animator'. As for direct experience, Clark and Gerrig mean the fact that 'we perceive the depicted aspects partly as we would the aspects they are intended to depict' (1990: 791). For example, the function of quotation in Example 7.6 is direct experience. In the example, it is as if A's addressees are being asked to experience the singing themselves. On the other hand, Example 7.4 is a case of detachment for solidarity purposes. Direct speech reporting serves solidarity purposes when, through it, participants assert 'I am demonstrating something we both can interpret correctly' (Clark and Gerrig, 1990: 793). In this example, quotation works effectively only because all participants can recognise that it is meant to elicit laughter. Unlike in Example 7.6, here participants are not being asked to experience the threat themselves. However, as Myers (1991: 379) says, in any quotation, 'there are elements of direct experience and of detachment'.

Thus the decision as to what aspect to report, rather than being random, is functional. In actual situations, speakers select to depict any aspect which can best serve the intended function. In Example 7.3, for example, the intended function is that of direct experience. Addressees are being invited to experience the intensity of the debates regarding bilingualism in Belgium. To achieve this function, A chooses to depict delivery, content serving as a supportive element while language choice is incidental. Also consider Example 7.7. Participants in the interaction are saying that some Rwandans' pronunciation of French has been strongly influenced by Kinyarwanda. To illustrate this, A uses the example of a Bishop who, he says, came to give a talk at his school. The specific aspect of the 'original' event he decides to depict, with a view to bring other participants to experience the Bishop's pronunciation of French, is the cluster [nt]. In French, [t] is dental occlusive and remains such in the context of the nasal [n]. In Kinyarwanda, on the other hand, in contact with [n], [t] moves back to the ridge and ceases to be occlusive, as a stream of air is allowed to go out through the nose. Thus, in the example, A reports the sentence 'Le roi Rwabugiri a éte' interonisé dans les montagnes de Ntongwe', stressing the cluster [nt]. In this case, pronunciation of this cluster is the depictive aspect, everything else including content becoming secondary.

*Example 7.7*

1. A: hari um- umusenyeri witwaga S yigeze kuza kuduha conference (.) à l' école cyera niga muri *secondaire* (.) araatubwira ngo (.) **le roi Rwabugiri a été in*te*ronisé dasn les mo*nta*nge to *nt*ongwe** ((laughter))
2. A&B] ((laughter))
3. A: ugash- ugashakisha niba ari igifaransa arimo avuga cyangwa niba ari ikinyarwanda
4. C: S ndamuzi
5. A: ngo *il a été in*te*ronisé* [((laughter))
6. B: [*in*te*ronisé*
7. A: *dans les mo*nt*anges* ((laughter))

1. A: One bishop called S one day came to give a talk at our school when I was still at secondary school and (.) he said King Rwabugiri was enthroned in the hills of Ntongwe ((laughter))

2. B:     ((laughter))
3. A:     and you'd wonder whether he was speaking French or Kinyarwanda
4. A&B:   ((laughter))
5. C:     I know S
6. A:     he was enthroned ((laughter))
7. B:     enthroned
8. A:     in the hills ((laughter))

To summarise, direct speech reporting or quotation must be understood as a demonstration because it has the two main aspects of any demonstration, namely being a selective and non-serious action. Direct speech reporting is a non-serious action, for it corresponds to what Goffman (1974) calls 'frame shift' at various levels or 'footing'. As a shift of frame, direct speech reporting is necessarily functional. As we have seen, the functions of direct speech reporting can be thought of either in terms of detachment or in terms of direct experience. On the other hand, direct speech reporting is selective and partial because it depicts some aspects of the event reported and disregards some others. The selection itself of what aspect to depict depends on the intended function. Once an aspect of the event reported has been selected, other aspects work either as supportive elements or as annotative elements. Alternatively, they may simply be incidental. The issue of language choice in direct speech reporting must be understood with reference to this general nature of quotations as demonstrations.

## 7.4. Language choice and direct speech reporting among bilingual speakers

### 7.4.1. Language choice as the depictive element

In Section 7.2, we saw that language choice in direct speech reporting must be seen as an issue of order. As we have seen, some of the questions that language choice in this interactional site raises are as follows: why is it that direct speech reporting is sometimes found to adopt the medium of 'original' event and to change it some other times? If the medium of 'original' event is not retained, what does it change into and why? In order to be able to address these questions, a respecification is necessary. As Clark and Gerrig argue, direct speech reporting is not a mere reproduction of a previous event. Rather, direct speech reporting must be seen as the creation of current speaker. That is to say, both questions above are based on the verbatim assumption, an assumption which, as we have seen, is unsupportable. If the verbatim assumption is rejected, the issue for research becomes, why is it that, in direct speech reporting, speakers sometimes stay within current medium and depart from it some other times? That is, current medium, rather than 'original' medium, must be seen as the point of reference. In turn, this is consistent with the ideas developed in Chapter 6 according to which the medium of an interaction is a 'scheme of interpretation' (Garfinkel, 1967). Thus, given two examples such as Example 7.3 and Example 7.4, the question to ask is, why is it that, in Example 7.3, Kinyarwanda–French language alternation, that is the medium of current conversation, is adopted in doing direct speech reporting and why is it that it is deviated from in Example 7.4? It is also why, in Example 7.4, deviance from the medium takes the specific direction of Swahili, for it could have gone in the direction of French as in Example 7.5.

Two initial situations may be observed. As Clark and Gerrig (1990) have noted, in direct speech reporting, language (choice) itself may be depictive, but it may also be incidental. If language choice is incidental, the default choice, that is current medium, is adopted. In turn, this is understandable because, as we have seen, the medium of a conversation is a norm, deviance from which must be accountable. Conversely, if language choice itself is the depictive aspect in direct speech reporting, 'original' medium must be used. Elsewhere, I have spoken of the contrast 'medium reporting' vs 'content reporting' (1997b, 1998), but this is a very gross simplification as we will see shortly. Language choice as a depictive aspect can be found in Example 7.7. As we have seen, the function of direct speech reporting in this instance can be characterised as direct experience. The aim is to get co-participants to experience the reported speaker's way of pronouncing French. Obviously, the only way this could be achieved is by medium reporting, by using the medium of original talk and, even then, selecting to emphasise specific aspects of it, namely the pronunciation of the cluster [nt]. Another example of medium reporting is Example 7.8, an extension of Example 7.2. As we have seen, A is narrating an event which occurred to his family when they came to join him in Brussels. Ongoing topic, which occasions the story, is that children are losing the use of Kinyarwanda (see Chapter 8). Participant A narrates a story illustrating this. He says that, after his family had gone through customs clearance, he took them in his car and they told him what had happened to them. In addition to the family, present in the car was a Belgian friend who had offered to help A pick up his family from the airport. Because of the presence of this

166  *Talk in Two Languages*

non-Kinyarwanda speaker, French was used (see Example 7.4), leading the child to complain about this choice of a language he did not understand and to threaten that, if they did not stop, he too would speak 'Zairian' (Swahili). In this case, the choice of Swahili in the highlighted quotation is meant to illustrate this use of 'Zairian' by the child, to get co-participants to experience directly the child's use of 'Zairian'. As in Example 7.7, the content of what is reported to have been said is irrelevant. Note that, precisely because content is irrelevant, medium reporting is always of the 'component part' type of quotation.

*Example 7.8*

1. A:    baki- bakigera ku kibuga rero aba baje
2. B:    nka wa mukobwa (X) [we rwose
3. A:                    [mbakubise mu modoka tugiye mu rugo (long talk omitted) atubwira ibibazo bari bagize kuko barahageze bakabaza (.) ngo ese ngo ese muje muzasubirayo (.) ngo mufite ama*tickets* yahe (.) [aba barituramira nyine
4. C:                    [umh
5. A:    noneho umwana aratubwira (.) ati ubu mvuye muri Zaire (.) ati murakomeza kuvuga ibyo bifaransa nanjye ndavuga [ikizayiruwa ((laughter))
6. C:    [ndavuga ikizayiruwa ((laughter))
7. A:    ati **Habari gani**? ((laughter))
8. B&D:  ((laughter))

1. A:    when they arrived at the airport when they came
2. B:    like that girl (X) [as for her
3. A:                    [I put them in the car to go home (long talk omitted) he told us the problem they had had for when they arrived they were asked are you going to go back (.) what kind of *tickets* do you have (.) [these of course kept quiet
4. C:                    [umh
5. A:    and then the child told us (.) I am coming from Zaire (.) he said if you keep on speaking French [I will speak Zairian
6. C:                    [I will speak Zairian
7. A:    he **How are you**? ((laughter))
8. B&D:  ((laughter))

As for the situation where language choice is incidental, the first possibility is when content is reported. Consider Example 7.2 again (part of Example 7.8). As we have seen, the aim of reporting is to give some examples of the questions A's family were asked when they arrived at Zaventem airport. That is to say, A is reporting the content of what was said, and how it was said is felt to be irrelevant. As a consequence, Kinyarwanda–French language alternation is adopted, even though it could not possibly have been used in the 'original' event. Likewise, consider Example 7.9. A is saying that he has nice and friendly neighbours. By way of illustrating this, comparing his neighbourhood to the Rwandan countryside, he says that they invite him for drinks and even for food. To make his narrative more vivid, he uses the strategy of direct speech reporting, phrasing the invitations as they would be by the neighbours. Here again, because the medium these invitations actually take is incidental, A uses current medium, namely Kinyarwanda–French language alternation, even though the Belgian neighbours cannot possibly use it.

*Example 7.9*

1. A: barantumira- akan*telephon*a ati **yayaya** (.) ni nk'iwacu mu giturage (.) ati **nabonye akadivayi wanyarutse tukagasogongera tukumva uko kameze**
2. B: *c'est vrai?*
3. A: eeh [((laughter))
4. B:         [((laughter))
5. A: abenshi b'ahangaha benshi ni abahinzi (unclear)
6. B: umh
7. A: ati **irukakanka twakoze bya***saucissons*- **yewe waje tukabyumva niba biryoshye?**

1. A: they invite me- they call and says **yayaya** (.) it's like home in the countryside (.) says **I have a small wine come and have a taste**
2. B: *really?*
3. A: eeh [((laughter))
4. B:         [((laughter))
5. A: most people around here are farmers (unclear)
6. B: umh
7. A: says **come quick we've made sausages – let's taste them and see if they are nice**

However, content need not be the depictive aspect for current medium to be adopted. In Example 7.3, for example, we have seen that delivery, that is the use of short utterances as if many people were talking at the same time, is the depictive element. The aim of direct speech reporting is to depict the reported debate as heated. Consequently, as the actual medium of the debates is irrelevant, Kinyarwanda–French language, the default choice for current interaction, is used. Thus, rather than the contrast content vs medium reporting, a more realistic contrast would be [+medium reporting] vs [− medium reporting].

### 7.4.2. Language choice as a supportive element

As the discussion above shows, in direct speech reporting, language choice can be depictive just as it may be incidental. A third possibility is for it to be used as a supportive element. In this case, without being the focus of direct speech as such, language choice either adds new meaning to what is being said or reinforces it in various ways. Consider Example 7.4 again. In this example, content is relevant. Therefore, we can speak of content reporting. However, language choice is also relevant. To understand the function of language choice in this example, I propose we start by observing that there is a feeling of disassociation between Zairians and Rwandan refugees, including participants in this interaction. These categories are associated with two different ways of speaking. Current participants use Kinyarwanda–French language alternation, Zairians use a different medium. Elsewhere, I have spoken of language preference as a membership categorisation device (Gafaranga, 2001b; Torras and Gafaranga, 2002). By enacting these linguistic identities, the speaker is able to evoke further category-bound features, further meanings associated with being Zairian, including that of laughable people. In this sense, language choice can be said to be used metaphorically (Blom and Gumperz, 1972; Gumperz, 1982). In other words, language choice is used as a supportive element, as an additional resource even though it is not itself the primary focus of direct speech reporting.

Also consider Example 7.10. In this episode, participants are saying that it is not good to live in the countryside, for one is easily identified as different. In the example, two stories are used by way of exemplifying this. In the course of the narratives, direct speech reporting occurs. As in Example 7.4, here the main focus is on what was said (content). However, here too, two categories of people are involved, namely current participants (and their Rwandan friends) and the people reported, white Belgians. In both cases, the thrust of talk is such that current participants have to distance themselves from the people whose talk they are reporting. In both cases, this identity contrast is reflected at the level of language choice, with current participants using Kinyarwanda–French language alternation, while the white community is attributed to the use of French.

*Example 7.10*

1. A: nagiye kumusura (.) nsigaje kilometero nk' icumi ngo ngere iwe (.) uwo mbajije wese (.) ngo ah ngo *tu vas chez monsieur* (.) *le monsieur là le noir*
2. B: ((laughter))
3. A: umh *tu t'imagines* ngo *tu vas chez le monsieur là* (.) *le monsieur le noir*
4. C: eh *donc* bose bamuzi
(talk omitted)
5. B: *oui* ejobundi nagiye mu nama ya (name omitted) (.) ejobundi *dimanche*
6. C: umh
7. B: numva abantu bari kumbwira S utuye (name omitted) muri region muri *région* ya (name omitted) (.) [bamuzi
8. A:                                                [*c'est ça*
9. B: twari mu nama gutya noneho ikizungu kiba kirambwiye ngo (.) *donc tu es Rwandais* (.) *il y a un Rwandais qui habite dans la mairie* (name omitted) *dans trente kilomètres* ngo *il était militaire*

1. A: I went to visit him (.) about ten kilometres before I got to his place everybody I asked would say *you are going to see mister* (.) *mister the black*
2. B: ((laughter))
3. A: umh *can you imagine* say *you are going to see mister* (.) *mister the black*
4. C: eh *so* everybody knows him
(talk omitted)
5. B: *yes* two days ago I went to the meeting of (name omitted) (.) two days ago on *Sunday*
6. C: umh
7. B: I heard people telling me about S who lives (name omitted) in the *district* of (name omitted) (.) [they knew him
8. A:                                              [*that's it*
9. B: we were sitting like this in a meeting and a white man told me (.) *so you are Rwandan there is a Rwandan who lives* (name omitted) (.) *thirty kilometres from here* (.) he said *he was in the army* (.)

It is at this level of language choice as a supportive aspect in direct speech reporting that the issue of whether to retain 'original' medium or not and, if not, what to change it into arises. And it arises precisely because both content and language choice are relevant. Because language choice is relevant, as in the case of medium reporting, ideally, 'original' medium will be retained. On the other hand, because content is relevant, language choice in direct speech reporting must take account of participants' 'competence-related language preference' (Torras and Gafaranga, 2002). Thus, when language preference is not an issue, 'original' medium is retained as in Example 7.4. As we have seen, among Rwandans, Zairians are associated with Swahili. In addition, current participants, just like any Rwandans, are competent enough in Swahili to be able to understand the meaning of *'fukuza munyarwanda'* (kick out the Rwandan). However, the same cannot be said of the choice of French in Example 7.10. It is not the case that, for Rwandans in Belgium, all Belgians speak French. How do we explain this choice of French?

One candidate answer could be that French was actually used as the medium in 'original' event. However, this answer has to be rejected on two grounds. First, the answer unjustifiably subscribes to the verbatim assumption, as 'original' interaction could actually have taken place in Flemish. Secondly, such an answer is falsified by instances of language choice in direct speech reporting as illustrated in Example 7.5 (reproduced as Example 7.11 for convenience).

*Example 7.11*

1. A: ikikwereka ukuntu ari ntuza- ari- badashaka abanyamahanga iwabo (.) baraza bakakubaza (.) **urikwiga iki**? ah ngo *c'est pour aller travailler dans ton pays*? ((laughter))
2. B: *il faut* kubasubiza uti *oui*
3. A: reka jye ndababwira nti **ubungubu nta muntu-** nti – jye ndababwira- jyewe ndabibabwira nti (.) *la situation* yo mu Rwanda ni *catastrophique* nta muntu ushobara gu gu gu*planifi*a (.) ubu (.) aho azaba ari

1. A: what shows you that they are- that they don't want foreigners is that they come and ask you (.) **what are you studying** ah say *is it to go and work in your country*? ((laughter))
2. B: *you should* tell them *yes*
3. A: no (.) I tell them **today nobody-** as for me I tell them- I tell them (.) *the situation* in Rwanda is *catastrophic* nobody can *plan* (.) today (.) where they will be

As we have seen, participants in the conversation are talking about the racism they suffer in the different countries where they live. Participant A, who lives in Germany, illustrates this saying that a typical question Germans ask foreign students is whether they will go back to their countries. In the example, three interesting situations can be observed. On the one hand, the native Germans are reported to typically ask two questions, namely 'uri kwiga iki?' (what are you studying?) and 'c'est pour travailler dans ton pays?' (is it to go and work in your country?). As it can be seen, one of the questions uses the medium of Kinyarwanda, while the other uses the medium of French. Obviously, the reported speakers could not have used any of these two languages. On the other hand, the report consists of a dialogue in which A himself typically gets involved. Again, as it can be seen, while one of the questions that the Germans are said to typically ask is in French, A's answers are reported in Kinyarwanda–French language alternation, the medium of current interaction, as if 'original' talk had taken place in what Gafaranga and Torras (2001) refer to as the 'parallel mode'. Finally, it is important to note that, in the report, the content is important.

In order for all three situations to be accounted for, the choice of French to report the second question must be seen as a case of language choice as a supportive element. On the one hand, the choice of French allows the speaker to contrast the two questions, the question which is neutral (Question 1), which service as context (Rae and Kerby, 2007) and the focal question, which denotes racism on the part of the people reported (Question 2). By deviating from the norm, A is able to highlight the second question. This is a case of what Chan (2004) calls 'textualization'. On the other hand, the contrast between the choice of French to report the Germans' talk and that of Kinyarwanda to report current speaker's own talk corresponds to the social categories 'racists' and 'victims' which underlie the ongoing talk. Through language choice, A is able to distance himself from the Germans whom he is affirming to be racist. As in Example 7.4, all of the above could have been achieved by using German, presumably the medium of 'original' interaction. However, participant B (myself) does not speak German. The choice of German would have hindered communication of content. Therefore, it is safe to say that French was adopted, not because it was used in 'original' event, but rather as a compromise strategy, allowing the speaker to highlight the above contrasts while, at the same time, attending to the relevance of content. And, if this analysis of language choice in Example 7.11 is accepted, a similar account can be proposed for language choice in Example 7.10 as well. In Example 7.10, French would have been chosen, not necessarily because it was the medium of 'original' talk, but rather because it allowed participants both to attend to content and to distance themselves from the people they are reporting. In short, language choice in direct speech reporting is neither a mere matter of reproducing the medium of 'original' talk nor is it that of contrasting the reported material and the surrounding interactional context. Rather, it is a matter of whether language choice itself is being reported or not and, if it is, of whether language choice itself is the depictive aspect or whether it is a supportive aspect.

## 7.5. Conclusion

In Chapters 5 and 6, I surveyed the main approaches which have been developed to account for the interactional dimension of language alternation. Following on from this, Chapter 7 has aimed to illustrate the use of those approaches in practice, focusing on a specific aspect of order in talk in two languages. The specific aspect of order I have examined is language choice in direct speech reporting. At the beginning of the chapter, I indicated that language choice in direct speech reporting can be seen as an issue of order, for, in some cases, the medium of 'original' talk is reproduced and, in some other cases, it is not. Furthermore, in those cases where the medium of 'original' talk is altered, in some cases, the overall medium of current interaction is adopted while, in some other cases, it is not. In order to address these issues, in line with Auer (1984), I maintained that two theories were needed: a theory of direct speech reporting as a conversational object and a theory of language alternation as an interactional object.

On this occasion, I adopted the 'demonstration theory' of direct speech reporting as developed by Clark and Gerrig (1990) and paired it with ideas from the overall order perspective on language alternation (see Chapter 6). Clark and Gerrig maintain that direct speech reporting or quotation is a 'non-serious' action inserted within a 'serious' action. In turn, this is in line with the ethnomethodological notions of norm and deviance from the norm in social action. In this sense, quotation is a case of functional deviance. A key aspect of the demonstration theory is the rejection of the verbatim assumption. According to this theory, direct speech reporting must be understood, not necessarily with reference to a previous event, but rather as the creation of current speaker. Therefore, the issue that direct speech reporting raises is: why does current speaker deviate from the norm? And this question can be asked whether one is dealing with language choice or not. The general answer to this question is that direct speech reporting is a strategy speakers use to communicate by depiction rather than by description. A second key aspect of the demonstration theory is that quotation is selective and partial. According to Clark and Gerrig, speakers select which aspect of the supposedly 'original' event to depict. They may depict content, they may depict delivery, but they may also depict language among other things. Finally, according to Clark and Gerrig, in direct speech reporting, an aspect of a supposedly 'original' event may be depictive, it may be supportive, but it may also be incidental.

If these ideas are applied to language choice, the following picture emerges. First, if language choice is seen as incidental, that is if the medium of 'original' talk is viewed as irrelevant for the purpose of the quotation, current medium is adopted. As we have seen, the medium of a conversation is the default choice, the choice speakers make when no special functionality is intended. It is in this sense that, in the data, people who could not have used Kinyarwanda-French language alternation were often reported using this medium. On the other hand, if language choice is the depictive aspect, the medium of 'original' event must be maintained. Again, this is in line with the ideas we developed in Chapter 6 according to which deviance from current medium must be accountable. Finally, if language choice is viewed as a supportive element, current medium must be deviated from, but deviance may or may not lead to the reproduction of 'original' medium. As we have seen, 'original' medium is reproduced if, given current participants' language preferences, it does not hinder communication of content. If on the other hand, 'original' medium is likely to hinder communication of content, speakers adopt compromise strategies whereby they can communicate content and at the same time depart from current medium. In the data I have examined, the need to attend to both requirements led participants to adopt French even though the speakers whose talk was reported could not plausibly (or necessarily) have spoken this language. The fact that this compromise strategy invariably goes in the direction of French is itself interesting as evidence of 'language ownership', but space does not allow me to look into this issue in any detail. In short, far from being random, language choice in direct speech reporting is orderly and its orderliness is accountable.

## Notes

1. Swahili is used as a lingua franca in Eastern Congo, where Rwandan refugees were camped.
2. For all these reasons, the term 'original' will be marked with apostrophes whenever it appears.

# 8
# Applying Language Alternation Studies

## 8.1. Introduction

In a most inspiring paper, Heap (1990: 42) writes that 'Any serious piece of scholarship presumes the existence of a compelling answer to the twin questions of Why Speak/Listen and Why Write/Read.' That is, any piece of scholarship presumes an answer to the question 'Why bother?'. In turn, a general answer to the question is that 'inquiry can deliver some of what we need to know in order to make reasoned judgements in particular situations about how to act to achieve some end' (1990: 39). To be sure, that end may be the advancement of knowledge per se, but it may also be, based on the knowledge developed, 'to make a difference to how we act'. In the first case, Heap speaks of 'straight-ahead Ethnomethodology' and, in the second, he speaks of 'applied Ethnomethodology'.

> Straight-ahead EM is done for, and reported to, other professional (including students) ethnomethodologists. It provides knowledge of some state of affairs, affairs chosen for study because of their value for furthering the development of ethnomethodological knowledge. Applied EM is done for, and reported to, persons perhaps having a nodding acquaintance with EM. The affairs studied are those whose formal structures may have consequences important to this audience of 'lay ethnomethodologists.' The affairs chosen for study have value for, and to, them. (1990: 44)

Although Heap refers particularly to Ethnomethodology, the reasoning behind his statement applies to other areas of scientific enquiry. Thus, distinctions such as between Linguistics and Applied Linguistics (see below), between Conversation Analysis and Applied Conversation Analysis (Ten Have, 1999; Richards and Seedhouse, 2005) and between Discourse Analysis and Applied Discourse Analysis (Gunnarsson, 1997) are nowadays very common.

So far in this book, I have looked at the various ways in which the phenomenon of language alternation, as an object of enquiry, has been approached. I have also used two case studies to illustrate how the various perspectives I have surveyed can be used in practice to address specific issues of order. In that sense, in Heap's framework, I have been doing straight-ahead science (Ethnomethodology, Linguistics, Discourse Analysis, etc). My aim has been to show how researchers view and talk about language alternation. In this chapter, I will be concerned with the question: 'why bother?'. Why do researchers bother investigating the orderliness of language alternation? Part of the answer is, of course, that understanding the orderliness of language alternation is in itself a fascinating topic for linguistic enquiry. The other part of the answer, with which I will be concerned in this chapter, is that understanding of the orderliness of language alternation can be of interest for 'lay linguists'. Knowledge about the orderliness of language alternation in talk in two languages can be used to address real-life issues.

## 8.2. From applied Linguistics to applied Language alternation studies

Many definitions of the term 'Applied Linguistics' are currently available. For example, Wilkins (1999: 7) writes,

> In a broad sense, Applied Linguistics is concerned with increasing understanding of the role of language in human affairs and thereby with providing the knowledge necessary for those who are responsible for taking language-related decisions whether the need for these arises in the classroom, the workplace, the law, or the laboratory.

The two most important elements of the definition are 'understanding of the role of language in human affairs' and 'providing the knowledge necessary' for decision-making. That is to say, Applied Linguistics is built on the premise that knowledge about language (linguistics) can 'make a difference to how we act' (Heap, 1990: 39). An even more explicit definition of Applied Linguistics, which I will adopt for the purposes of this chapter, is the following by Schmitt and Celce-Murcia (2002: 1):

> 'Applied Linguistics' is using what we know about (a) language, (b) how it is learned and (c) how it is used, in order to achieve some purpose or solve some problem in the real world.

Although, as Wilkins implies, knowledge about language can be used to address issues in a variety of domains of social life (e.g. classroom, the workplace, the law court, etc.), a long tradition in Applied Linguistics has been to use findings of linguistic analysis to contribute to educational issues, particularly language educational issues (1st and 2nd language teaching). As Davies and Elder (2004: 7) say, in the 1960s and 1970s, 'it was largely taken for granted [...] that Applied Linguistics was about language teaching'. Only relatively recently has the scope of Applied Linguistics widened to cover any 'language-based problems that people encounter in the real world.' (Grabe, 2001, cited in Davies and Elder, p. 7). Nowadays, the main difference between Linguistics and Applied Linguistics seems to be that of focus, with Applied Linguistics, unlike Linguistics, focusing, 'not on language per se – whatever that might be – but on language in use in authentic contexts' (Gunnarsson, 1997: 285).

An issue in Applied Linguistics is the nature of its application and the kind of solutions Applied Linguistics can bring to real world problems. As Roberts (2003: 133) notes, the relationship between linguistic knowledge and real world problems should be seen as a continuum ranging from 'the most indirect and hypothetical to the most direct and actual'. As for Richards (2005), referring specifically to Applied Conversation Analysis, he distinguishes between two ways of conceptualising the relationship between linguistic analysis (CA in this case) and the real world, one of which he finds to be problematic. These are the 'discovery-prescription framework' and the 'description-informed action framework'. The discovery-prescription framework is one where, once a linguistic regularity has been described using linguistics tools, it is translated into 'a standard operating procedure', prescribing and proscribing courses of action in the real world (Richards, 2005: 4). Here is an example. As we have seen, among bilingual speakers, some instances of language alternation can be described in terms of competence-related language preference (Auer, 1995; Torras and Gafaranga, 2002), that is in terms of lexical gaps. Bilingual speakers often use language alternation to overcome lexical gaps. A prescriptive model of Applied Linguistics (language alternation studies in this case) would prescribe the use of language alternation as a strategy for overcoming lexical gaps. The inadequacy of the prescriptive framework in this case is obvious for language alternation is only one of the many aspects of 'strategic competence' (Canale and Swain, 1980), the set of strategies that speakers draw on in order to avoid communication breakdowns. On the other hand, the description-informed action framework is one where knowledge about language is used as evidence in deciding appropriate courses of action. For example, knowing that, among bilingual speakers, language alternation often occurs because of competence-related problems and as a way of overcoming them, that is aware that language alternation among bilingual speakers is an aspect of their strategic competence, a teacher in a bilingual classroom may decide to accept this type of language alternation in his or her classes or to reject it.

As implied in Wilkins' definition above, most Applied Linguistics work has been conducted in institutional contexts, particularly in contexts where professionals must interact constantly with members of the general public. In such contexts, effective communication, between the professionals and the general public as well as between sections of the institutions, is of such crucial importance that, in some cases, explicit language policies are adopted. The issue for Applied Linguistics is how it can best contribute to such institutions. In this respect, sociologists make a distinction between research which targets the policy community as its audience and practitioner-oriented research (Bloor, 1997). In the first case, the aim is to achieve policy change, either by 'engineering' it or by 'enlightening' policy makers. In the second, the aim is to get practitioners to be reflexive about their own practices. This second alternative is felt to be most effective. '... the real opportunities for sociological influence lie closer to the coalface than they do to the head office [...] the real opportunities for sociological influence lie in relations with practitioners, not with the managers of practice' (Bloor, 1997: 234). In line with the discovery-informed action framework (see above), Applied Linguistics work is mostly practitioner-oriented. In this respect, under the eloquent title of 'Applied Linguistics applied', Roberts writes,

> I want to suggest that most applied researchers are more likely to have an impact by trying to change practice with practitioners rather than through grand attempts at engineering policy change. There are researchers who have influenced policy, but qualitative research has particular insights, grounded in the everyday reality that practitioners live by, which makes it appealing to practitioners. (2003: 135)

That is to say, in Applied Linguistics, there is a preference for research to aim to influence actual practices on the ground rather than 'grand' policies.

As we have seen above, a long tradition in Applied Linguistics has been to use linguistic analyses to contribute to educational issues. Following in this tradition, applied studies of language alternation have mainly focused on classroom contexts (see Martin-Jones, 1995, 2000 for an overview). According to Ferguson (2004), this body of research identified three main categories of functions that language alternation serves in the classroom, namely (i) curriculum access, (ii) classroom management and (iii) management of interpersonal relations in the classroom. In identifying these functions, classroom research used existing models of language alternation. For example, issues of class management drew on the idea that language alternation is a contextualisation cue (Gumperz, 1982; Auer, 1984). Likewise, the idea that language alternation in the classroom serves in the management of interpersonal relations was facilitated by the models of language alternation I have referred to as identity-related explanations. Finally, it was possible to appreciate the role of language alternation in curriculum access thanks to notions such as competence-related language preference (Auer, 1984, 1995; Torras and Gafaranga, 2002).

Because language alternation in the classroom was found to be functional, researchers drew implications about 'how to act differently'. Since, as Roberts (2003: 135) says, qualitative 'researchers are more likely to have an impact by trying to change practice rather than through grand attempts at engineering policy change', researchers' recommendations were first and foremost addressed to teachers. More importantly, in line with the description-informed action perspective in Applied Linguistics, researchers recommended that activities meant to raise teachers' awareness of the functions of language alternation in the classroom be included in teacher training. Ferguson (2004: 48) summarises the recommendation as follows:

- Draw trainees' attention to the existence of language alternation in communities and classrooms and to reassure them that this is very common, in fact normal behaviour in these settings
- Highlight some of the functions that code-switching has in multilingual classrooms, and to make the point that it can be a useful communicative resource for helping pupils understand lesson content, for managing pupil behaviour and for maintaining a good classroom climate

- Inform teachers that code-switched talk, like most talk, can be more or less helpful depending on when and why it occurs.

Briefly, there is evidence of applied language alternation studies in educational contexts. And this is not surprising as education has always been the main field of application of language studies. However, language alternation can also be studied in order to contribute to non-educational real world issues. By way of an example, the rest of this chapter is based on a piece of research I have conducted among bilingual Rwandans in Belgium with a view to contribute to the community's concern with its language maintenance/shift.[1]

## 8.3. Investigating language shift and maintenance among bilingual Rwandans in Belgium

### 8.3.1. Language shift as a real world concern

As indicated in the Introduction, the sociolinguistics of Rwanda was one of superposed bilingualism in which one language, Kinyarwanda, was spoken by everybody, and the other, French, was spoken only by the educated elite minority. The Rwandans in Belgium originally belonged to this bilingual elite. For reasons which are still to be clarified, the children of these bilingual Rwandans started losing the use of Kinyarwanda as soon as they settled in Belgium. As early as 1996, 2 years after they left Rwanda, Rwandans in Belgium could be heard complaining about their children's declining competence in Kinyarwanda and, in actual interaction, there was evidence of choices indicative of language shift. Maybe because language shift was very abrupt, the community immediately noticed it and organised themselves to resist it. Thus, some started cultural organisations aimed to preserve the culture and the language of Rwanda, while others started centres specifically meant to teach Kinyarwanda to children. Today, over half a dozen of such organisations can be found in the Brussels area alone.

In setting out to resist language shift, community members followed their own, often lay, understanding of how language works and how it can be maintained. Thus, in undertaking to investigate language shift in this community, our aim was to use our expertise as linguists and contribute to the community's own effort towards language maintenance. More specifically, our aim was to describe language choice and language alternation practices in the community because we believe that language shift is talked into being in everyday interaction and that certain patterns of language choice and language alternation mediate language shift. In line with the description-informed action perspective, the hope was that, once the community was made aware of the patterns of language choice and language alternation which mediate language shift in day-to-day interaction, they would be in a better position to address the issue however they decided to. In other words, the hope was to make available to the community the knowledge they needed in order 'to act differently' if they so chose. Thus, one group of our research questions was as follows:

(1) Ten years after bilingual Rwandans arrived in Belgium, (a) has language shift firmly set in or (b) has the community succeeded in stopping it?
(2) If (a), what interactional practices mediate language shift?
(3) If (b), what interactional strategies do members adopt towards language maintenance?

Drawing on my previous work in the community, we held each of the following situations, if it were observed, to be evidence of language shift in progress.

(1) Adoption of French-based language alternation itself as the medium, in lieu of Kinyarwanda-based language alternation as used to be the case in Rwanda (see Myers-Scotton, 1998a for the phenomenon of the ML (Matrix Language) *turn-over* as evidence of language shift in progress).
(2) Adoption of a *'composite ML'* (Myers-Scotton, 1998a) whereby the base language for alternated elements is found to be either French or Kinyarwanda
(3) Adoption of the *parallel medium* (Gafaranga and Torras, 2001) whereby, in the same conversation, some participants use French while others are using Kinyarwanda (-for-all-practical-purposes)
(4) Adoption of French as the medium.

Conversely, the following situations, if observed, would be taken as evidence of language maintenance:

(1) adoption of Kinyarwanda-based language alternation as the medium
(2) adoption of Kinyarwanda as the medium.

Briefly, our strategy was to compare current language choice and language alternation practices to those I had observed in my previous work in the community. As already indicated, in that previous work, I had observed that choices formed a continuum ranging from the use of Kinyarwanda to the use of French as the medium. In between these extremes, a form of Kinyarwanda-based language alternation, referred to elsewhere as 'Kinyarwanda-for-all-practical-purposes' was used (Gafaranga, 1998, 2001a). Therefore, divergence from these patterns could be seen as evidence of language shift.

### 8.3.2. Research design

In order to implement the objectives of the project, we used a combination of qualitative methodologies. To gain access to the community, we used already existing contacts who introduced us to leaders of community organisations (see below). These community leaders in turn introduced us to the membership of their organisations, out of which we selected 25 families with children aged 10 years and below. This age criterion was necessary because anybody aged above 10 years would have been born in Rwanda and therefore their language preference might not be a good indication of what is happening. We obtained consent from these families and went on to observe interaction in them, focussing on interaction involving children in the target age group. Afterwards, we recorded naturally occurring conversations in those families, transcribed them and analysed them for language choice patterns. After analysis, we took our results back to the community. Particularly, we held meetings with participating families in which we looked at their language choice practices and considered how these were mediating language shift.

Since, as I have shown throughout this book, many approaches to the orderliness of language alternation are currently available, in analysing the conversations we collected among the Rwandans in Belgium, we used the model I have referred to in Chapter 6 as the Overall Model of language alternation for two main reasons. First, it is this very same model that I had previously used in describing the choices Rwandans used to make before they settled in Belgium. Therefore, the first reason it was adopted is that it allowed easy comparison of the data. Secondly, we used this model for reasons of convenience, as it is the one I am most comfortable with, having developed it myself. As we have seen, the most important concept in this model is the notion of medium or linguistic code, the 'scheme of interpretation' (Garfinkel, 1967) at the level of language choice. As I have shown, the medium need not be monolingual; it may also be bilingual. If the medium is bilingual, at least two options are available, namely the parallel mode and the mixed mode. Some of the language choice practices we have observed and which, we believe, mediate language shift are discussed below.

### 8.3.3. Language alternation, language shift and maintenance

The view that language alternation can be used as evidence of language shift in progress is obviously not new, although it might not have been stated so explicitly before. Among non-linguists, this view translates into the generally negative attitudes towards language alternation (see Section 2.2). Similarly, as we have seen, researchers such as Fishman and Gumperz (see Sections 5.2 and 5.3) explain frequent language alternation among bilingual speakers in terms of language shift in progress. Along the same lines, Gal (1979: 173), in her discussion of language shift in the bilingual community of Oberwart, writes,

> ...conversational language-switching can be explained as the middle and variable step in the process by which (communities) change from categorical use of one language to categorical use of the other. It occurs in contexts where the old form is no longer invariably used and the new form is not yet invariably used.

A number of other authors who have worked in specific settings (e.g Wei, 1994; Rindstedt and Aronsson, 2002) corroborate this general observation.

Yet, other researchers, for example Poplack (see Chapter 3), maintain that language alternation is evidence of a high degree of competence in both languages, and by implication, that it can be seen as evidence of language maintenance. Even, there are researchers who, while recognising that there is a relationship between language alternation and language shift, also indicate that it is not a straightforward one. For example, in relation with the situation of Sardinian–Italian bilingualism, Schjever (1998: 246) writes that the 'frequency of switch alone cannot be taken as a sign of language shift', and that, although

> It is true that codeswitching often goes hand in hand with language shift, the evidence of the Sardinian/Italian language pair would seem to suggest though, that codeswitching should not be seen as a mechanism which accelerates the shift. On the contrary, the present data indicate that codeswitching should be understood as a bridge

by which the continuum of the two languages and the bicultural competence of the Sardinians are being kept intact for the time being. (1998: 247)

Briefly, there seems to be a consensus that language alternation and language shift/maintenance interact, but the nature of that relationship is yet to be specified. Therefore, at the theoretical level, an interesting question for researchers is, when is language alternation evidence of language shift in progress and when is it evidence of a high degree of competence in both languages and, by implication, of language maintenance? The problem, in part at least, seems to me to be that the nature of language alternation itself has not always been specified.

As for the study of language shift and maintenance itself, two perspectives can be identified, if only for the sake of presentation. On the one hand, there are studies which aim to understand language shift as a linguistic phenomenon per se. In turn, as Pauwels (2004: 721) says, research in this tradition draws on a variety of disciplines, including sociology, sociology of language, anthropology, sociolinguistics, psycholinguistics and so on. Some of the questions that research in this perspective asks are, what factors and forces are conducive to language shift? Why do some groups of people tend to retain their languages where others are losing theirs? How to explain variability within the same linguistic group? Some of the factors that have been found to affect language shift, either by precipitating it or by slowing it, are pre-emigration experience with language maintenance, educational level of immigrants, numerical strength of the group, attitudes of the dominant group, whether the group sees language as a 'core value' or not, the ethnolinguistic vitality of the group, the market value of the language and so on (see Pauwels, 2004 for a discussion of these factors). Also, inside particular ethnolinguistic groups, tendencies either towards shift or towards maintenance have been associated with the kind of social networks in which members of those groups operate (Wei, 1994). On the other hand, there are studies with a more applied agenda. For these, the issue is, 'how can LS (language shift) be halted or reversed and/or how can LM (language maintenance) be effected' (Pauwels, 2004: 725). Drawing on the knowledge developed under the first perspective, researchers seek to 'inform and assist individuals, groups, communities, and indeed governments' (Pauwels, 2004: 725) involved in language maintenance efforts. Our work in the Rwandan community in Belgium fits in this second tradition.

*Table 8.1* Stages of reversing language shift (Read from bottom up)

---

1. Education, work sphere, mass media and governmental operations at higher and nationwide levels
2. Local/regional mass media and government services
3. Lacal/regional (i.e. non-neighbourhood) work sphere, both among the Xmen and among Ymen
4a. Public schools for Xish children offering some instructions via Xish, but substantially under Yish curricular and staff control
4b. Schools in lieu of compulsory education and substantially under Xish curricular and staffing control

*II RLS to transcend diglossia, subsequent to its attainment*

5. Schools for literacy acquisition, for the old and for the young, and not in lieu of compulsory education
6. The intergenerational and demographically concentrated home–family–neighbourhood: the basis of mother tongue transmission
7. Cultural interaction in Xish primarily involving the community-based older generation
8. Reconstructing Xish and adult acquisition of XSL

*I RLS to attain diglossia (assuming prior ideological clarification)*

---

Note: Xish refers to minority language, Yish refers to the majority language

One of the most known model for language maintenance, known as the 'Reversing Language Shift Model' (RLS), has been developed by Fishman (1991, 2000) and comprises eight stages as in Table 8.1 (taken from Fishman, 1991: 395).

A number of assumptions in this model must be highlighted. As can be seen, central to Fishman's RLS model is his own understanding of language choice in bilingual settings, namely diglossia (see Chapter 5). In reversing language shift, communities must aim first to re-establish diglossia and then to overcome it. And this is so because, as we have seen, diglossia is a factor of language shift. Secondly, the RLS model was developed with indigenous territorially based minority language groups in mind (Edwards, 2004). The aim is to get the language to be used as the main language, if not nationally, at least regionally and by everybody (Stages 1, 2 and 3). Thirdly, for all the stages to apply, the target language must have reached the point where it is no longer used in the community and is not used anywhere else in the world (Stages 8 to 5). Therefore, the model is meant to help the community revive its language.

In the context of immigrant minorities, such as the Rwandans in Belgium, most of the above assumptions do not obtain, making the model itself difficult to apply. First, at the theoretical level, it seems unrealistic to hope that, in the context of immigrant minorities, diglossia can be overcome. Therefore, the issue is how to effect language maintenance despite diglossia since, as we have already seen, diglossia is a factor of language shift. Secondly, immigrant minority languages often lack territoriality. Dispersal, rather than territorial concentration, due either to government policies or to socio-economic realities, is the norm. Of course, in some cases, such as the phenomenon of Chinatowns, it is possible to have some degree of concentration, but, even then, contact with the majority group and other immigrant minorities prevails. Even the possibility of creating demographically concentrated neighbourhoods itself might not be desirable. In immigrant minority contexts, the aim of social policies is usually integration, often accompanied by/understood as assimilation. The creation of linguistic enclaves would go against these policies. The issue therefore is how to maintain a language without adequate neighbourhood concentration since, as Fishman says, a 'demographically concentrated home-family-neighbourhood' is the 'basis of mother tongue transmission' (1991: 395). Thirdly, immigrant minority languages, unlike indigenous minority languages, must be protected, not from extinction, but rather from shift. That is the language to protect is still used in the country of origin and often in the community by older members. For example, Kinyarwanda is still the national language and one of the official languages of Rwanda and, in Belgium, adult members of the community still use it for internal communication. Therefore, the problem is not to revive the language, but rather to make sure it is transmitted from one generation to the next. The fact that the language is still used outside (and possibly inside) the community should, in principle, facilitate the task of language maintenance. In reality, however, it actually makes the task even harder. An important factor in minority language maintenance is active support from the majority group. From the majority group's point view, continued internal use of the minority language is often viewed as a mark of difference, difference which must be levelled in the name of integration (understood as assimilation). On the other hand, the fact that the language is used by another community leads to the view that the language is a foreign language even if its speakers are legally and often by birth members of the new community.

However, in Fishman's model of RLS, a couple of points can be retained in immigrant minority contexts. First, it is possible to promote activities at Stage 7. Minority groups can organise themselves for cultural activities to take place. As we have seen, the Rwandans in

Belgium have started cultural organisations meant to preserve the Rwandan culture. Almost all cultural events performed in Rwanda are performed in Belgium. For example, birth, marriage and death events are performed among the Rwandans in Belgium exactly as they are in Rwanda. Also Stage 5 of the RLS model is possible. Communities can, and indeed do, organise themselves to teach literacy in the minority language to children. As we have seen, the Rwandans in Belgium have started after-school centres to teach Kinyarwanda to children. In the literature, these two kinds of actions are referred to as 'bottom-up strategies' for language maintenance (Nettle and Romaine, 2000). It is argued that one of the advantages of such bottom-up strategies is that they can be adopted even in the absence of support from the majority group. However, numerous studies show that language shift can take place despite community members' attachment to their cultures (Odisho, 1993; Papapavlou and Pavlou, 2001; Rindstedt and Aronsson, 2002). According to Fishman (2001), a major problem at this level is that of the 'linkage' between cultural activities as 'special events' and everyday interaction in the 'home, family and community'. Rindsedt and Aronsson speak of the 'ethnic revitalization paradox'. That is, use of the language in everyday interaction is the single most important factor in language maintenance. In immigrant minority contexts in particular, in the absence of a linguistic community and neighbourhood, the use of the language in family interaction becomes crucial.

Research in language maintenance at the level of the family, also referred to as 'child bilingualism', has mainly been concerned with describing the strategies that parents can adopt in order to bring up their children bilingually. Six such strategies have been identified as in Table 8.2 (taken from Piller, 2001: 64).

Of the six, Types 3 and 6 seem to be the most relevant for language maintenance in minority contexts. Type 3 is when both parents, monolingual, come from the same language background and want to preserve their language. To achieve this, they decide to use it consistently in interaction with the child. On the other hand, Type 6 is when parents are bilingual and, in interaction between themselves as in interaction with the child, they use language alternation. Clearly in this case, the aim is not to maintain one of the languages only, but both languages. The situation of the Rwandans in Belgium is closer to this last type. As we already know, in this community, in interaction among themselves, adult members use Kinyarwanda–French language alternation. The issue is whether they also consistently use Kinyarwanda–French language alternation in interaction with children.

*Table 8.2* Strategies for language maintenance in bilingual families

|        | Parental languages | Community language(s) | Strategies |
|---|---|---|---|
| Type 1 | Different L1s | The L1 of one parent | Each parent speaks their language to the child |
| Type 2 | Different L1s | The L1 of one parent | Both parent speak the non-dominant language to the child, who is exposed to the dominant language outside the home, particularly in day care and preschool |
| Type 3 | Same L1 | The L1 of neither parent | Both parents speak non-dominant language to the child, who is exposed to the dominant language outside the home, particularly in day care and preschool |
| Type 4 | Different L1s | The L1 of neither parent | Each parent speaks their language to the child, who is exposed to the dominant language outside the home, particularly in day care and preschool |
| Type 5 | Same L1 | L1 of both parents | One parent speaks an L2 to the child |
| Type 6 | Bilingual (either L1s or L2s) | May or may not be bilingual | The parents code-switch and mix languages with the child |

In addition to the above comment, the following two can be made on the research into bilingual language acquisition strategies. First, in the strategies, there is a strong assumption of a nuclear family (father–mother–child) as the setting for language development. Little attention is paid to the role of third parties such as siblings, neighbours, relatives and so on. The limits of such a view of the context for language development are currently widely acknowledged. Furthermore a number of studies have highlighted the role of other parties in the child's language maintenance (Fishman, 1991; Zentalla, 1997; Clyne, 2001). A study of the interactional strategies for language maintenance should not limit itself to child–parent interaction. Rather it should be extended to all interactional events and all interactional partners. The project on language maintenance among the Rwandan diaspora in Belgium aimed to go beyond the nuclear family unit. In the project, we put a particular focus on interactional events which, although taking place in the home, involved participants from outside the family. The idea was that, in their interaction with children, these members of the 'public' would draw on and therefore reflect community-wide norms. Secondly, as Piller (2001) says, in undertaking to raise their children bilingually, parents often have more or less clear ideas of what bilingualism is and how to achieve it. And this is precisely the reason she speaks of 'private language planning'. The idea that language maintenance in the family is a case of language planning highlights the element of consistency and that of determination as sine qua non conditions for language maintenance.

### 8.3.4. Language choice and language shift among the Rwandans in Belgium

As I have indicated above, this project was undertaken on the assumption that language shift is talked into being, that it takes place out of sight and out of mind, through the choices that speakers make in day-to-day interaction. In the following, for lack of space, only three of the language choice practices we have observed among the Rwandans in Belgium are examined.

#### 8.3.4.1. Initiation of conversation in French

In the Rwandan community in Belgium, conversations involving children in the target group are routinely initiated in French. An example of this practice is the following piece of talk. Conversation takes place in A's family. Also present are two visitors, B and D, and A's 7-year-old son (C). Conversation has mostly been between the adult participants and we join it at the point where B initiates talk to C (turn 2). As the transcript shows, B initiates talk to C in French without any further thought as if this was the only available option.

*Example 8.1*

1. A: mpe mperutse no kubona ntuza avuga ho – avuga kuri *télévision* (.) simenya (.) *ministre* wa finance
2. B: (to C) *papa a dit papa a dit va t'asseoir là-bas*
3. C: *non*
4. B: *si si c'est ce que papa a dit parce que tu as fait des bêtises.*
5. A: umh R ni nde ra R
6. D: eh warayibonye
7. B: (to C) *là-bas là-bas*
8. A: yje narayibonye (.) sinzi ukuntu nafunguye hano mbona agezweho
9. C: *là là*

10. B: *tu as fait des bêtises*
11. D: jye buri gihe saa mbiri n' igice (.) ndeba kuri ART

1. A: I recently saw that man talking on television (.) I don't know (.) finance minister
2. B: (To C) papa said papa said go and sit there
3. C: no
4. B: yes yes that's what papa said because you've been naughty
5. A: umh R who's R
6. D: eh did you watch it (programme)
7. B: (to C) over there over there
8. A: I watched it (.) I switched on just like this and there he was
9. C: over there
10. B: you've been naughty
11. D: every 8:30 (.) I watch ART

Even more explicit in this respect is Example 8.2. In the conversation, A and D are visitors and B and C are sisters, aged 4 and 17 years respectively. A, C and D have been talking using Kinyarwanda–French language alternation. We join the conversation at the point where A attempts to engage a conversation with B. Here again, French is seen as the default choice. The example is interesting in two other respects. First, in turn 12, C starts talking to B and she too initiates the conversation in French. That is the choice of French in interaction with children is demonstrably not an isolate incident. Secondly, in turn 13 and 15, A and C depart from their use of Kinyarwanda-for-all-practical purposes in talk among themselves and use French. However, close inspection of the data reveals that this choice of French is significant. It is a case of what Bell (1997) has called 'audience design', the fact of adjusting one's language in response to the presence of an 'auditor', defined as somebody who is 'present in the group but not directly addressed' (1997: 246). In this case, talk is actually designed for B to follow exactly what A and C are saying, even though she is not being directly addressed. And this indirect way of talking to B is felt to be possible only if French is used.

*Example 8.2*

1. A: B, **qui t'as tressée?**
2. B: (.)
3. A: **c'est maman?**
4. B: (.)

5. A: Hmm?
6. C: Uri *connecté* kuli SGM?
7. A: oya
8. D: Iyo *téléphone* iragwa
9. A: hmm?
10. D: iyo *téléphone* yaza kugwa
11. A: nta kibazo
12. C: ça va... viens... je vais te donner quelque chose... viens
13. A: ne lui donne pas mes biscuits parce qu'elle ne veut pas me dire bonjour
14. A: B?
15. C: elle ne veut pas

1. A: B, who did your hair?
2. B: (.)
3. A: is it your mum?
4. B: (.)
5. A: Hmm?
6. C: Are you connected to GSM?
7. A: No
8. D: Careful, you might drop your phone
9. A: Hmm?
10. D: you might drop your phone
11. A: No problem
12. C: That's okay... come .. I'll give you something... come
13. A: Don't give her my biscuits because she's refused to say hallo to me
14. A: B!
15. C: She doesn't want to

Literature from two sources can be referred to in order to appreciate the role of this practice of initiating conversation with children in French in ongoing language shift. First, research in CA has amply highlighted the role of the opening sequence in talk-in-interaction. Researchers, Schegloff (1968) in particular, have convincingly argued that the opening sequence is an opportunity for participants to negotiate different kinds of conversational relevancies. In the opening sequence, participants ascertain the readiness of each other to engage in conversation, they negotiate what the interaction is going to be about, they confirm to each other who they are doing being, etc. To give just one example, Gafaranga and Britten (2003, 2005) have examined the opening sequence in doctor–patient interaction and demonstrated that participants use it to negotiate whether the consultation they are about to engage in is to be viewed as a new consultation or whether it is to be viewed as a follow-up consultation. Secondly, research in language choice shows that, among bilingual speakers, the opening sequence is an opportunity for participants to negotiate the medium they are going to adopt in the interaction. The notion of 'language negotiation sequence' has been adopted in this respect (see Chapter 6). Among the factors that participants take into account in negotiating the medium is language preference (see Chapter 6). In other words, by initiating talk to children in French as if by default, adult members of the community define them as being monolingual in French. Furthermore, as argued in Gafaranga and Torras (2001), in approaching language choice, bilingual participants either draw on already shared expectations or they negotiate the medium on the spot. That is to say, over time, repetition of the practice of initiating conversation in French leads to a situation where French is taken to be the expected choice, the norm. Language shift consists precisely in this normalisation of French as the default medium.

### 8.3.4.2. Accommodation in French

As Auer (1984) rightly points it out, the notion of language negotiation implies potentially divergent language preferences on the part of speakers. To resolve this divergence, one speaker accommodates to the other, thus concluding the negotiation. The issue of who accommodates and why is a very complex one because various factors are involved in 'speech accommodation' (Giles *et al.*, 1973), but there is no doubt that language preference is an important one. Unless there are reasons not to accommodate, in case of divergent language preferences, participants converge towards a shared language, if there is one. In the Rwandan community in Belgium, accommodation always goes in the direction of French. Consider Example 8.3.

Example 8.3

1. A: Wowe urashyira iki ku meza?
2. B: *Le couvert. on est combien? un, deux, trois, [quatre, cinq..*
3. C:                                            [Abadahali ni bande, B?
4. B: *Oui quatre cinq*
5. C: Ni bande badahali- **qui qui qui ne sont pas ici**?
6. B: *Ah oui quatre le monsieur*
7. C: *Non le monsieur est là. qui ne sont pas ici?*

8. B: *Il y a papa et tonton Benoît, donc [on est-*
9. C: [*Donc on est combien?*
10. B: *un, deux, trois, quatre, cinq, six, sept- on est sept.*

1. A: what are you putting on the table?
2. B: forks, knives and spoons. How many are we? One, two three four five
3. C: Who's not present, B?
4. B: yes four, five
5. C: who's not present- who's not present?
6. B: ah yes four the man
7. C: no. the man is here. Who's not here?
8. B: daddy and uncle Benoît, so we are
9. C: how many are we?
10. B: one, two, three, four, five, six, seven. We are seven.

Participants in the conversation are a visiting relative (A), a mother (C) and her 4-year-old daughter (B). The family is getting ready for their evening meal and B is 'helping' to set the table. We join the interaction at the point where A asks B, in Kinyarwanda, what she is putting on the table. In turn 2, using French, B answers A's question (*le couvert*) and starts to count how many people she should prepare for. In turn 3, C interrupts the counting by asking her, in Kinyarwanda, how many people are not present. Ignoring C's question, B goes ahead with her counting, recycling the bit of her talk that C's turn has obscured. As her question has not received any response, in turn 5, C reiterates it in Kinyarwanda and, interrupting herself, she reformulates it in French, that is, she accommodates to B's choice. From this point onwards, the conversation is conducted in French. Also consider Example 8.4.

*Example 8.4*

1. A: Mwicare hariya ku meza (.) mukine (.) muganire. None se Christelle wamubajije ibibazo byose?
2. B: *Je lui ai posé toutes les questions que j'avais*
3. A: Byose?
4. B: *Oui*
5. A: None se wamubwiye ko wagiye muli *vacances*
6. B: *Oui Je lui ai tout dit*
7. A: ***Il faut savoir apprécier et raconter une histoire. Il faut écouter les gens*** (.) ***il faut parler aux gens*** (talk goes on in French)

1. A: Sit over there (.) play (.) talk (.) Did you ask her all the questions, Christelle?
2. B: I asked her all the questions that I had.
3. A: All of them?
4. B: Yes
5. A: Did you tell her that you went for a holiday
6. B: Yes. I told her every thing.
7. A: You need to know how to tell a story (.) you have to listen to people (.) you have to talk to people

In the example, a mother (A) is talking to her daughter (B). As the transcript shows, A is using Kinyarwanda while B is using French. In turn 7, A shifts from her use of Kinyarwanda and accommodates to B's use of French. With reference to language shift, the importance of these unidirectional accommodation practices is clear. Through them, children are defined and redefined as monolingual in French. Because parents are bilingual in French and Kinyarwanda, French offers itself as the shared language. Furthermore, the frequency of these accommodation practices creates expectations on the part of children that interlocutors, even when they start their contribution in Kinyarwanda, will eventually shift to French. In other words, these accommodation practices encourage children to stick to their choice of French.

Analysis of the above extracts in terms of accommodation, although relevant, misses out a crucially important element. In both examples, a communication problem arises and, in both cases, participants blame the choice of Kinyarwanda. In Example 8.3, C's talk in turn 3 is a request for information, that is a first pair part in an adjacency pair (Schegloff and Sacks, 1973). Conversation analysts have amply demonstrated that, after a request for information, the preferred second part of the adjacency pair is the granting of the requested information. If the requested information is not provided, dispreference markers such as delays, hesitation and accounts of why the preferred second is not provided are used (Levinson, 1983). Obviously, the use of these markers presupposes and confirms that the first part of the adjacency pair has been received and understood. In this particular case, none of these are found, leading C to conclude that a transmission problem of some sort has occurred. Therefore, she reiterates her request to try and overcome the problem. In the middle of the repair, she realises that the problem might be the choice of Kinyarwanda itself and, therefore, switches to French. In extract 4, on the other hand, although B provides relevant second parts to A's initiations, A feels her contribution to the talk to be less than satisfactory. B is rather unenthusiastic. The first attempt to overcome the problem takes the form of asking a confirmation question in turn 3, which only receives a minimal answer (oui). The answer to the question in turn 5 reveals that the strategy of reiteration has not solved the problem. Therefore, in turn 7, A adopts a different strategy. She switches from Kinyarwanda to French as if blaming the choice of Kinyarwanda for the interactional difficulty. Similar observations whereby interactional problems are interpreted as 'the wrong choice of language' have been attested elsewhere in the literature (Auer, 1995: 130). In other words, what we are witnessing is not just accommodation, but rather a type of medium repair (Gafaranga, 2000b) in favour of French. In short, by constantly viewing the choice of Kinyarwanda as the one to blame when interactional problems arise in conversation involving children, adult members of the community unwittingly reinforce the view that the choice of Kinyarwanda is potentially problematic, and therefore to be avoided, while that of French is unproblematic, and therefore to be encouraged.

### 8.3.4.3. The parallel mode

The third language choice pattern we have observed among the Rwandan community in Belgium is the parallel mode. As indicated above, this is the possibility for conversation to be conducted in two languages, with each of the two participants speaking a different language. An example of this pattern is the following:

*Example 8.5*

1. A: B, nakubwiye ngo murye *glace*?
2. B: *Non, tu ne l'as pas dit*
3. A: Kuki wabeshye papa? Wamubwiye ngw'iki?
4. B: *Je n'avais pas entendu très bien.*
5. A: Wamubwiye ngw'iki papa?
6. B: *Rien*
7. A: Ni papa ubeshya noneho (.) papa arabeshya?
8. B: *Oui*
9. A: Wabwiye papa ngo nababwiye ngo mufate *glace*.
10. B: *Non.*

1. A: B, did I tell you to eat ice cream?
2. B: No, you didn't
3. A: why did you lie to daddy then? What did you tell him?

4. B: I hadn't understood correctly
5. A: What did you tell daddy?
6. B: Nothing
7. A: So daddy is lying. Daddy is lying?
8. B: Yes
9. A: you told daddy I had told you to take ice cream
10. B: No

In the example, a mother (A) is talking to her 7-year-old daughter (B). As the transcript shows, the mother consistently uses Kinyarwanda while the daughter consistently uses French. Also consider Example 8.6:

*Example 8.6*

1. A: Kuki mugiye?
2. Vis: **On doit rentrer**
3. A-D: Lili ntimwahishije se?
4. D: **Oui, tout est prêt**
5. A-Vis: Mwaretse se mukarya hanyuma mukagenda
6. Vis: **Non, nous devons partir. Nous savons quand il faut être à la maison.**

1. A: Why are you leaving now?
2. Vis: *We must go home*
3. A-D: Haven't you finished cooking, Lili?
4. D: *Yes, every thing is ready*
5. A-Vis: Why can't you wait and eat first and then go
6. Vis: *No, we have to go. We know when we must be home.*

Participants in the extract are the father of the family (A), his daughter (B) and two visiting children (Vis). By the time we join the conversation, the visitors are saying goodbye. The father attempts to make them stay a bit longer so they can eat before leaving, speaking to them first (turns 1 and 5) and then to his daughter to check if the food is ready (turn 3). As the transcript shows, while, in both cases, he uses Kinyarwanda, in both cases, children respond in French. To be sure the fact that this pattern is routine in the community can be seen in other instances as well. For example, in extract 4, both participants seem to be happy to conduct the conversation in two languages in this fashion until it becomes clear that there is a problem and it is only at this point that the pattern is abandoned. Likewise, in Example 8.3, the fact that the child answers A's question using French without any sign of hesitation seems to indicate that this is something she does all the time. And indeed C herself can be seen to orient to the routine nature of this pattern because, while there is evidence at her disposal that B is speaking French, she talks to her in Kinyarwanda until she realises that there is a problem.

The significance of this pattern of language choice in terms of language shift cannot be underestimated. As we have seen, in immigrant minority contexts, language maintenance in the family requires a great deal of determination and consistency. The pattern of the parallel mode works precisely against these requirements. In adopting this pattern, participants show more concern for the transmission of content than for consistent language choice. That is, the pattern is an easy solution to a communication problem. The result is that the availability of this pattern actually takes away the need, on the part of children, to speak Kinyarwanda. That is to say, by allowing this pattern to develop into a normal way of talking, the community indirectly encourages children to abandon Kinyarwanda.

## 8.4. Conclusion

The orderliness of language alternation can be investigated for two main reasons. Language alternation can be studied as a linguistic phenomenon which is interesting in its own right. In fact it would not be difficult to find arguments in support of this position as, at first sight, language alternation appears to be a disorderly phenomenon. Showing that it is actually orderly responds either to what Heap refers to as 'the critical news' or to what he calls the 'positive news' or else to both (1990: 42). But language alternation can also be studied because of the applications the gained understanding can be put to. In this chapter, I have identified education as the most common domain of application of language alternation studies. As I have said, research in classrooms shows that language alternation is a resource that classroom participants draw on in accomplishing teaching and learning as interactional events. Because language alternation is seen as a resource, researchers recommend its inclusion in teacher training so that future practitioners are made aware of it.

However, most of the chapter has been devoted to yet another domain of application, that of language shift and maintenance. Using the specific case of the Rwandan community in Belgium, I have shown that and how the study of language alternation can be used to address a real world issue. Studying language choice and language alternation in this community, I have been able to identify and describe some of the patterns of language choice which mediate language shift currently underway in the community. These include routine initiation of conversation with children in French, frequent accommodation to French and the parallel medium. After these patterns had been identified and described, and as planned in the design of the project, community members were made aware of them. Briefly, this case study along with the vast literature on language alternation in educational contexts shows that, in the case of language alternation, a 'compelling answer' exists 'to the twin questions of Why Speak/Listen and Why Write/Read' and that the study of language alternation meets the requirements for 'any serious scholarship' (Heap, 1990: 42).

## Notes

1. Research for this chapter was kindly supported by the ESRC through grant res-000-22-1165. Dr Jean Baptiste Munyandamutsa worked on the project as the research assistant. Thus, where appropriate, I will be referring to the project using 'we' for both myself and J.B.

# 9
# Summary and Conclusion

My main aim in this book has been to find common grounds among studies of language alternation. The common ground I have identified and clarified is that they all address essentially the same issue, namely the orderliness, that is the possibility of language alternation in talk in two languages. In turn, the notion of order I have adopted comes from Ethnomethodology, where order is defined as the very possibility of social action. According to Ethnomethodology, without order, social action is impossible. This notion of order goes hand in hand with that of social norm, itself defined as any 'scheme of interpretation' (Garfinkel, 1967). Social norms are schemes of interpretation for any action points to a norm that has made it possible and with respect to which participants make sense of that action. In this perspective, an act refers to a relevant social norm in either of two ways. An act can be a direct application of the norm (normative behaviour), but it can also be an instance of deviance from it (deviant behaviour). In turn, two types of deviant behaviour can be observed. Deviance from the norm is either repairable or functional. These ideas of the orderliness and normativity of social action have found their way into CA, the study of the organisation of talk itself as social action.

One of the most striking aspects of language alternation is that, from the outside, it is very noticeable although, for bilingual participants involved in talk in two languages, it may pass unnoticed. As we have seen, wherever language alternation is frequent in conversation, community members assign labels (e.g., Kinyarwançais in Rwanda, Spanglish in the USA, Singlish in China, etc.) to it as evidence of their noticing. Some even go further and develop accounts, functional and otherwise, for its occurrence. Thus, language alternation is said to occur out of laziness, because of an inadequate mastery of the target language, because of gaps in the system of one of the languages involved, and so on. In this book, I have referred to these and similar accounts of language alternation as lay explanations.

The mere fact that these accounts exist indicates that, for ordinary everyday people, language alternation is an issue of order. To be sure, language alternation is noticeable and accounts are developed because ordinary everyday people use what I have referred to as the monolingual ideology as a scheme of interpretation. According to this ideology or social norm, monolingual language choice is normative and, by implication, the use of two languages within the same conversation is deviant. Of course, nobody denies that some aspects of language alternation may be explained in terms of linguistic competence or competence-related language preference – indeed, in this book I have shown how this is possible – and nobody denies that language alternation may occur because of gaps in the linguistic system of one of the languages in contact. However, it is also true that not every instance of language alternation can be explained in these terms. Even more importantly, lay explanations of language alternation do not have anything to say about the fact that, as indicated above, participants themselves may not be aware of language alternation while producing it, an attitude which seems to indicate that language alternation, some of it at least, is normative language choice.

Although, in Chapter 2, I have mentioned lay explanations, this book has mostly focused on professional explanations or fully-fledged theories of language alternation. Chapter 3 has looked at grammatical perspectives on language alternation, arguing that these can be seen as accounts of order. As I have indicated, at the grammatical level, language alternation is an issue of order, for, in principle, it deviates from the organisational norm Myers-Scotton (2002, 2006) refers to as the Uniform Structure Principle. This principle has it that, in language, any constituent has a uniform structure and always takes this structure whenever it is used. As we have seen, this principle works only as a scheme of interpretation, as, in actual use, the principle may be deviated, but deviance is interpreted either as repairable or as functional. Given this principle, language alternation in the same conversation is 'impossible in principle' (Muysken, 1995: 196). Therefore, the task for grammatical theories of language alternation is to explain how talk in two languages is possible despite this impossibility.

Research has shown that, globally, two types of language alternation can be observed. Language alternation can be alternational, but it can also be insertional (Muysken, 1995, 2000). However, we have also observed that this distinction is not an absolute one as both types can be found in the same corpus of data. In Chapter 3, I have surveyed two grammatical models, one alternational and the other insertional, as accounts of order in talk in two languages. The alternational model of language alternation I looked at, namely Poplack's constraints model, starts by establishing an important pre-theoretical distinction between code-switching and borrowing. Borrowing is defined as consisting of elements of one language that have been integrated, at whatever level, in the system of the other. As such, borrowing does not represent any challenge to the Uniform Structure Principle, and is therefore uninteresting. Code-switching, on the other hand, consisting of elements of one language that have not been integrated, is potentially a serious challenge to the Uniform Structure Principle. How is a sense of uniformity maintained despite diversity? The model's account of the orderliness of code-switching is that it occurs at equivalence sites, at sites where the syntactic structures of the two languages 'map onto each other' (Poplack, 1980/2000: 228). Poplack speaks of the equivalence constraint in this case. A number of criticisms against the model have been raised and counter examples have been presented, leading Poplack to readjust the model, but I will not venture into this area as my aim in this book has only been to show how the model can be read as an account of order in talk in two languages. Suffice it to mention that many of the objections against the model result from the fact that the model, being alternational, has difficulty dealing with insertional aspects of language alternation.

The insertional model of language alternation we have looked at is Myers-Scotton's Matrix Language Frame. The starting point for this model is that the two languages involved in language alternation 'do no participate equally' (Myers-Scotton and Jake, 1995/2000: 282). One language is dominant, the Matrix Language, while the other, the Embedded Language, is less dominant. The dominance of the Matrix Language shows in two respects. The Matrix Language provides the syntactic frame and it provides outsider late system morphemes. Thus, according to the model, it is through the dominance of the Matrix Language that a sense of structural uniformity is maintained in talk in two languages. More concretely, according to the Matrix Language Frame model, the norm is for content items from the Embedded Language to be inserted in grammatical slots provided by the Matrix Language and to be integrated in the morphological system of the Matrix Language. In this case, as in the case of borrowing, language alternation does not threaten the Uniform Structure Principle. Myers-Scotton speaks of Embedded EL items. However, this norm is often deviated from and deviance takes either of two forms, namely bare forms or singly occurring items, which are not integrated, and EL islands, that is longer EL constituents that remain internally consistent with EL grammar. Interestingly enough, in both cases of deviance, Myers-Scotton suggests, although as in passing, that functional motivation might be the reason for deviance. Briefly, formally at least, the Matrix Language Frame model is a complete account of the orderliness of language alternation.

After this survey of grammatical models of language alternation, in Chapter 4, I presented a case study, in which some of the ideas developed in the survey were used to account for a specific aspect of order in talk in two languages. The specific aspect of talk organisation I focused on in the case study is that of class agreement in Kinyarwanda–French language alternation. As we have seen, language alternation between these two languages presents a serious issue of order, for the two systems are drastically different. Kinyarwanda is a class language while French is not. So, given this difference, the first issue is: how is a sense of structural uniformity maintained? A casual look at the data reveals that, in my data, Kinyarwanda is the Matrix Language in the sense that, like in Kinyarwanda, in Kinyarwanda–French language alternation, class agreement is observed. In other words, at this level, it can be said that the sense of structural uniformity is maintained through the dominance of Kinyarwanda. However, a closer look reveals that class agreement in Kinyarwanda–French language alternation is not completely similar to class agreement in Kinyarwanda. For example, while, in Kinyarwanda, adjectives agree in class with nouns, that is take outsider late system morphemes, in Kinyarwanda–French language alternation, French adjectives in structural positions where they would normally refer to Kinyarwanda nouns for agreement remain bare. Likewise, while, in Kinyarwanda, there are 16 classes of nouns, when French bare nouns are in agreement commanding positions, they pattern differently. They subdivide into two major categories along semantic lines. Nouns with the feature [+HUMAN] command agreement of CL1 and CL2, whether they are bare or not, while nouns with the feature [–HUMAN] command agreement of CL9 and CL10 for the singular and the plural, respectively.

A first conclusion from this case study was that, although, in Kinyarwanda–French language alternation, there is a Matrix Language, this Matrix Language should not be equated with the natural language known as Kinyarwanda. Following from this, the second conclusion was that the orderliness of Kinyarwanda–French language alternation at the level of class agreement could be accounted for, not with reference to Kinyarwanda, but to this actually oriented-to Matrix. Thirdly and following from the above, the case study highlighted the need to approach the issue of the orderliness of language alternation from this perspective of specific aspects of order rather than from a 'grand-theory' perspective. Meanwhile, the case study shed light on important concepts, especially those adopted by the Matrix Language Frame. We have just seen that the case study allowed me to respecify the notion of Matrix Language. The second concept on which the case study brought some light is that of bare form. As we have seen, in Myers-Scotton, there is a suggestion that the occurrence of bare forms can be explained in terms of functional motivation. The case study revealed one instance where this is not a satisfactory explanation. As indicated above, in Kinyarwanda–French language alternation, French adjectives that would normally agree in class with Kinyarwanda nouns systematically remain bare. Because this is a regularity, it must be seen not as a case of deviance and therefore as functional, but rather as normative language use.

The orderliness of language alternation has been approached from a grammatical perspective, but it has also been examined from a socio-functional perspective. In turn, socio-functional accounts divide into two traditions, namely the identity-related explanation and the organisational explanation. Chapters 5 and 6 covered models of language alternation representative of these two traditions of research. Under the identity-related explanation, I examined the model developed by Gumperz in the context of his Interactional Sociolinguistics and Myers-Scotton's Markedness Model of Codeswitching. Both models were said to adopt the functional differentiation of languages as their scheme of interpretation. To clarify this notion of functional differentiation of language varieties, I made a digression into models of diglossia as developed by Ferguson (1959) and, especially, by Fishman (1967). One of the key notions in Fishman's work is that of domain congruency, the fact that, in a diglossic community, language varieties and social contexts in which they are appropriately used are co-selective. That is to say, under diglossia, normative language choice consists of choosing the right language variety in the right situation. However, functional differentiation being only a social norm, proponents of diglossia themselves recognise that this norm can be deviated from, but that deviance must be interpreted with reference to the norm either as functional or repairable. In the first case, borrowing a term from Gumperz (see below), Fishman speaks of 'metaphorical code-switching' and in the second he sees language alternation as evidence of language shift in progress. Here again, formally at least, diglossia can be seen as a complete account of the orderliness of language alternation: there is normative language choice, there is functional deviance and there is repairable deviance.

After this digression, I looked at the two models of language alternation listed under the identity-related explanation, starting with Gumperz. Gumperz's scheme of interpretation is the distinction he makes between we- and they-codes. According to Gumperz, the we-code is the variety associated with intimacy, sharedness, same social belonging and so on, while the they-code is the variety associated with social distance, formality, power and so on. The similarity between Gumperz's we-/they-codes on the one hand and Fishman's Low (L)/High (H) languages is obvious. In Gumperz, as in Fishman, three types of language alternation can be observed, namely normative language choice, functional deviance and repairable deviance. In Gumperz, normative language choice, the one that occurs according to appropriate changes in the speech situation, is referred to as 'situational code-switching'. Functional deviance, on the other hand, consists of deviating from the norm for specific expressive purposes. Gumperz uses the term 'metaphorical code-switching'. Finally, the third type, which Gumperz refers to as 'conversational code-switching', can properly be seen as repairable deviance, for, like in Fishman, it is said to occur in situations of change. Here again, a formally complete model of the orderliness of language alternation is presented.

I have just said that both Fishman's and Gumperz's models are formally complete accounts of the orderliness of language alternation. However, this does not necessarily mean they are adequate. One of the key aspects of the notion of order as used in Ethnomethodology is that order is 'lived order'. It is order as experienced by participants themselves. Therefore, to be adequate, any account must describe order in social action as it is actually lived by participants themselves while accomplishing that same social action. Elsewhere in this book, I have spoken of the 'emic perspective'. As indicated above, an important aspect of language alternation, especially language alternation of the type Gumperz and Fishman see as a case of repairable deviance, is that, while producing it, participants themselves seem to be involved in normative action. By portraying this type of language alternation as deviant while participants themselves orient to it as normative language use, both Fishman's and Gumperz's accounts would appear to be, in ethnomethodological terms, 'ironical', that is detached from participants' own reality.

The second model that I examined under the identity-related explanation is the Markedness Model of Codeswitching as developed by Myers-Scotton. Myers-Scotton's scheme of interpretation is what she refers to as the indexicality of language choices, the fact that each choice signals a specific set of rights and obligations. It must be stressed here that, according the Myers-Scotton, no set of rights and obligations can normatively be signalled by two different choices, and that this is precisely the reason why the languages are maintained in the community. Here again, this functional differentiation of languages is only a scheme of interpretation in the sense that, according to Myers-Scotton, given a particular set and obligations set, speakers need not use the congruent language variety. Thus, Myers-Scotton identifies essentially two types of language alternation, normative language choice and deviant language choice, referring to them as unmarked and marked choices, respectively. Two types of choices are listed under the unmarked category, namely sequential unmarked choice and codeswitching itself as an unmarked choice. As for the category of marked choices, it also divides into two subcategories, although Myers-Scotton does not identify them as such. On the one hand, there is the case where switching signals the negotiation of a new rights and obligations set, the proposed language, if adopted, becoming the unmarked choice for the new set of rights and obligations. And as such, one could also say that language choice in this case is normative. On the other hand, there are momentary departures into another language, which does not lead to a renegotiation of the relevant rights and obligations set. The parallelism between this and Gumperz's category of metaphorical code-switching is clear, and therefore one can speak of functional deviance.

Myers-Scotton's most important contribution to the identity-related perspective lies in her category of codeswitching itself as an unmarked choice. In Gumperz as in Fishman, as we have seen, there is a category of language alternation that can properly be characterised as a case of repairable deviance, for it denotes the lack of a well-established norm. We have also seen that Fishman's and Gumperz's accounts of the orderliness of this type of language alternation are ironical, for they do not correspond to participants' own reality. As we have said, speakers' attitudes while producing this type of language alternation indicates that they experience it as normative behaviour. Myers-Scotton's account goes some way towards overcoming this problem, for she says that language alternation, in this case, is itself an unmarked, that is normative, choice. However, as we have seen, this explanation is unsatisfactory. For language alternation itself to be an unmarked choice capable of indexing a specific set of rights and obligations, it must first of all be shown to exist as a variety in the community. Only in this case can members' markedness evaluator be able to recognise it, that is only in this case would members be able to use it confidently that other members will recognise it for what it means. Unfortunately, recognising language alternation as a variety in its own right would run against the initial scheme of interpretation, which is that of language separateness.

As indicated above, socio-functional perspectives to language alternation divide into the identity-related explanation and the organisational explanation. The first organisational explanation I examined is the Local Order Model as developed by Peter Auer. Drawing on Conversation Analysis, Auer states his scheme of interpretation as that of preference for same language talk. In this framework, normative language choice is when language choice in a particular turn or turn constructional unit is the same as the one in the turn or turn constructional unit immediately before it. However, because the preference for same language talk is only a scheme of interpretation, it allows for accountable deviance from it. Auer identifies two types of deviance from the preference for same language talk, namely code-switching and transfer. As we have seen, code-switching is when language alternation leads to the adoption of a new language-of-interaction and transfer, usually consisting of identifiable items (single words, fixed expressions), and is only a momentary departure away from the adopted language-of-interaction. According to Auer, such departures are functional. Here again, the parallelism between code-switching and transfer (discourse-related) on the one hand and situational code-switching and metaphorical code-switching on the other is clear. Of course, Auer is aware that his account of the orderliness of language alternation would be incomplete if he limited himself to this, that is if he did not deal with the issue of frequent language alternation.

According to Auer, order in frequent language alternation cannot be accounted for by reference to the preference for same language talk. Rather, he tentatively suggests that, in this case, one is dealing with a 'new code'. In mentioning this possibility, Auer can be seen to have opened the way for alternative accounts of the orderliness of language alternation from an organisational perspective. Gafaranga took this opportunity to put forward one such alternative account, an account we have referred to as the Overall Order Model of language alternation. In all the previous models, the notion of 'code' and that of 'language' had been taken as if they were equivalent. Drawing on more recent studies, Gafaranga argues that the two notions are actually different.

'Language' is a grammatical notion, while 'code' is a semiotic notion. On the basis of this specification, Gafaranga argued that, in actual interaction, the code, referred to as medium, need not be monolingual, but rather that it can also be bilingual. Following this, he respecified Auer's scheme of interpretation saying that, in talk, there is a preference not for same language talk, but rather for same medium talk, whether that medium be monolingual or bilingual. Here again, because this preference is only a scheme of interpretation, it allows for normative conduct as well as for deviance from it. In this framework, normative conduct is when the medium is maintained, whether it be monolingual or bilingual. As for deviance, it occurs when an already established medium is departed. Two ways of departing from an established medium are provided for. The first is referred to as medium switching and corresponds in many ways to situational code-switching, except that, in this case, the departed-from medium just like the deviated-into medium need not be monolingual. The second category, corresponding to what Auer calls transfer, divides into two, namely medium repair and medium suspension. Medium repair is when deviance is oriented to as repairable, and medium suspension is when, not being perceived as requiring any repair, deviance is necessarily functional.

As in the case of grammatical perspectives, at the end of the discussion of socio-functional accounts of the orderliness of language alternation, a case study was proposed in order to show how ideas and concepts surveyed can be used to address specific issues of order in talk in two languages. The specific issue of order I focused on is that of language choice in direct speech reporting. Language choice in direct speech reporting can be seen as an issue of order because, as other researchers have observed, in direct speech reporting, speakers need not reproduce the medium of 'original' talk. The question therefore that I set out to address is why, in direct speech reporting, speakers sometimes reproduce 'original' medium and sometimes do not. To answer this question, I drew on the 'Demonstration Theory' of direct speech reporting as developed by Clark and Gerrig (1990). According to Clark and Gerrig, any significant aspect of talk organisation can be reported. In turn, there are three ways in which a significant aspect of talk organisation can be handled in direct speech reporting. In direct speech reporting, an aspect of 'original' talk can be the depictive element; it can work as a supporting element or it can simply be ignored as an incidental element. As regards language choice, I took as my starting point that language choice itself is a 'significant aspect of talk organisation' (Gafaranga, 1999) as maintained in the organisational accounts of language alternation. Therefore, I posited that language choice itself can be reported. Inspection of the data revealed that, when language choice itself is the depictive element, 'original' medium must be reproduced. In this case, I spoke of medium reporting. On the other hand, when the medium of 'original' talk is incidental to direct speech reporting, current medium is used. As I said, this is normal because the medium is a social norm and is departed from only if there are reasons to. In this case, I spoke of content reporting. Finally, if the medium of 'original' talk serves as a supporting element, 'original' medium may, but need not, be maintained depending on participants' language preferences.

After the round of existing accounts of order in talk in two languages and some case studies that show how those models can be used to address specific aspects of order, in Chapter 8, I turned to the question of 'why bother' to study the orderliness of talk in two languages. I indicated that most applied studies of language alternation have been conducted in classroom contexts, and that such studies have amply shown that, in the classroom, language alternation is an important resource. However, the main bulk of the chapter focused on another area of application of language alternation studies. Drawing on my recent work in the Rwandan community in Belgium, I showed that the study of language alternation can be applied to address the issue of language shift and maintenance. More specifically, drawing on existing accounts of language alternation, especially the Overall Model, I have been able to describe some of the patterns through which this community is talking its language away. As detailed in the chapter, some, but by no means all, of the language choice patterns through which language shift is taking place are constant initiation of talk to children in French, constant accommodation in French and the frequent use of the parallel medium. In describing these language choice patterns that mediate language shift, the hope was that, aware of them, community members might begin to go about resisting language shift in an informed manner.

Where to from here? Current models of language alternation as I have discussed them in this book might not be perfect, but, as I have said elsewhere, they must be recognised for at least one achievement. They have rehabilitated talk in two languages (Gafaranga, 2007). Together they make a strong case for the orderliness of language alternation. Three paths, the basis of all of which has been laid in this book, are open for future work on language alternation. In view of the weaknesses found in current models, some researchers might aim to refine them and even to develop alternative ones. Applied linguists will continue to draw on models of language alternation and use them to address real-life issues in traditional domains of application such the educational domain and some will even want to apply studies of language alternation to ever new domains. Thirdly, and more urgently in my view, there is a need for studies of language alternation that focus on specific aspects of order in talk in two languages. As the two case studies I have included in this book show, a focus on specific aspects of order allows us to judge the validity of existing theories and even to refine them. More importantly, it is my view that safe theory-building should proceed from a sufficiently large collection of cases.

# References

Agard, J. (1985) Listen Mr Oxford Don. In *Mangoes and Bullets*. London: Serpent's Tail (www.images.hachette-livre.fr/media/contenuNumerique/036/3482565790.pdf, accessed 30 April 2007).

Alfonzetti, G. (1998) The conversational dimension of code-switching between Italian and dialect Sicily. In P. Auer (ed.) *Code-switching in Conversation*. London: Routledge, 180–211.

Alvarez-Caccamo, C. (1996) The power of reflexive languages: Code displacement in reported speech. *Journal of Pragmatics*, 25, 33–59.

Alvarez-Caccamo, C. (1998) From 'switching code' to 'code-switching': Towards a reconceptualisation of communicative codes. In P. Auer (ed.) *Code-switching in Conversation*. London: Routledge, 29–48.

Auer, P. (1984) *Bilingual Conversation*. Amsterdam: John Benjamins.

Auer, P. (1988) A conversation analytic approach to codeswitching and transfer. In M. Heller (ed.) *Codeswitching*. Berlin: Mouton de Gruyter, 187–214 (Reprinted in L. Wei (ed.) (2000), 166–187).

Auer, P. (1991) Bilingualism in/as social action: A sequential approach to code-switching. In *Papers for the Symposium on Code-switching in Bilingual Studies: Theory, Significance and Perspectives*, Barcelona: European Science Foundation, 21–23 March 1991, 319–352.

Auer, P. (1995) The pragmatics of code-switching: A sequential approach. In L. Milroy and P. Muysken (eds) *One Speaker Two Languages*. Cambridge: Cambridge University Press, 115–135.

Auer, P. (ed.) (1998) Introduction: Bilingual Conversation revisited. In *Code-switching in Conversation*. London: Routledge, 1–24.

Auer, P. (1999) From codeswitching via language mixing to fused lects: A dynamic typology of bilingual speech. *International Journal of Bilingualism*, 3, 309–332.

Auer, P. (2000) Why should we and how can we determine the 'base language' of a bilingual conversation? *Estudios de Sociolingüística*, 1, 129–144.

Backus, A. and Van Hout, R. (1995) Distribution of code-switching in bilingual conversations. In *Summer School Code-Switching and Language Contact*. Network on Code-Switching and Language Contact, Ljouwert/Leeuwarden 14–17 September 1994, 16–28.

Bangamwabo, F. X. (1984) Les problèmes de bilinguisme au Rwanda: Situation actuelle. *Miniprisec* (vol. and pp not recorded).

Baynham, M. (1996) Direct Speech: What is it doing in non-narrative discourse? *Journal of Pragmatics*, 25, 61–81.

Bell, A. (1997) Language style as audience design. In N. Coupland and A. Jaworski (eds) *Sociolinguistics: A Reader and Coursework*. London: Macmillan Press, 240–250.

Bentahila, A. and Davies, E. (1991) Constraints on code-switching: A look beyond grammar. In *Papers for the Symposium on Code-Switching in Bilingual Studies: Theory, Significance and Perspectives*. Barcelona: European Science Foundation, 369–403.

Bentahila, A. and Davies, E. (1998) Codeswitching: An unequal partnership? In R. Jacobson (ed.) *Codeswitching Worldwide*. Berlin: Mouton de Gruyter, 25–49.

Berk-Seligson, S. (1986) Linguistic constraints on intra-sentential code-switching: A study of Spanish/Hebrew bilingualism. *Language in Society*, 15, 313–348.

Bilmes, J. (1988) The concept of 'preference' in Conversation Analysis. *Language in Society*, 17, 161–181.

Blom, J. P. and Gumperz, J. (1972) Social meaning in linguistic structure: Codeswitching in Norway. In J. Gumperz and D. Hymes (eds) *Directions in Sociolinguistics*. New York: Holt, Rinehart and Winston, 407–434 (Reprinted in L. Wei (ed.) (2000), 111–136).

Bloor, M. (1997) Addressing social problems through qualitative research. In D. Silverman (ed.) *Qualitative Research: Theory, Methods and Practice*. London: Sage Publications, 221–238.

Boeschton, H. E. (1990) Asymmetrical code-switching in immigrant communities. *Papers for the Workshop on Constraints, Conditions and Models*, Network on code-switching and language contact, Strasbourg: European Science Foundation, 85–100.

Button, G. (1991) Conversation-in-a-series. In D. Boden and D. H. Zimmerman (eds) *Talk and Social Structure*. Cambridge: Polity Press, 251–277.

Cameron, D. (2001) *Working with Spoken Discourse*. London: Sage Publications.

Canale, M. and Swain, M. (1980) Theoretical bases of communicative approaches to second language teaching and testing. *Applied Linguistics*, 1, 1–47.

Chan, B. (2004) Beyond 'contextualisation': Code-switching as a 'textualization cue'. *Journal of Language and Social Psychology*, 23, 7–27.

Chomsky, N. (1965) *Aspects of the Theory of Syntax*. Cambridge, Massachusetts: The MIT Press.

Clark, H. and Gerrig, R. (1990) Quotations as demonstrations. *Language*, 66, 764–805.

Clift, R. and Holt, E. (2007) Introduction. In E. Holt and R. Clift (eds) *Reporting Talk: Reported Speech in Interaction*. Cambridge: Cambridge University Press, 1–15.

Clyne, M. (1987) Constraints on code-switching: How universal are they? *Linguistics*, 25, 739–764 (Reprinted in L. Wei (ed.) (2000), 257–280).

Clyne, M. (2001) Can the shift of immigrant languages be reversed in Australia? In J. Fishman (ed.) *Can Threatened Languages Be Saved?* Clevedon, UK: Multilingual Matters, 364–390.

Coates, J. (ed.) (1998) Gossip revisited: Language in all-female groups. In *Language and Gender: A Reader*. Oxford: Blackwell, 226–253.

Codó, E. (1998) *Analysis of Language Choice in Intercultural Service Encounters*. Unpublished MA dissertation, Lancaster University.

Cummins, J. (1979) Linguistic interdependence and the education of bilingual children. *Review of Educational Research*, 49, 222–251.

Davies, A. and Elder, C. (ed.) (2004) General introduction. Applied Linguistics: Subject to discipline? In *The Handbook of Applied Linguistics*. Oxford: Blackwell, 1–16.

Eckert, P. (1980) Diglossia: Separate and unequal. *Linguistics*, 18, 1053–1064.

Edwards, J. (2004) Language minorities. In A. Davies and C. Elder (eds) *The Handbook of Applied Linguistics*. Oxford: Blackwell, 451–475.

Elster, J. (1979) *Ulysses and the Sirens*. Cambridge: Cambridge University Press.

Elster, J. (1989) *The Cement of Society*. Cambridge: Cambridge University Press.
Fasold, R. (1984) *The Sociolinguistics of Society*. Oxford: Blackwell.
Ferguson, C. (1959) Diglossia. *Word*, 15, 325–340 (Reprinted in L. Wei (ed.) (2000), 65–80).
Ferguson, G. (2004) Classroom code-switching in post-colonial contexts: Functions, attitudes and policies. *IALA Review*, 16, 38–51.
Firth, A. (ed.) (1995) Talking for change: commodity negotiating by telephone. In *The Discourse of Negotiation: Studies of Language in the Workplace*. Oxford: Pergamon Press, 183–222.
Fishman, J. (1967) Bilingualism with and without diglossia; diglossia with and without bilingualism. *Journal of Social Issues*, 23, 29–38 (Reprinted in L. Wei (ed.) (2000), 81–88).
Fishman, J. (1972a) *The Sociology of Language*. Rowley: Newbury House Publishers.
Fishman, J. (1972b) The relationship between micro- and macro-sociolinguistics in the study of who speaks what language to whom and when. In J. B. Pride and J. Holmes (eds) *Sociolinguistics*. Harmondsworth: Penguin Education, 15–32.
Fishman, J. (1991) *Reversing Language Shift*. Clevedon, UK: Multilingual Matters.
Fishman, J. (ed.) (2000) *Can Threatened Languages be Saved?: Reversing Language Shift, Revisited*. Clevedon: Multilingual Matters.
Fuller, J. M. and Lehnert, H. (2000) Noun phrase structure in German-English codeswitching: Variation in gender assignment and article use. *International Journal of Bilingualism*, 4, 399–420.
Gafaranga, J. (1987a) Code-switching ou le vernaculaire du locuteur bilingue au Rwanda. *Langage et Société*, 41, 24–25.
Gafaranga, J. (1987b) *Towards an Integrative Model of Societal Bilingualism: Rwandan Speech Continua*. Unpublished MA dissertation, Lancaster University.
Gafaranga, J. (1997a) Code-switching, code mixing or Kinyarwanda for all practical purposes: The base language issue. *First International Symposium on Bilingualism*, Vigo, Spain, 21–25 October, 1997.
Gafaranga, J. (1997b) Direct speech reporting and code-switching in bilingual conversation: Kinyarwanda-French language alternation. Unpublished conference paper, *First International Conference on Bilingualism: Bilingual communities and individuals* (Vigo, 21–25 October, 1997).
Gafaranga, J. (1998) *Elements of Order in Bilingual Talk: Kinyarwanda-French Language Alternation*. Unpublished PhD Thesis, Lancaster University.
Gafaranga, J. (1999) Language choice as a significant aspect of talk organisation: The orderliness of language alternation. *TEXT: An Interdisciplinary Journal for the Study of Discourse*, 19, 201–226.
Gafaranga, J. (2000a) Language separateness: A normative framework in studies of language alternation. *Estudios de Sociolingüística*, 1, 65–84.
Gafaranga, J. (2000b) Medium repair vs. other-language repair: Telling the medium of a bilingual conversation. *International Journal of Bilingualism*, 4, 327–350.
Gafaranga, J. (2001a) Code-switching, code mixing or Kinyarwanda for all practical purposes: The base language issue. *Actas Do i Simposio Internacional Sobre o Bilingüismo*, 504–514.
Gafaranga, J. (2001b) Linguistic identities in talk-in-interaction: Order in bilingual conversation. *Journal of Pragmatics*, 33, 1901–1925.
Gafaranga, J. (2005) Demythologising language alternation studies: Conversational structure vs. social structure in bilingual interaction. *Journal of Pragmatics*, 37, 281–300.

Gafaranga, J. (2007) Code-switching as a conversational strategy. In P. Auer and L. Wei (eds) *Handbook of Multilingualism and Multilingual Communication.* Berlin: Mouton de Gruyter, 279–313.

Gafaranga, J. and Britten, N. (2003) 'Fire away': The opening sequence in general practice consultations. *Family Practice*, 20, 242–247.

Gafaranga, J. and Britten, N. (2005) Talking an institution into being: The opening sequence in general practice consultations. In K. Richards and P. Seedhouse (eds) *Applying Conversation Analysis.* New York: Palgrave Macmillan, 75–90.

Gafaranga, J. and Torras, M. C. (1998) Do speakers speak a language? Evidence from two bilingual settings. *Working Paper Series*, 94, Centre for Language in Social Life, Lancaster University.

Gafaranga, J and Torras, M. C (2001) Language versus medium in the study of bilingual conversation. *International Journal of Bilingualism*, 5, 195–220.

Gafaranga, J. and Torras, M. C. (2002) Interactional otherness: Towards a redefinition of codeswitching. *International Journal of Bilingualism*, 6, 1–22.

Gal, S. (1979) *Language Shift: Social Determinants of Language Change in Bilingual Austria.* New York: Academic Press.

Gardner-Chloros, P. (1995) Code-switching in community, regional and national repertoires: The myth of the discreteness of linguistic systems. In L. Milroy and P. Muysken (eds) *One Speaker Two Languages.* Cambridge: Cambridge University Press, 68–89.

Garfinkel, H. (1967) *Studies in Ethnomethodology.* Englewood Cliffs, NJ: Prentice Hall.

Garfinkel, H. (1968) The origin of the word 'Ethnomethodology'. In R. J. Hill and K. S. Crittenden (eds) *Proceedings of the Purdue Symposium on Ethnomethodology.* Institute for the Study of Social Change, Purdue University: Institute Monograph Series, 1, 5–11 (extract in R. Turner (ed.) (1974), 15–18).

Gasana, A. (1984) Bilinguisme et traduction: Le cas du kinyarwanda et du français. *Miniprisec* (vol. and page numbers not recorded).

Giles, H., Taylor, D. and Bourhis, R. Y. (1973) Towards a theory of interpersonal accommodation through language: Some Canadian data. *Language in Society*, 2, 177–192.

Goffman, E. (1974) *Frame Analysis: An Essay on the Organization of Experience.* Boston: Northeastern University Press.

Goffman, E. (1981) *Forms of Talk.* Oxford: Blackwell.

Grice, P. (1975) Logic and conversation. In P. Cole and J. Morgan (eds) *Syntax and Semantics: Speech Acts.* New York: Academic Press, 41–58.

Grosjean, F. (1982) *Life with Two Languages: An Introduction to Bilingualism.* Cambridge: Harvard University Press.

Grosjean, F. (1986) The bilingual as a competent but specific speaker-hearer. *Journal of Multilingual and Multicultural Development*, 6, 467–477.

Grosjean, F. (1989) Neurolinguists, beware: The bilingual is not two monolinguals in one person. *Brain and Language*, 36, 3–15.

Gumperz, J. (1977) Sociocultural knowledge in conversational inference. In M. Saville-Troike (ed.) *Linguistics and Anthropology.* Washington, DC: Georgetown University Press, 191–211 (Reprinted in Adam Jaworski and Nikolas Coupland (eds) (1999), 98–120).

Gumperz, J. (1982) *Discourse Strategies.* Cambridge: Cambridge University Press.

Gunnarsson, B.-L. (1997) Applied Discourse Analysis. In T. A. Van Dijk (ed.) *Discourse as Social Interaction.* London: Sage Publications, 285–312.

Haakana, M. (2001) Laughter as a patient's resource: Dealing with delicate aspects of medical interaction. *TEXT*, 21, 187–219.
Haakana, M. (2007) Reported thought in complaint stories. In E. Holt and R. Clift (eds) *Reporting Talk: Reported Speech in Interaction*. Cambridge: Cambridge University Press, 150–179.
Haugen, E. (1956) *Bilingualism in the Americas: A Bibliography and Research Guide*. Publications of the American Dialect Society 26.
Haugen, E. (1966) Dialect, Language, Nation. *American Anthropologist*, 68, 922–935 (Reprinted in J. B. Pride and J. Holmes (eds) (1972), 97–111).
Heap, J. L. (1990) Applied ethnomethodoloy: Looking for the local rationality of reading activities. *Human Studies*, 13, 39–72.
Heath, C. (1981) The opening sequence in doctor-patient interaction. In P. Atkinson and C. Heath (eds) *Medical Work: Realities and Routines*. Aldeshot: Gower, 71–90.
Heller, M. (1982) Negotiation of language choice in Montreal. In J. Gumperz (ed.) *Language and Social Identity*. Cambridge: Cambridge University Press, 108–118.
Herbert, R.K. (2001) Talking in Johannesbourg: The negotiation of identity in conversation. In R. Jacobson (ed.) *Codeswitching Worldwide II*. Berlin: Mouton de Gruyter, 223–250.
Heritage, J. (1984) *Garfinkel and Ethnomethodology*. Cambridge: Polity Press.
Heritage, J. (1988) Explanations as accounts: A conversation analytic perspective. In C. Antaki (ed.) *Analyzing Everyday Explanation: A Casebook of Methods*. London: Sage Publications, 126–144.
Holmes, J. (1999) *Introduction to Sociolinguistics* (11th edition). London: Longman.
Holt, E. (1996) Reporting on talk: The use of direct reported speech in conversation. *Research on Language and Social Interaction*, 29, 219–245.
Holt, E. (2007) 'I'm eyeing your chop mind': Reporting and enacting. In E. Holt and R. Clift (eds) *Reporting Talk: Reported Speech in Interaction*. Cambridge: Cambridge University Press, 47–80.
Hutchby, I. and Wooffit, R. (1998) *Conversation Analysis: Principles, Practices and Applications*. Oxford: Polity Press.
Jakobson, R. (1953) Results of the conference of anthropologists and linguists. *IJAL* supplement. Memoir No 8: 18–22.
Jaworski, A. and Coupland, N. (eds) (1999) *The Discourse Reader*. London: Routledge.
Jones, J. and Wareing, S. (1999) Language and politics. In L. Thomas and S. Wareing (eds) *Language, Society and Power*. London: Routledge, 31–47.
Kachru, B. (1978) Towards structuring code-mixing: An Indian perspective. *International Journal of the Sociology of Language*, 16, 27–47.
Kimenyi, A. (1980) *A Relational Grammar of Kinyarwanda*. Berkely: University of California Press.
Labov, W. (1972) *Sociolinguistic Patterns*. Philadelphia: University of Pennsylvania Press.
Lerner, G. H. (1991) On the syntax of sentences-in-progress. *Language in Society*, 20, 441–458.
Levinson, S. (1983) *Pragmatics*. Cambridge: Cambridge University Press.
Livingston, E. (1987) *Making Sense of Ethnomethodology*. London: Routledge.
Mackey, W. F. (1962) The description of bilingualism. *Canadian Journal of Linguistics*, 7, 51–85 (Reprinted in L. Wei (ed.) (2000), 26–54).

Martin-Jones, M. (1995) Code-switching in the classroom: Two decades of research. In L. Milroy and P. Muysken (eds) *One Speaker Two Languages.* Cambridge: Cambridge University Press, 90–111.

Martin-Jones, M. (2000) Bilingual classroom interaction: A review of recent research. *Language Teaching,* 33, 1–9.

Martin-Jones, M. and Romaine, S. (1985). Semilingualism: A half-baked theory of communicative competence. *Applied Linguistics,* 6, 105–117.

Meechan, M. and Poplack, S. (1995) Orphan categories in bilingual discourse: A comparative study of adjectivization strategies in Wolof/French and Fongbe/French. *Summer School Code-Switching and Language Contact* (Ljouwert/ Leeuwarden, 14–17 September 1994). Ljouwert/ Leeuwarden, The Netherlands: Fryske Akademy, 179–191.

Meeuwis, M. and Blommaert, J. (1998) A monolectal view of code-switching: Layered code-switching among Zairians in Belgium. In P. Auer (ed.) *Code-switching in Conversation.* London: Routledge, 76–100.

Milroy, L. and Wei, L. (1995) A social network approach to code-switching: The example of a Chinese community in Britain. In L. Milroy and P. Muysken (eds) *One Speaker Two Languages.* Cambridge: Cambridge University Press, 136–157.

Mkilifi, A. M. H. (1978) Triglossia and Swahili-English bilingualism in Tanzania. In J. Fishman (ed.) *Advances in the Study of Societal Multilingualism.* The Hague: Mouton, 129–152.

Morimoto, Y. (1999) Making words in two languages: A prosodic account of Japanese-English language mixing. *International Journal of Bilingualism,* 3, 23–44.

Murray, P. S. (3 October 2006) Kids talk 106 languages. wwwdailyrecord.co.uk, accessed 5 October 2006.

Muysken, P. (1995) Code-switching and grammatical theory. In L. Milroy and P. Muysken (eds) *One Speaker Two Languages.* Cambridge: Cambridge University Press, 177–198.

Muysken, P. (2000) *Bilingual Speech: A Typology of Code-mixing.* Cambridge: Cambridge University Press.

Myers, G. (1991) Functions of reported speech in group discussions. *Applied Linguistics,* 20, 376–401.

Myers-Scotton, C. (1983) The negotiation of identity in conversation: A theory of markedness and code choice. *International Journal of the Sociology of Language,* 44, 115–36.

Myers-Scotton, C. (1988) Codeswitching as indexical of social negotiation. In M. Heller (ed.) *Codeswitching.* Berlin: Mouton de Gruyter, 151–186 (Reprinted in Wei, (ed.) (2000), 137–165).

Myers-Scotton, C. (1993a) *Duelling Languages: Grammatical Structure in Codeswitching.* Oxford: Clarendon.

Myers-Scotton, C. (1993b) *Social Motivations for Codeswitching: Evidence from Africa.* Oxford: Clarendon Press.

Myers-Scotton, C. (1995) A lexically based model of codeswitching. In L. Milory and P. Muysken (eds) *One Speaker Two Languages.* Cambridge: Cambridge University Press, 233–256.

Myers-Scotton, C. (1998a) A way to dusty death: The Matrix Language turnover hypothesis. In L. A. Grenoble and L. J. Whaley (eds) *Endangered Languages: Language Loss and Community Response.* Cambridge: Cambridge University Press, 289–316.

Myers-Scotton, C. (1998b) A theoretical introduction to the markedness model. In C. Myers-Scotton (ed.) *Codes and Consequences: Choosing Linguistic Varieties*. Oxford: Oxford University Press, 18–42.

Myers-Scotton, C. (1999) Explaining the role of norms and rationality in codeswitching. *Journal of Pragmatics* 32, 1259–1271.

Myers-Scotton, C. (2001) The matrix language frame model: Development and responses. In R. Jacobson (ed.) *Codeswitching Worldwide II*. Berlin: Mouton de Gruyter, 23–58.

Myers-Scotton, C. (2002) *Contact Linguistics: Bilingual Encounters and Grammatical Outcomes*. Oxford: Oxford University Press.

Myers-Scotton, C. (2006) *Multiple Voices: An Introduction to Bilingualism*. Oxford: Blackwell.

Myers-Scotton, C. and Bolanyai, A. (2001) Calculating speakers: Codeswitching in a rational choice model. *Language in Society*, 30, 1–28.

Myers-Scotton, C. and Jake, J. L. (1995) Matching lemmas in a bilingual competence and production model: Evidence from intrasentential code-switching. *Linguistics*, 33, 981–1024 (Reprinted in Wei (ed.) (2000), 281–320).

Myers-Scotton, C. and Jake, J. L. (2000) Four types of morpheme: Evidence from aphasia, codeswitching and second language acquisition. *Linguistics*, 38, 1053–1100.

Nettle, D. and Romaine, S (2000) *Vanishing Voices: The Extinction of the World's Languages*. Oxford: Oxford University Press.

Nortier, J. (1990) *Dutch-Moroccan Arabic Code-Switching*. Dordrecht, The Netherlands: Foris.

Odisho, E. Y. (1993) Bilingualism and multilingualism among Assyrians: A case study of language erosion and demise. *Journal of Assyrian Academic Studies*, 7, 76–83.

Papapavlou, A. and Pavlou, P. (2001) The interplay of language use and language maintenance and cultural identity of Greek Cypriots in the UK. *International Journal of Applied Linguistics*, 11, 92–113.

Pauwels, A. (2004) Language maintenance. In A. Davies and C. Elder (eds) *The Handbook of Applied Linguistics*. Oxford: Blackwell, 719–737.

Peräkylä, A. and Vehveläinen, S. (2003) Conversation analysis and professional stocks of interactional knowledge. *Discourse and Society*, 14, 727–750.

Piller, I. (2001) Private language planning: The best of both worlds. *Estudios de Sociolingüística*, 2, 61–80.

Pomerantz, A. (1984) Agreeing and disagreeing with assessment: Some features of preferred/dispreferred turn-shapes. In J. M. Atkinson and J. Heritage (eds) *Structures of Social Action: Studies in Conversation Analysis*. Cambridge: Cambridge University Press, 79–101.

Poplack, S. (1980) 'Sometimes I'll start a sentence in Spanish *y termino en español*': Toward a typology of code-switching. *Linguistics*, 18, 581–618 (Reprinted in L. Wei (ed.) (2000), 221–256).

Poplack, S. (1990) Variation theory and language contact: concept, methods and data. In *Papers for the Workshop on Concepts, Methods and Data* (Basel 12–13/ January/ 1990). Strasbourg: European Science Foundation, 33–66.

Poplack, S., Sankoff, D. and Miller, C. (1988) The social correlates of linguistic processes of lexical borrowing and assimilation. *Linguistics*, 26, 47–104.

Poplack, S. and Meechan, M. (1995) Patterns of language mixture: Nominal structure in Wolof-French and Fongbe-French bilingual discourse. In L. Milory and

P. Muysken (eds) *One Speaker Two Languages*. Cambridge: Cambridge University Press, 199–232.

Psathas, G. (1995) *Conversation Analysis: The Study of Talk-in-Interaction*. Thousand Oaks, CA: Sage Publications.

Psathas, G. (ed.) (1990) *Interactional Competence*. Washington, DC: University Press of America.

Rae, J. and Kerby, J. (2007) Designing contexts for reporting tactical talk. In E. Holt and R. Clift (eds) *Reporting Talk: Reported Speech in Interaction*. Cambridge: Cambridge University Press, 179–194.

Reershemius, G. (2001) 'Token codeswitching' and language alternation in narrative discourse: A functional-pragmatic approach. *International Journal of Bilingualism*, 5, 175–194.

Richards, K. (2005) Introduction. In K. Richards and P. Seedhouse (eds) *Applying Conversation Analysis*. New York: Palgrave Macmillan, 1–18.

Rindstedt, C. and Aronsson, K. (2002) Growing up monolingual in a bilingual community. The Quichua revitalization paradox. *Language in Society*, 31, 721–742.

Roberts, C. (2003) Applied Linguistics applied. In S. Sarangi and T. van Leeuwen (eds) *Applied Linguistics and Communities of Practice*. London: Baal in association with Continuum, 132–149.

Robinson, J. D. (2006) Soliciting patients' presenting concerns. In J. Heritage and D. Maynard (eds) *Communication in Medical Care: Interaction between Primary Care Physicians and Patients*. Cambridge: Cambridge University Press, 22–47.

Romaine, S. (1995) *Bilingualism* (2nd edition). Oxford: Blackwell.

Ryave, A. L. and Schenkein, J. N. (1974) Notes on the art of walking. In R. Turner (ed.) *Ethnomethodology: Selected Readings*. Harmondsworth: Penguin, 265–274.

Sacks, H. (1972) On the analysability of stories by children. In J. Gumperz and D. Hymes (eds) *Directions in Sociolinguistics*. New York: Holt, Rinehart and Winston, 329–45.

Sacks, H., Schegloff, E. and Jefferson, G. (1978) A simplest systematics for the organization of turn-taking in conversation. In J. N. Schenkein (ed.) *Studies in the Organization of Conversational Interaction*. New York: Academic Press, 7–55.

Sankoff, G. (1972) Language use in multilingual societies: Some alternative approaches. In J. B. Pride and J. Holmes (eds) *Sociolinguistics*. Harmondsworth: Penguin Education, 33–51.

Saussure, (de) F. (1995) *Course in General Linguistics*. London: Duckworth (Translated and annotated by Roy Harris).

Schegloff, E. (1968) Sequencing in conversational openings. *American Anthropologist*, 80, 1075–1095 (Reprinted in J. Gumperz and D. Hymes (eds) (1972), 346–380).

Schegloff, E. (1979) Identification and recognition in telephone conversational openings. In G. Psathas (ed.) *Everyday Language: Studies in Ethnomethodology*. New York: Irvington, 23–78.

Schegloff, E. (1982) Discourse as an interactional achievement: Some uses of 'uh huh' and other things that come between sentences. In D. Tannen (ed.) *Analyzing Discourse: Text and Talk*. Washington, DC: Georgetown University Press, 71–93.

Schegloff, E. (1988) On a virtual servo-mechanism for guessing bad news: A single-case juncture. *Social Problems*, 35, 442–457.

Schegloff, E. and Sacks, H. (1973) Opening up closings. In *Semiotica*, 8, 289–327 (Reprinted in R. Turner (ed.) (1974), 233–264).

Schegloff, E. Jefferson, G. and Sacks, H. (1977) The preference for self-correction in the organization of repair in conversation. *Language*, 53, 361–382 (Reprinted in G. Psathas, (ed.) (1990), 31–61).

Schjever, R. (1998) Codeswitching as an indicator of language shift? Evidence from Sardinian-Italian bilingualism. In R. Jacobson (ed.) *Codeswitching Worldwide*. Berlin: Mouton de Gruyter, 221–247.

Schmitt, N. and Celce-Murcia, M. (2002) An overview of Applied Linguistics. In N. Schmitt (ed.) *An Introduction to Applied Linguistics*. London: Arnold, 1–18.

Searle, P. (1969) *Speech Acts*. Cambridge: Cambridge University Press.

Sebba, M. (1998) A congruence approach to code-switching. *International Journal of Bilingualism*, 2, 1–20.

Sebba, M. and Wootton, A. (1998) We, they and identity: Sequential versus identity-related explanation in code-switching. In P. Auer (ed.) *Code-switching in Conversation*. London: Routledge, 262–286.

Shin, S. and Milroy, L. (2000) Conversational code-switching among Korean-English bilingual children. *International Journal of Bilingualism*, 4, 351–584.

Sperber, D. and Wilson, D. (1995) *Relevance* (2nd edition) Oxford: Blackwell.

Tannen, D. (1989) *Talking Voices: Repetition, Dialogue and Imagery in Conversational Discourse*. Cambridge: Cambridge University Press.

Ten Have, P. (1989) The consultation as a genre. In B. Torode (ed.) *Text and Talk as Social Practice*. Dordrect, Holland: Foris Publications, 115–135.

Ten Have, P. (1999) *Doing Conversation Analysis: A Practical Guide*. London: Sage Publications.

Thompson, G. (1996) Voices in the text: Discourse perspectives on language reports. *Applied Linguistics*, 17, 501–530.

Torras, M.C. (1998) *Code Negotiation and Code Alternation in Service Encounters in Catalonia*. Unpublished MA thesis, Lancaster University.

Torras, M. C. (2002) *Language Choice, Social Identity and the Order of Service Talk-in-Interaction*. Unpublished PhD, Lancaster University.

Torras, M. C. (2005) Social identity and language choice in service talk. In K. Richards and P. Seedhouse (eds) *Applying Conversation Analysis*. New York: Palgrave Macmillan, 107–123.

Torras, M. C. and Gafaranga, J. (2002) Social identities and language alternation in non-formal institutional bilingual talk: Trilingual service encounters in Barcelona. *Language in Society*, 31, 527–548.

Treffers-Daller, J. (1990) Towards a uniform approach to code-switching and borrowing. *Papers for the Workshop on Constraints, Conditions and Models*. Strasbourg: ESF Network on Code-Switching and Language Contact, 259–277.

Ventola, E. (1987) *The Structure of Social Interaction: A Systemic Approach to the Semiotics of Service Encounters*. London: Frances Printer.

Wei, L. (1994) *Three Generations, Two Languages, One Family: Language Choice and Language Shift in a Chinese Community in Britain*. Clevedon, Avon: Multilingual Matters.

Wei, L. (1998) The 'why' and 'how' questions in the analysis of conversational code-switching. In P. Auer (ed.) *Code-switching in Conversation*. London: Routledge, 156–176.

Wei, L. (2001) Lemma congruence checking between languages as an organizing principle in intrasentential codeswitching. *International Journal of Bilingualism*, 5, 153–174.

Wei, L. (2002) 'What do you want me to say?' On the Conversation Analysis approach to bilingual interaction. *Language in Society*, 31, 159–180.

Wei, L. (2005) 'How can you tell?' Towards a common sense explanation of conversational code-switching. *Journal of Pragmatics*, 37, 375–389.

Wei, L. (ed.) (2000) *The Bilingualism Reader*. London: Routledge.

Weinreich, U. (1953) *Languages in Contact*. The Hague: Mouton.

Whalen, J., Zimmerman, D. H. and Whalen, M. R. (1988) When words fail: A single case analysis. *Social Problems*, 35, 435–462.

Whalen, M. R. and Zimmerman, D. H. (1990) Describing trouble: Epistemology in citizen calls to the police. *Language in Society*, 19, 465–492.

Wilkins, D. A. (1999) Applied Linguistics. In B. Spolsky (ed.) *Concise Encyclopedia of Educational Linguistics*. Amsterdam: Elsevier, 6–17.

Winford, D. (2003) *An Introduction to Contact Linguistics*. Malen, MA: Blackwell.

Zentella, A. C. (1997) *Growing up Bilingual: Puerto Rican Children in New York*. Oxford: Blackwell.

# Index

Agard, J., 36
Alfonzetti, G., 151
alternational approach
   and constituent insertion, 44–7
   later developments, 41–7
   and lone L2 incorporations, 41–4
   original constraints model, 38–41
   *versus* insertional, 27–32, 34
Alvarez-Caccamo, C., 21, 81, 151
Applied Conversation Analysis, 176
applied language alternation studies, 174–9
Applied Linguistics, 174–9
   definitions, 175–6
   and description-informed action framework, 176, 177, 178
   and discovery-prescription framework, 176–7
   and education, 176, 179, 196
   institutional context, 177
   practitioner-oriented, 177–8
   and real world problems, 176
Arabic, 87
Aronsson, K., 182
asymmetrical approach, *see* insertional approach
Auer, P., 8, 16, 21, 23, 24, 27, 35, 100, 109, 116, 120–1, 123–5, 127, 128, 130, 130–5, 138–9, 142, 145–6, 148, 151, 156, 172, 176, 178, 191, 194

Backus, A., 28
Bantu, 52
base language, 138–40, 142–5
Baynham, M., 157
Bell, A., 189
Bengali, 1
Bentahila, A., 41
Berk-Seligson, S., 41

bilingualism
   balanced, 48
   and diglossia, 88–9
   and division of labour between lexicon/grammar, 2
   emic perspective, 120
   and language alternation, 3
   language/dialect boundary, 1–2
   local order in, 120–35
   overall order in, 135–49
   as problem of linguistics, 2
   as set of activities, 120
   as the norm, 4
   and understanding of language itself, 3
   as world-wide phenomenon, 1
Bilmes, J., 117
Blom, J. P., 24, 84
Blommaert, I., 21
Bloor, M., 177
Boeschton, H. E., 19
Bolanyai, A., 102, 103
borrowing, 38
   appropriateness of, 14–15
   and code-switching, 18–22
   implications of term, 14
   psycholinguistic view, 15–16
   and semilingualism, 15–17
Britten, N., 4, 5, 137, 190
Button, G., 136

Canale, M., 177
Cantonese, 2, 126
Castilian, 16, 29, 83–4, 96, 112, 124
Catalan, 16, 29, 83–4, 124, 126, 127, 128–30, 142, 147
Celce-Murcia, M., 176
Chan, B., 171
Chinese, 1, 2, 6, 11, 52
Chomsky, N., 47

Clark, R., 157, 158, 160, 162–3, 164–5, 172–3, 206
class agreement, 2
  and bare forms, 63–4, 80
  and constituent insertion, 80–1
  and focusing on specific aspects of order, 81–2
  French adjectives and verbs, 66–70
  French nouns, 70–5
  in Kinyarwanda and French, 64–79
  and Matrix Language, 80, 81
  and multi-word fragments, 76–9
  and nature of language alternation, 81
  significance of, 62, 62–3
  and singular occurring elements, 80
  and structural uniformity, 79
classical Arabic, 87
Clift, R., 157
Clyne, M., 187
Coates, J., 121
code-switching, 2, 132
  and borrowing, 18–22
  and code-mixing, 22–7
  conversational, 102
  definition, 19, 47
  and language mixing, 134–5
  as locally functional, 25–7
  markedness model, 102–8
  metaphorical, 96, 97–9, 101–2, 113
  and sequential environment, 6
  situational, 96–7
  and social meaning, 7
  and transfer, 134
Codó, E., 128, 140
communication, *see* Interactional Sociolinguistics
Conversation Analysis (CA), 4–5, 6, 92–3, 116–17, 120, 149, 176
  as misunderstood, 6
  and notion of preference, 117–19
Cooperative Principle, 102
Cummins, J., 15

Davies, A., 176
Davies, E., 41
demonstration theory, 157
  delivery, 161
  detachment, 162
  and direct experience, 162–3
  and direct speech reporting, 157–64
  indices, symbols and icons, 158
  language, 161
  linguistic acts, 161–2
  non-serious actions, 158–9, 160
  partial and selective, 158, 159–60
  and verbatim assumption, 157–8, 172–3
Dhimotiki, 87
diglossia, 14, 86–91, 114–15, 185
direct speech
  as demonstration, 157–64
  depictive element, 164–8
  and discourse-related transfer, 156
  language choice as issue of order, 151–7
  supportive element, 168–72
  and use of original medium, 156
dominance approach, *see* insertional approach

Eckert, P., 90
education, 176, 179, 196
Edwards, J., 184
Elder, C., 176
Elster, J., 102, 103
Embedded Language (EL), 50–1, 57–8
en-résumé practices, 17–18, 32
  borrowing *versus* code-switching, 18–22
  code-mixing *versus* code-switching, 22–7
  insertional *versus* alternational, 27–32
English, 6, 11, 14, 29, 50, 51, 52, 90, 100, 111–12, 113–14, 126, 127, 128, 128–9, 130–1, 138–9, 140, 142–3
equivalence approach, *see* alternational approach
Ethnomethodology, 3–5, 116, 120, 142, 149
  applied, 174
  straight-ahead, 174, 175

face-to-face communication, 92–3
Fasold, R., 90

Ferguson, C., 14, 86–7, 96, 114, 178, 202
Firth, A., 5
Fishman, J., 14, 88–90, 94–5, 96, 97, 109, 115, 184, 185–7, 202, 203
Flemish, 154
Fongbe, 42–3
Franglais, 11
French, 9, 11, 14, 15, 18, 19, 21, 27, 37, 40, 42–3, 45, 50, 52, 53–4, 86, 87, 88, 101, 126, 129, 130, 130–1, 139, 142, 144, 146, 147, 154, 155, 166, 171
*see also* Kinyarwanda-French bilingualism
French-English bilingualism, 13, 14
Fuller, J. M., 60
functionalism, 85–91, 99–102, 113–14

Gafaranga, J., 4, 5, 6, 8, 12, 21, 27, 29, 34, 81, 83, 96, 100, 116, 137, 138, 144–5, 149, 153, 168, 170, 171, 176, 178, 180, 181, 190, 191, 194, 205–6, 207
Gal, S., 90, 97, 182
Gardner-Chloros, P., 12
Garfinkel, H., 3, 4, 43, 107, 198
Gasana, A., 12
German, 60, 97–8, 100, 144, 155, 171
Gerrig, R., 157, 158, 160, 162–3, 164–5, 172–3, 206
Goffman, E., 158, 164
grammar, 62
alternational model, 38–47
insertional model, 47–57
and MLF/EL approaches, 50–60
and orderliness, 34–8
as system, 35
Grice, P., 102
Grosjean, F., 14, 16–17, 18
Gumperz, J., 24, 81, 84, 91, 92–4, 96, 97, 98, 101–2, 108, 109, 114, 132, 151, 156, 168, 202
Gunnarsson, B.-L., 175, 176

Haakana, M., 5, 158
Haitian Creole, 87, 88
Haugen, E., 1, 13
Heap, J. L., 174, 175, 196, 197

Heath, C., 137
Hebrew, 29
Heller, M., 130
Herbert, R. K., 23
Heritage, J., 117, 126
High German, 29
Holmes, J., 92
Holt, E., 156, 157, 160
Hungarian, 97–8

identity-related explanation, 84–5, 114–15, 149
diglossia, 85–91
and Interactional Sociolinguistics, 91–102
and language choice as rational act, 102–4
markedness model, 104–14
we-/they-codes, 91–102
insertional approach
asymmetry principle, 49–57
constituent insertion, 44–7
mentalistic model, 47–9
*versus* alternational, 27–32, 34
Interactional Sociolinguistics, 84, 91–4
and contextualisation cues, 93–4
and domain congruency, 95
functional/non-functional, 99–102
and inference, 92, 93
language alternation in, 94–102
and language variation, 92–3
and participant-related transfer, 100–2
and repairable deviance, 100–1
and situated interpretation, 93
successful, 93
we-code/they-code, 95–6, 101–2
Italian, 100, 182

Jake, J. L., 48, 50, 56, 63, 200
Japanese-English bilingualism, 22
Jones, J., 11

Kachru, B., 24, 99, 109
Katharévusa, 87
Kerby, J., 171
Kinyafrançais, 11
Kinyarwanda, 2, 9, 18–21, 24, 26–7, 31, 38, 40–1, 43, 45, 52–3, 56, 59,

Kinyarwanda – *continued*
    101, 139, 144, 146, 147, 152–3,
    165, 179–81, 185–6
Kinyarwanda-French bilingualism, 2,
    8, 9, 12, 30, 31, 62–4, 86, 98–9,
    152–3, 156, 163, 165, 167–71,
    173, 186
  accommodation, 191–4
  adjectives-verbs in
    agreement-governed position,
    66–70
  class agreement in, 66–79
  and concept of order, 79–82
  grammatical agreement in, 64–6
  initiation, 188–91
  and multi-word fragments, 76–9
  nouns in agreement-commanding
    position, 70–5
  parallel mode, 194–6
Kirundi, 2

L2 incorporations, 41–4
Labov, W., 91
Labovian (Variationist)
  Sociolinguistics, 92
language alternation
  already established medium, 148–9
  categories, 131–5
  class agreement in, 8, 62–82
  as code-switching, 132
  common grounds in studies of, 5–7
  as contextualisation cue, 125–6
  data on, 8–9
  as deviation from the medium,
    146–7
  and direct speech, 8, 151–73
  discourse-related, 131–3
  as disorderly phenomenon, 11, 13
  doctor-patient analogy, 10
  grammatical perspective, 8, 34–61
  identity-related perspective, 8,
    83–115
  and language shift/maintenance,
    182–8
  local order of talk, 134
  model of, 7
  negotiation, 148
  organisational perspective, 116–50
  participant-related, 131, 132, 133

  as problem of order, 3–5, 31–2,
    174–97
  professional/non-professional
    views, 10–17
  quasi-theories of, 7, 10–32
  sequential analysis of, 120–1
  significance of, 6
  socio-functional perspective, 8,
    83–150
  as the norm, 9
  theoretical impossibility, 3
  as transfer, 132–3, 134
  turn-by-turn/TCU-by-TCU analysis,
    133–4
  *see also* code-switching
language choice
  and conventionalised
    exchange/intraction type,
    106–7
  as depictive element, 164–8
  and direct speech, 151–7, 164–72
  and felicity conditions/social
    closeness, 106
  indexicality of, 105–6
  marked, 111–14
  and markedness
    metric/evaluator, 107
  monolingual, 108
  optimal, 109
  orderliness of, 109–11
  as rational act, 102–4
  and reciprocity of perspectives,
    107–8
  sequential unmarked
    codeswitching, 108–9, 113
  structural view, 104–5
  as supportive element, 168–72, 173
  types of, 108–14
  unmarked, 108–11
language-of-interaction, 135
  and alignment, 140–2
  base language, 138–40, 142–5
language separateness, 12, 14
language shift
  acquisition strategies, 186–7
  applied agenda, 183
  and child bilingualism, 186
  and language choice, 188–96

as linguistic phenomenon per se, 183
and maintenance, 182–8
as real world concern, 179–81, 196
research design, 181–2
reversing model, 184–6
lay explanations
and borrowing, 14–17
disorderly phenomenon, 11–13
and interference, 13–14
and monolingual ideology, 11–12
negative attitude, 12–13
pseudo-scientific terms, 11, 13–17
Lehnert, H., 60
Lerner, G. H., 26, 81, 122
linguistics, 2, 174–5, 176
Livingston, E., 116
Low German, 29
Luya, 95–6, 108–9
Lwidakho, 105–6, 141–2

Mackey, W. F., 13
Mandarin, 2
Markedness Model of Codeswitching, 84, 147
and language choice, 104–8
language choice as rational act, 102–4
premises, 104–8
and 'the why' of language, 103–4
types of language choices, 108–14
Martin-Jones, M., 16, 178
Matrix Language Frame (MLF), 62
as abstract morphosyntactic frame, 58
asymmetry principle, 50–1
development, 47–9
difficulties with, 58–9
morpheme order principle, 51–5
and orderliness, 58–9, 60
predictions of, 57–60
system morpheme principle, 51, 55–7
as taken for granted, 59–60
Meechan, M., 19, 38, 41, 42
Meeuwis, M., 21
Milroy, L., 6, 28, 126, 132
Mkilifi, A. M. H., 90

monolingualism, 1, 87, 88, 108, 146, 182
Morimoto, Y., 21
morpheme order principle, 51–5
Murray, P. Scots, 1
Muysken, P., 3, 8, 17, 19, 21, 23, 28, 30–1, 34, 36, 41, 43, 66, 199
Myers, G., 157, 163
Myers-Scotton, C., 2, 3, 6, 11, 15, 18, 19, 35–6, 47–50, 53, 55–9, 63, 76, 80–1, 84, 95, 102–5, 107–14, 141, 180, 200, 201–2, 204

norms, 4, 9, 117
and base language, 138–9, 142
and bilingualism, 12, 89
community, 188
and Conversational Analysis, 119
and deviance, 103–4, 109, 113, 119, 128, 142, 148, 149, 165, 171, 172
and diglossia, 89–91
equivalence, 47
and immigrant minority languages, 185
and language alternation, 9, 145, 146, 149
and language negotiation, 142
and language repair, 144
and language separateness, 83
and language shift, 191
and markedness, 107–11, 114
and MLF framework, 58, 60, 80
and monolingualism, 11
one-situation-one-language, 96, 113, 114–15
and position of prepositional phrase, 53
and preference, 118, 133, 138
and situational/metaphorical code-switching, 97, 101–2
social actor/social action, 49, 117
and Standard English, 36
and TCU, 122, 124
Nortier, J., 41
Norwegian, 94

One-Situation-One-Language
Principle, 83–5, 89–91, 96, 113,
114–15, 116
orderliness, 31–2, 116, 145, 198
accounts of, 3, 4, 8, 22, 34, 38,
82, 84
and code-mixing, 109
and code-switching, 46
and constituent insertion, 47
and conversation analysis, 4
dealing with, 10, 31
en-résumé practices, 17,
32, 40
ethnomethodological, 3–5
and grammar, 34–8
identity-related, 114–15
and language choice in direct
speech, 151–7
lay explanations, 11
and markedness model, 102
and Matrix Language Framework,
52, 57, 58–9, 60
and metaphorical
code-switching, 99
problem of, 3
and situational code-switching,
101–2
social action, 117
and sociolinguistics, 91
switch-points, 39–40
and Uniform Structure Principle,
36, 38
and use of dichotomous
categories, 31
organisational explanation,
116–17
local order in bilingual
conversation, 120–35
and notion of preference,
117–19
overall order in bilingual
conversation, 135–49

Pauwels, A., 183
Peräkylä, A., 8
Piller, I., 188
Pomerantz, A., 21, 117
Poplack, S., 19, 28, 38, 39–40, 41, 42,
46, 49, 76, 80
preference, 117–19
and external ideological factors, 128
and language negotiation,
130–1, 134
and linguistic competence, 128
for same language, 116, 123–8, 149
for same medium, 116, 138–45, 149
production-based model, *see* Matrix
Language Frame (MLF)

quotation, *see* direct speech

Rae, J., 171
rational choice model, 102–4
Reershemius, G., 29
relevance, 102
repair of language, 144, 146
Reversing Language Shift Model (RLS),
184–6
Richards, K., 175, 176
Rindstedt, C., 182
Roberts, C., 176, 177, 178
Robinson, J. D., 137
Romaine, S., 2, 16, 18
Russian-English bilingualism, 13
Rwandan, 9
Ryave, A. L., 49

Sacks, H., 4, 35, 106, 118, 121, 122,
135, 137, 193
Sankoff, G., 24, 99
Sardinian, 182
Saussure, (de) F., 3, 85–6
Schegloff, E., 117
Schegloff, E., 4, 6, 35, 118, 135, 137,
140, 190, 193
Schenkein, J. N., 49
Schjever, R., 182–3
Schmitt, N., 176
Searle, P., 106
Sebba, M., 6, 8, 43
Second Language Acquisition
(SLA), 13
semilingualism, 15–17
Shin, S., 6, 28, 132
Singlish, 11
social action/social actor, 3–5, 117
social norm, 4, 7, 198, 199, 202,
206, 207

sociology of language, 85–91
Spanish, 124, 128, 129, 130, 132–3, 147
Sperber, D., 102
Standard English, 36
Standard German, 87
structural uniformity principle, 83
structuralism, 85–6, 101–2
Swahili, 19, 25–6, 51–2, 90, 95–6, 105–6, 108–9, 111–12, 113–14, 141–2, 147, 154–5, 166
Swain, M., 177
Swiss German, 87
system morpheme principle, 1, 55–7

talk-in-interaction, 4
talk in two languages, *see* code-switching
Tannen, D., 157, 158
Ten Have, P., 3, 82, 117, 122, 175
Thompson, G., 157, 158
Torras, M. C., 8, 21, 29, 34, 81, 96, 116, 138, 140, 144–5, 170, 171, 176, 178, 180, 191
transfer, 132
Treffers-Daller, J., 19, 41

'triglossia', 90
turn constructional unit (TCU), 121–7, 133–4, 135, 149

Uniform Structure Principle, 3, 35–8, 60–1
Urdu, 1

Van Hout, R., 28
Variationist (Labovian) Sociolinguistics, 92
Vehviläinen, S., 8

Wareing, S., 11
Wei, L., 6, 7, 23, 28, 103, 126, 132, 149, 182, 183
Weinreich, U., 13, 83, 96
Whalen, M. R., 135, 136
Wilkins, D. A., 175, 177
Wilson, D., 102
Winford, D., 43
Wolof, 42–3
Wootton, A., 6, 8

Yiddish, 29

Zairian, 166
Zentella, A. C., 187
Zimmerman, D. H., 135